I've travelled the world twice over,
Met the famous: saints and sinners,
Poets and artists, kings and queens,
Old stars and hopeful beginners,
I've been where no-one's been before,
Learned secrets from writers and cooks
All with one library ticket
To the wonderful world of books.

© Janice James.

The wisdom of the ages
Is there for you and me,
The wisdom of the ages,
In your local library.

There's large print books
And talking books,
For those who cannot see,
The wisdom of the ages,
It's fantastic, and it's free.

Written by Sam Wood, aged 92

A TIME TO REMEMBER

This is a collection of some of Marie Joseph's most outstanding short stories — previously published in magazines in the 1960s and 1970s — exploring the theme of love: its dreams, hopes, disappointments and the joy of its discovery. There is unexpected holiday romance for a woman resigned to caring for her mother; the anticipation of motherhood for a newly-wed; a child's joy at Christmas; a schoolgirl who brings together her elder sister with the boy next door; a birthday surprise for a lonely girl; and childhood friends who don't realise that love is right in front of them.

Books by Marie Joseph
Published by The House of Ulverscroft:

FOOTSTEPS IN THE PARK
MAGGIE CRAIG
A LEAF IN THE WIND
EMMA SPARROW
GEMINI GIRLS
THE LISTENING SILENCE
LISA LOGAN
THE GUILTY PARTY
THE CLOGGER'S CHILD
POLLY PILGRIM
A BETTER WORLD THAN THIS
PASSING STRANGERS
A WORLD APART
THE TRAVELLING MAN
WHEN LOVE WAS LIKE THAT
SINCE HE WENT AWAY
THE WAY WE WERE

MARIE JOSEPH

A TIME TO REMEMBER

A collection of short stories

Complete and Unabridged

CHARNWOOD
Leicester

First published in Great Britain in 1997 by
Century Books
London

First Charnwood Edition
published 1998
by arrangement with
Century a division of
Random House UK Limited
London

The right of Marie Joseph to be identified as
the author of this work has been asserted by her
in accordance with the
Copyright, Designs and Patents Act, 1988

British Library CIP Data

Joseph, Marie
    A time to remember: a collection of
    short stories.—Large print ed.—
    Charnwood library series
    1. Love stories
    2. Large type books
    I. Title
    823.9′14 [F]

ISBN 0–7089–9023–1

Published by
F. A. Thorpe (Publishing) Ltd.
Anstey, Leicestershire
Set by Words & Graphics Ltd.
Anstey, Leicestershire
Printed and bound in Great Britain by
T. J. International Ltd., Padstow, Cornwall

This book is printed on acid-free paper

Super Bird

Tom and I first met at Angie's wedding.

It was in a register office, and Angie wore a long purple dress, lilac clogs and a big hat with a nodding bronze chrysanthemum pinned to the front. Paul, her bridegroom, wore a braid-trimmed smoking jacket and velvet trousers, picked up at the Portobello Road market, and his rimless spectacles, through which he peered at her most fondly.

They had been living together for two years, and I had never discovered just why they were getting married, as neither of them professed any faith in the matrimonial state, but as reasons for doing anything were not considered to be necessary in the crowd I went around with, I never questioned their motives . . .

They loved each other; that much was obvious, and when the short, simple ceremony was over, we all piled into cars and drove back to their house for champagne drunk out of coffee mugs and tooth glasses.

Tom shared the back seat of the car with me and another much-whiskered stranger, and he told me that he worked in an advertising agency.

It followed. All the men we knew seemed to work either in advertising, journalism or television, and his appearance was quite in keeping too.

1

His trousers were satin, and as he put out a hand to steady himself as the car swung round a corner on two wheels, the lace on his shirt cuff fell across his hand.

The much-whiskered stranger told me that *his* name was Adrian and that he was a fashion photographer, and that made sense too.

'And you are?' they said together, and we all laughed.

'I'm Gillian,' I said.

'Then I shall call you Esmeralda,' said Tom, and I hid a sigh.

Once, just once, I'd have liked to meet a man in this crazy set-up who called me by my right name, and accepted me for what I was. But it seemed it was not to be . . .

And what was I? Now there was a very good question.

Gillian Barnes, twenty-two years old, a tri-lingual secretary, fluent in French and fairly fluent in Spanish, because of a Spanish grandmother on my mother's side. Brought up in Westmorland, with a background hilariously puritanical, according to Vera, with whom I'd shared a flat in Hampstead ever since coming to London three months ago. Hidebound, with principles so rigid as to be almost archaic, and with what she called a sweetly naïve outlook on life.

But I'd tried.

I mean, look at me, on that drizzly day in November, attending a wedding in what my mother would have considered to be fancy dress.

A granny-printed maxi-dress, a fringed woolly shawl, topped with a cloche pulled down low on my forehead, with a bunch of red plastic cherries pinned just above my left eyebrow.

And there in my wardrobe was a perfectly good silk suit, and a pair of leather court shoes with matching handbag.

Vera had soon taken me in hand, after promptly having what she called one of her shocking-pink fits when she saw the contents of my wardrobe.

Apparently the only clothes I had which were in the least suitable for the kind of life I would be expected to lead from then on were my twinsets and tweed skirts, and that was because they were so out-dated as to be in fashion again, if you see what I mean.

'Staying on for the party, Esmeralda?' Tom was saying, and I said: 'But of course,' and the bit of his face that I could see through the whiskers looked glad, and I turned to smile at him and saw his eyes, and they were brown and gentle, and I had an irresistible urge to stretch out my hand and touch him.

He looked vulnerable somehow, and that was silly because, as far as I could see, he wasn't the vulnerable type. All the men I'd met since coming down to London were completely self-sufficient.

Angie's husband, Paul, had a house in the less fashionable part of Highgate; a huge, tall house, bought for him by his wealthy parents, and he and Angie lived in two rooms, letting out the rest to any of their friends who were in

3

need of shelter at the time.

It was a perfect house for parties, containing as it did only the bare necessities of furniture, and completely uncarpeted, apart from a strip in the living room and an opulent Chinese rug in the lavatory.

My mother would have died a thousand deaths if she'd seen it, her idea of comfort being wall-to-wall carpeting and white-painted walls, and seeing Paul's parents standing together amongst the guests, drinking white wine out of plastic cups, and trying to look as if they *understood*, I suppressed a fit of the giggles.

Just then a boy in skin-tight jeans, with long hair tied back in a pigtail, came in, leading by the hand a girl in equally form-fitting trousers, with *her* hair tied back in a matching pigtail, and I noticed Paul's father flinch.

'There's a thought bubble coming out of the top of his head, and it says: 'What is the world coming to?'' Tom said, appearing suddenly by my side. 'But you have to admire them, for at least they came.'

'Angie isn't telling her parents that they're married until Christmas,' I said, saying it casually, as if I thought it the most natural thing in the world, and as I'd known he would, Tom nodded.

'Wise,' he said and, like the hypocrite I'd become, I agreed with him at once.

Paul's mother, still bewildered in her silk dress and matching jacket and little feathered toque, her fur stole slipping from her plump shoulders, was gallantly going the rounds, saying goodbye to her son's wedding guests.

'We're going to the theatre. *Do* have a lovely party,' she was saying to a huge Jamaican, wearing a satin shirt as black and shiny as his face.

'Sure will,' he promised her with a gleam of white teeth before she turned politely to me.

'And you are a friend of Angie's, dear?'

So much did she remind me of my own mother that I knew a moment of homesickness so acute that, to my horror, I felt the prick of tears behind my eyelids.

'Yes,' I said, 'and please don't worry about them. Angie loves Paul very, very much. They're so happy together.'

Then I remembered that their being together was only supposed to be, officially, as from that day, and blushed, but Paul's mother gave me the sweetest smile, and leaning forward, kissed my cheek.

'Thank you, my dear,' she said with feeling.

The stereo equipment had been set up in the big drawing room at the front of the house, and people were drifting through. At Paul and Angie's parties, people did just that; moving as the will took them, from one room to another.

Tom and I, leaving more room for friends arriving to greet the happy pair, drifted in the direction of the loud, pulsating music.

The only light came from a single green bulb set in the high ceiling, and couples were dancing, their faces thrown into sickly relief. In the total absence of anything remotely resembling a chair,

Tom and I sat down on the floor, leaning against the wall.

'Tell me about it,' he said, and I glanced at him, startled, though I had thought that in the last three months nothing could startle me again.

'Tell you what?' I shouted into a sudden lull in the loud music, and a boy clad in a tartan blanket raised a comical eyebrow at me.

'Everything,' Tom said, unperturbed. 'Where you come from, what you do and, more important, what you think.'

And if I'd told him the truth I would have said that I didn't know what I thought, that I was in reality as bewildered as Paul's poor mother had been, but I told him I came from Westmorland, that I lived in Hampstead with Vera, and that I worked in an office tucked away between a gown shop and a shoe shop in Oxford Street, travelling there every day by bus.

'And you've sloughed off your former life?' Tom asked. 'Like a snake sloughs off its dead skin?'

'Yes,' I said firmly, 'something like that.' And I thought that tomorrow was Sunday and I would write my weekly letter to my mother and tell her that I'd been to a wedding, and then on to a party, knowing she would imagine me sitting in church on the bride's side, in my silk suit and leather shoes with matching handbag; going back to the flat to change into my little black dress, with the pearls my parents had given me for my twenty-first birthday present.

Poor Mother . . .

And the party afterwards. Well, in her fond innocence there I'd be, standing around 'chatting' to my friends, drinking innocuous glasses of sweet sherry, eating pâté on toast and nibbling little squares of pineapple paired off with cubes of cheese.

Tom turned to me. 'Happy?' he asked.

I sighed, but only inwardly, of course. Now was the moment when I would be expected to say something like: 'What is happiness? Can it ever be defined? Surely it's an ephemeral thing? A living for the moment, a state of mind, only indulged in by the sentimental or the searcher for an experience, which stales before it becomes remotely tangible?'

And he, in his turn, would tell me how he despaired of simply everything in general, and the whole world in particular, and how he was considering throwing up his job at the agency because he was in danger of becoming materialistic, and was going to bum around Europe, or Mexico, until he got things more into perspective and himself sorted out.

We would sit there on the hard floor with that horrible green light bulb etching our respective profiles into bilious relief and together we'd put the universe to rights. Then he'd take me home and expect to make love to me, and I'd fend him off with one of the excuses at which I was becoming more than adept.

Suddenly I knew I couldn't do it. Suddenly I knew I'd had enough . . .

'At this particular moment I'm not all that

7

happy,' I said. 'For one thing, this floor is too hard; for another I find the music too loud and this bunch of cherries is somewhat obstructing my vision. How about you?'

'Let's go,' he said. So we did.

First we went in search of Angie and Paul. Angie was in the kitchen warming up a family-sized tin of baked beans, still wearing the large, floppy hat with the nodding bronze chrysanthemum pinned to the front of it; Vera was making the toast, whilst in the hall Paul was demonstrating the second yoga position.

We said goodbye to the pair in pigtails, who were sharing the bottom stair and a carton of natural yoghurt.

The night air smelled cool and fresh. Tom took my hand, and for no reason at all, we started to run.

Down the hill, across the road, and up the short path leading to the Heath we ran, and only when we were out of breath did we stop, leaning against each other, laughing, with the trees waving dark branches, bending into nebulous shapes, and a sluggish moon glinting silver on the small pond.

'You're quite a girl, aren't you, Esmeralda?' Tom said, and I looked up at him.

'My name is Gillian,' I told him firmly. 'I like my job, I love my parents, I am perfectly aware that the world is in a mess, but as far as I can see, there is precious little I can do about it. You can take me home if you'd like to, but I have no intention of sharing my bed with you.'

He started to say something, but I held up my hand. 'I am a good cook and I make perfect scones, and worse than that, I saw *The Sound of Music* three times, and cried every single time, so now you know.

'Yes, and something else . . . when I marry, *if* I marry, it will be in church, and I will wear white, and my mother will sit in the front pew, and I won't be satisfied with baked beans on toast for my wedding supper, oh dear no. A candlelit dinner for two, and I won't wear a hat.'

And with that, I took off my silly hat, and threw it as far away as I could, and heard it land with a satisfying plop in the pond. Then I shook my hair loose.

Very serious was Tom; so serious that the contours of his face, surrounded by all that hair, seemed etched into a kind of nobility.

For a long moment I wondered what he was going to do. Then, solemnly, he stretched out an arm, and with little ripping sounds, tore the ruffled lace from the cuffs on his shirt, hanging them ceremoniously on the branches of the nearest tree.

'Esmeralda will kill me. It took her ages to sew them on,' he said.

Aghast, I said: 'But I thought *I* was Esmeralda?'

He started to untie his long, flowing silk tie. 'All the girls I know are called Esmeralda,' he assured me gravely. 'But you are Gillian, and I too saw *The Sound of Music* and was overcome when the Mother Superior swelled out her chest

9

and sang about climbing every mountain.

'I, too, like my job. I don't write poetry on the quiet, and I wouldn't have expected to go to bed with you on our first acquaintance because you, as my dear mother would have said, are obviously 'not that kind of girl'.'

Then he held my hands, and started to swing them gently, and the wind caught my long hair and blew it round my face. The lights of London twinkled in blue formation to our left, and from the road came the hum of traffic.

'Thank you, Gillian,' Tom said in a soft voice.

'For what?' I whispered back.

'For reminding me of something my father once said to me: 'Best be yourself . . . "

"Imperial, plain and true',' I said, delighted because I knew my Browning too, and then he laughed out loud.

'And now I'm going to take you home, and on your doorstep I will plant a kiss on your forehead, chaste and pure, and tomorrow being Sunday, I will present myself for tea, and you will feed me buttered scones and we will start to get acquainted. Right?'

'Right!' I said, and we walked back down the path together, away from the Heath and on to the busy road. Still holding hands, our steps matching, not talking any more, not needing to, because somehow I knew that there was all the time in the world to say what we had to say.

And I thought about Vera's face when I told

her that Tom was coming for Sunday tea, and
how she would stare when I donned an apron
and started to bake.

One of her shocking-pink fits, she'd have
— that much was absolutely certain.

Father of the Bride

When I told my mother that I'd like my father to come to the wedding, her expression stiffened, the way it always did whenever his name was mentioned.

So often in the past had I seen it happen, I'd stopped talking about him, but now, uncaring, I was determined to get my own selfish way.

'You haven't seen him for twelve years,' she reminded me with sad reproach. 'If he walked through that door now, this minute, I doubt if you'd recognize him.'

I stared at the door, imagining him standing there, suddenly materializing, like a genie in a whiff of smoke, a huge genie, because I remembered him as a big man with a shout of a laugh, so tall he had to bend his head as he came through our cottage door. An exaggeration, surely? I blinked the image away, and returned to the fray.

'It's not as if it would matter. I mean, all your friends know he exists, and nowadays no one would bat an eyelid. And he needn't actually give me away. Just *be* there, that's all.'

My mother's face had gone pink, the way it does when she tries to assert herself, which isn't often, being the way she is. Guilt began to prick uncomfortably, but I ignored it.

'He's married again,' she was reminding me, 'with two children. An invitation could embarrass him.' She corrected herself. 'Well, embarrass his wife, perhaps. Can't you see that, Jan?' Then, seeing that I couldn't, or wouldn't, she turned to her prospective son-in-law. 'Can't *you* talk some sense into her?'

'Gave up trying to do that long ago,' he grinned. Then he closed his eyes and opted out of a situation he obviously felt to be between me and my mother.

★ ★ ★

It was funny really. There we'd been, Laurie and me, living together for a year, taking for granted my mother's shocked acceptance of it; happy, so happy it wasn't true. And there was Laurie one day saying it was time we got married. Not the other way round, as it's always supposed to be.

'We're all right as we are,' I said, and he reminded me of the children we intended to have some day, and the house we meant to buy when we'd scraped a deposit together.

'And besides, I love you,' he said, 'and I want it all tied up and legal. One man, one woman. For ever and ever, amen. Does that make me some kind of freak?'

I'd tried to put into words the way I felt, and failed utterly. I was scared, full of doubts, misgivings; *frightened*, the way my mother is frightened. All of the time. Even as I spoke I knew I was echoing her thoughts. If I'd looked in a mirror I swear I would have looked like her at that moment. Scared to turn a corner, to take a chance in case something lurks there to disturb the shelled-in safety of her days.

'Look at my parents,' I said. 'They got married, and what happened? I was only eight years old when they divorced, but I can still remember the awful silences when I was with them, the terrible arguments when they thought I was too young to understand. I was only eight, but I *knew*. How can we be sure that the same won't happen to us?'

Laurie is wise. Laurie is seven years older than me, slow to anger, quick to love. One of my clever friends had suggested to me that I used him as a father substitute, but then she didn't know the way his touch sent shivers of delight through me, the way his just being there lit every corner of a room with sunlight.

'We can't be sure,' he said at once, 'but we have to take that chance. Marriage is a chancy thing, and at least we've had a trial run.'

He smiled at the phrase and pulled me closer to him, outlining the shape of my mouth with his finger, but before my senses swam, I said: 'My father *must* come to the wedding . . . '

★ ★ ★

My mother gave in, as I knew she would. Not for my gentle, sweet mum the sitting on her bottom in the middle of the road, protesting. Not for her the waving of banners to proclaim her rights. She wrote to my father and he replied at once, accepting with pleasure, adding that he would be alone.

14

'Which is perhaps as well,' my mother said, and I knew her imagination had boggled at the thought of introducing his wife to her friends. Conventional to an old-fashioned degree, she would, I guessed, have lain awake in the night over the phrasing of the introductions.

'This is my husband's, my *ex*-husband's wife . . . ' Poor little Mother. What was I doing to her?

And still I didn't care.

Never quick to criticize, always willing to see the other side, yet she sometimes pilloried my father, trying, I knew, to stop me from investing him with glamour; a mythical figure to whom I would run with outstretched arms should I meet him on the street. How well she knew me, my timid little mother. Or was it that she saw too much of him in me?

'He gave you *nothing*,' she reminded me the day before the wedding, the morning of the rehearsal. 'With money he was always generous, a fool to himself, but you were my sole responsibility, remember that.'

The fear again, this time tempered with a terrible jealousy that I might transfer some of my affection from her. The uncertainty, the trembling indecision.

Suddenly I loved her so much I put my arms round her and hugged her. I couldn't say what was in my heart, but she knew, for when we drew apart, her eyes were damp with tears.

'You're a little beast, do you know that?' Laurie told me as we set off for the church that evening for the rehearsal.

'You wouldn't think that if you loved me truly,' I told him, but he disagreed.

'If I didn't see you as you are, warts and all; if you didn't see me as I am, then we'd merely be in love with love, not with each other at all.'

'There's a difference then?'

'And you know it,' he said, taking one hand from the wheel of our shabby car and squeezing my knee. 'Otherwise I wouldn't be marrying you.'

We were meeting my mother at the church, and my father, staying overnight at the Rose and Crown, was to join us there. It wasn't to be a big wedding, no veil, no bridesmaids, but to please my mother, to make up, I suppose, for my insistence on my father being there, I had given in to her wishes for the organ music, the flowers and my long cream dress.

She was waiting for us in the porch, sheltering from the rain, sweeping down now from a darkened sky.

'He's in there,' she said at once, 'talking to the vicar,' and I swear her fingers were trembling as she laced them together.

'See what you've done?' Laurie's glance said, loud and very clear.

And he *was* larger than life, my father, just as I remembered from so long ago. An exuberant extrovert in a brown light-weight suit, with dark hair a trendy length, and a handshake that made my armpits tingle. No kiss, not just then, I noticed, and was glad.

Laurie liked him, I could see that. It wouldn't be long before they were on a shoulder-thumping, the next-one's-on-me kind of terms. And the vicar liked him too, so much was obvious by the way he smiled through our little preparation of a ceremony. Our vicar is not given to smiling, taking his role as mediator between God and his congregation very seriously.

'Now when I say this, you do this,' he told my father, who winked at me as he took my hand, in the traditional way, and behind me, sitting alone in the pew on the left, I actually felt my mother flinch.

It was soon over. The vicar wished us luck, made an uncharacteristic joke about me turning up on time, and left us, walking slowly, head bent, as if in procession, to the vestry.

We stood there awkwardly for a moment, and then a friend of my mother's from the Women's Institute came in with the flowers, and as we walked back up the aisle they stopped to have a word together.

'Now what?' my father said, rubbing his hands together as we stood in the porch. 'Would you care to come back with me for a bite to eat?' He looked backwards over his shoulder, suddenly uncomfortable. 'I asked your mother, but she says she has a lot to do. An independent woman, your mother.'

And a brave one, I thought. Independent and courageous and proud; too proud to take from this man now that my education was finished.

This man, I thought, not my father, and was appalled.

He was talking to Laurie, laughing, throwing

17

his head back and roaring as if he were coming apart at the seams.

I stepped back and there in the church, by the altar, my little mother was in earnest conversation with the lady of the flowers. Pointing, advising, listening, making sure that everything was perfect. For me.

'I must go back with her,' I told him, 'it wouldn't be fair,' and immediately he shrugged his shoulders, understanding, or too hurt to try to understand? It was hard to tell.

'See you tomorrow then,' he said and walked away, and as I watched him go something in me grieved so much it was an actual physical pain.

'Surely Mother could have . . . what could I do?' I asked Laurie, putting my hand on his arm, pleading, I suppose, for understanding.

* * *

Back at the cottage there was so much to do, so many last-minute things to see to, it was half past nine before we ate.

'If I don't sit down I swear my feet will burst into flames,' my mother said, and it was then I said I was going to go for a walk.

'And I'll go back to the flat,' Laurie said, and my mother nodded, not seeing anything in the least hypocritical in the fact that for the night before our wedding Laurie and I, who had lived together for a year, would be sleeping apart.

'You're going to see your father,' Laurie said as soon as we got outside, and when I nodded he merely opened the door of the car and told me to get in.

'Don't be too hard on him,' was all he said as he kissed me good night, then his arms went round me, holding me tight, and he confessed that he felt as nervous as a bridegroom — 'the genuine article,' he grinned.

'Then that makes two of us,' I confessed, leaving him reluctantly, and going into the bar parlour of the Rose and Crown.

And there he was, my father, not alone as I'd imagined he would be, but sitting at a table with a couple of the regulars, swapping stories judging by the sound of the laughter which greeted me.

But his face when he saw me gave him away, and I knew I'd been right to come.

'What'll you have?' he asked me, and after he'd collected our drinks we found a quiet corner and sat down, facing each other across a small table with a pot of wilting Michaelmas daisies dead centre.

'I can't stay,' I told him. 'Mother thinks I've gone for a short walk and she'll alert Sergeant Watkins at the station if I'm not back soon. She's always worrying about me.'

'Once a worriter, always a worriter,' he said.

My quick flash of temper surprised me.

'She's had a lot of worrying to do. Twelve years of it. Remember?'

'Touché,' he said, and now the smile was rueful.

There wasn't enough time to lead into what I had to say. No time to hedge, to be circumspect and tactful, to weigh each word.

'You must have loved her once,' I said, and could have added, 'just as I love Laurie', but to my surprise, I admit, he understood at once.

Putting his beer mug down on the table and moving the daisies to one side, he leaned across and took both my hands in his own.

'And you're scared that the same might happen to you and Laurie?' he said straight out, and I nodded, biting my lip. I might have known, I told myself, that to this big man, smiling at me now with a kind of tenderness, a spade was a spade and nothing else.

Gently he caressed my wrist with his thumb.

'Marriage is a gamble,' he told me, just as Laurie had said. 'I married your mother after knowing her for a few weeks.' He had a glint of mischief in his eyes. 'In those far-off days it wasn't done to live together. No trial runs. Just a dive in at the deep end, and heaven take the consequences.'

'So you approve of what Laurie and I have been doing? Living together, I mean.'

He shook his head. 'Not for me to approve or disapprove, Jan. What I'm trying to tell you is that I couldn't make your mother happy. She is the way she is and I am the way I am. Oil and water, unable to mix.' He gave my hands a little squeeze. 'It wasn't easy to walk out and leave you both, believe me, but to stay would have been worse. And so I went . . .

'Tell me something,' he went on, pitching his voice so low I had to strain to hear it. 'Has

20

your mother been unhappy all these years? Honest now.'

I wanted to hurt him but I could only tell the truth.

'She's what I'd call a happy worriter,' I said, and he laughed out loud.

It was true. I thought about her, going quietly about her days, working for the Church, the Women's Institute, turning down at least one proposal of marriage, afraid to change the even tempo of her life. Nursing her bitterness about her failed marriage as a kind of shield.

Now, for the first time, I saw that some of her cautious apprehension had rubbed off on me.

'Life doesn't come all wrapped up neat and tidy, complete with a marriage certificate as a kind of guarantee form,' my father was saying now, 'but that doesn't say you have to steer clear of it. There are times when you have to dive in at the deep end, just as you are going to do tomorrow. You have to do what you feel to be right. At the time.'

He let go of my hands and trailed his fingers lightly down my cheek. 'I've only just met your Laurie, but from what I can see there's good chemistry there. Don't be afraid, Jan.'

'And you're happy now?' I whispered.

He patted his top pocket. 'If there was time, and if it wouldn't be too damned tactless for words, I'd show you some snaps.' One thick eyebrow raised itself quizzically. 'Perhaps not. Perhaps another time.'

And I knew he was thinking, as I was thinking, that there would probably never be another time.

He would give me away in the morning, then walk out of my life, just as he'd done before.

My loyalty lay with my mother, and however misguided she might be in some things, that was the way it had to be.

And his loyalty lay with his wife and his new-found happiness; no sentimental reaching back to a past that was dead and gone.

Now, I saw how alike we were, my father and I. Realized why I'd defied my mother to go and live with Laurie — answering when life beckoned instead of staying with her and watching it go by.

'I must go now,' I said, and immediately my father stood up and said he'd walk back with me as far as the cottage door.

And the rain had stopped; the sky had lightened, giving the promise of a fine day to come. He walked by my side, this man I hardly knew, moving with a loping stride, jingling loose coins in his pocket, the stride of a man who knows exactly where he is going, and why.

We didn't speak. We'd said all there was to say. Nothing had changed really, and yet, in a subtle way, everything had changed.

The next time my gentle little mother reminded me that he had given me nothing, I wouldn't argue with her, but I would know differently.

Tonight, he had given me everything, this tall stranger by my side — this stranger who just happened to be my father . . .

Head in the Clouds

Rosie's seat on the huge plane was one of two almost in line with the tiny kitchen place from which food and drinks were served. And right up to take-off the seat next to her managed to remain unoccupied.

Then, at the very last moment, just before the heavy door was swung into position, a tall fair man rushed on, showed his boarding pass, glanced at the number and came to sit beside her.

'Made it!' he gasped. 'Thank heaven for that.'

Then he fastened his black seat belt, leaned back and closed his eyes as the bright orange plane taxied to the runway ready for take-off.

He was, unlike the vast majority of the three hundred and sixty passengers, English. There was no mistaking his dark business suit and neatly striped tie.

Late thirties probably, Rosie thought, and so used to flying round the world that he could sleep even as they soared above the clouds, then levelled out.

He opened his eyes as an air hostess in her brown patterned silky dress, a beautiful girl with blusher worn high on her cheekbones, came round with the first drink.

'David Garson, en route for Dallas — strictly business,' he said, and held out a hand.

'Rosie Travers, en route for Fort Worth — purely pleasure,' she said, and he laughed. She noticed the way his whole face changed, its craggy solemnity smoothing out as his blue eyes crinkled into boyish amusement.

'Staying with friends?'

'With my sister actually. She married a captain in the American Air Force.'

He nodded. 'First trip?'

'Yes. But not yours?'

'No. I spend two weeks out of every six in Dallas. I reckon if the guys up front there all succumbed to some mysterious virus I could just about pilot this plane myself.'

There was more than a hint of a southern drawl in his deep voice, and Rosie immediately identified. After two weeks in Texas she knew she would probably come back with more than a touch of the romantic slurring in her own accent.

'I do hope they *don't* succumb,' she confided. 'I'm not sure about flying. It seems unnatural to be sitting here drinking gin and tonic with all that space beneath us.'

'You surprise me.' He gave her a quizzical stare. 'I had you categorized as a jump-on-a-plane-and-go-anywhere kind of girl.' She saw the way he glanced at her ringless left hand. 'You know: a conference in Hong Kong, a quick survey of the firm's branches in New Zealand, then back with a briefcase jammed with constructive notes.'

She shook her head. 'Oh, no. You have me all wrong — entirely. I live with my widowed invalid mother in Watford, and work in the reference library. It must be the gear,' she explained, glancing down at the neat navy skirt with matching jacket. 'Plus the hair. I went mad last week and told my hairdresser to do me like Kate Bush. My real image is probably a dirndl and a bun at the nape of my neck.'

Now what on earth had made her tell him that?

She sat back in her seat as one of the beautiful hostesses slotted a tray in front of her in readiness for the evening meal.

In another minute she would be telling him that she was still a virgin at twenty-four, and that the man she had just made up her mind at last to go to bed with had gone to share a flat with a girl called Victoria whose spontaneous surrender had been, she felt, at some variance with her name.

For a while they ate in companionable silence, unwrapping the tiny pats of butter and squeezing mustard on their ham from the miniature tubes.

'Then what would you say my image was?'

He opened a small bottle of red wine and insisted on sharing it with her.

'Go on. Let's see just how wrong *you* can be about me.'

She hesitated then spoke freely. There seemed no reason for doing anything but, with all that space outside and around them. She had the feeling that they were somehow suspended in time.

'You are an executive in a firm specializing

in computers or maybe office equipment. You live south of London in a heavily mortgaged house with a wife who is longing for your youngest child to go to big school so that she can stop playing about with pottery classes and yoga, and take up her career again. She watches your cholesterol by making you eat margarine on your toast, and she owns four pairs of jeans, umpteen little tops, but only one good dress and jacket.'

To her surprise, instead of grinning, he reached over and took her hand.

'Partly right, Rosie. But all in the past. My wife divorced me last year because she could not come to terms with my half-life with her. Two weeks away, two days overcoming jet lag, then working the clock round to prepare for going away again. No children, thank God; but even so, it was, at the time, the very bottom of my life.'

Already she felt she knew him too well to murmur a trite 'sorry', but she ached for the sadness in his face and, to her astonishment, laid his hand for a fleeting moment against her cheek.

'Why aren't you eating your trifle?' he asked her a few minutes later. 'There won't be anything else but a sort of brunch before we land.'

'Because I am ten pounds overweight,' she told him. And he assured her solemnly that it was her glorious Renoir-like proportions that had made him feel so comfortable with her straight away like that.

He went to sleep when the trays were taken away, and his head slipped sideways from the small white pillow provided by the airline, to rest on her shoulder.

And it came to her that this was the first time she had been so close to a sleeping man. She watched him tenderly, and when his lean face twitched in what could have been a bad dream, she moved to settle him more comfortably, then saw his mouth smile again.

She was a plumpish, calm, undemanding girl, and at that moment a wave of compassion engulfed her, so that she sat quite still, grieving for the time he had suffered at the very bottom of his life . . .

When he awoke he leaned across her and told her that they were flying over Greenland and there, far below them, was a frozen sea with icebergs floating majestically about on it.

'Now I am at the very *summit* of my life,' she told him, and he took her hand again and agreed that she could not hope to get much higher, and the Kate Bush hairdo swung forward just a fraction and tickled his cheek.

As they flew into cloud again he told her that the first thing she would notice in Texas would be the lack of pavements and the preponderance of fat bottoms, as the women — the vast majority of them — wore brightly coloured pants and skimpy tops.

Rosie laughed out loud. 'Fatter than mine?'

'Yours will fade into insignificance,' he assured her.

There were earphones in plastic bags and he

fixed them on for her, tuned her in, and later, as they flew over Canada at four hundred miles an hour, there was a sob-throated tenor singing into her ears.

'Now you must sleep,' he said, but it was no good. She told him she had never been able to sleep while travelling; so they sat together in silence for the next hour, savouring their pleasure in each other's company . . . or so it seemed to Rosie.

When the drinks came round again, they touched glasses and he drank to her holiday.

'At first you will revel in the sun,' he told her, 'then all you will want to do is scuttle from one air-conditioner to another. But it will be a visit you will never forget. The American way of life is so . . . so vital.'

Then for a while she thought about the loneliness that would clamp down on her own life when she came back home. She knew that somehow, over the Atlantic, they had gained six hours; but then, what an odd factor was time.

For her, it merely added a fourth dimension to an escape from a troubled world in general, and her own uneventful life in particular. She would go back to Mother, whose dependence on her was compounded, not of love, but of a clinging fear of losing her.

And this man sitting next to her? To what was he going back? A lonely flat, or maybe some girl who would not mind sharing a half-life with him?

For all his candour he had really given very little of himself away.

She stared down at a sea of rippled clouds, and reminded herself of the frequent regularity of his flights to America; of the many times he must have sat next to a total stranger, and even fallen asleep with his head on a receptive shoulder.

'You are frowning. Why?' he asked her then, and as naturally as if they had known each other for a long, long time, he gently removed the frown with the cushion of his thumb.

'That's better. You have the sort of face that was meant to be glad,' he told her softly. 'Did you know that?'

★ ★ ★

By the time he had slept some more, and the brunch had been served and eaten, she knew that he watched television only rarely, read voraciously, and that his office in Dallas was round the bend in the main road outside the tall building from where the fatal shot had been fired at President Kennedy.

'What do you read? You haven't read one word for the past nine hours,' she teased him as the 'Fasten Your Seat Belts' sign came on as they lost height and began to circle over Dallas.

'Talking to you was far more interesting than the paperback book in my bag,' he told her. Then just before the slight shudder that told her the plane had landed, he leaned across and kissed her lightly on her cheek.

'Er . . . thank you,' she said.

29

'You're welcome,' he said right back.

As they moved slowly towards passport control, he asked her which flight she was booked back on, and idiotically glancing at her watch, she told him the six-thirty flight two weeks today.

'No, two weeks tomorrow,' she amended, feeling the heat of an afternoon sun enclose her as if she had suddenly been wrapped in an electric blanket.

Then her sister Thea was there — as American as blueberry pie in her white pants and scarlet top — and Thea's husband, Gary, was shaking her hand and grinning; and when Rosie turned round, David Garson had disappeared.

'You sure do surprise me, Rosie,' Thea told her three times during the first three days. 'I imagined you arriving pale and wan, with the sorrows of a thousand summers on your shoulders; and yet here you are looking younger than me, honey. What happened? Have you gotten over the guy you were always telling about in your letters already?'

'It's the warmth,' Rosie said. 'The glorious bone-soaking warmth that never goes away. And the food.' She raised both arms above her head luxuriously. 'Why did nobody tell me before how good bacon and strawberry jam tasted spread on the same piece of hot toast?'

'And Momma?' Thea glanced through the window to where Gary was lovingly tending the vegetable patch in his beloved yard before the sun rose high in the wide, wide sky. 'Are you still letting her walk all over you? For heaven's sake,

30

honey, she's only sixty-four! There's nothing to stop her hopping on a plane and coming over. Diabetes isn't an illness nowadays. She could still have her shots here. It would give you a break.'

She got up and poured the second of endless cups of coffee. 'C'mon, go get your face fixed and we'll get in the car and drive down to Austin and see the L. B. J. Museum. It's only two hundred miles down the freeway.'

Into the car went the huge vacuum flask filled with coffee and, sitting in the backseat, watching the myriad signs flash by, Rosie marvelled at the sight of Gary sipping coffee as he drove along at the regulation fifty-five miles an hour.

'I met a man on the plane coming over,' she told Thea on the day they stopped over at San Antonio and had their photographs taken outside The Alamo, the landmark to the heroes of Texas liberty. 'He was . . . he was rather nice.'

'Oh, glory be!' Thea gave her a sisterly shove. 'That's what accounts for the stars in your eyes? Honey, you sure haven't changed: still the same romantic Rosie. The guy probably has a wife and four kids back home.'

Rosie nodded as if to agree, remembering for a sharp moment his kiss on her cheek.

But when they moved inside The Alamo, her eyes were suddenly black and her face had lost the glad look David Garson had remarked upon.

For the rest of her stay, the memory of him receded to the far corner of her mind — receded, but refused to go away. And yet the sun-filled

31

days took on a shape and colour of their own as she shopped in air-conditioned splendour, marvelling at the prices, the cleanliness and the open-spaced luxury of everything.

Just before she was due to fly back home again, Gary told her: 'This visit has done you a power of good, honey. We feel guilty, you know, Thea and me, about you having full responsibility for your momma. Try to persuade her to take a long vacation with us over here soon, huh?'

'It's been like a dream,' Rosie told him. Especially the flight over, her mind whispered. Then she reminded herself of how quickly dreams can fade.

'You will be able to sleep on the way back,' Thea assured her as they stood in line at Dallas airport waiting for her to be checked in for the six-thirty flight to Gatwick.

'Oh, no. I can't sleep on a train or a plane.'

Rosie, who hated goodbyes — and had once, to her shame, felt tears spring to her eyes when their regular milkman had told her he was retiring the next day — shook her head.

'You go away now. I would rather you did — truly.'

So they went — with Thea holding her head too high and nice kind Gary with his arm round her shoulders — as Rosie waited, her cases bulging with gift-wrapped presents, to be passed through to the Departure area.

And as before, when she got on the plane, the seat beside her was empty — the same seat, next to the place from where the drinks and food were served.

She watched the air hostesses — a different crew this time, but still all of them startlingly beautiful, with their gold chains gleaming against brown throats and the horseshoe-shaped blusher on their cheeks.

The position of her seat was such that she could see a group of hopeful standbyers waiting for a last-minute chance of a place. She had just reconciled herself to the company of a grizzled little man with a huge Stetson swamping his foxy features, when it happened.

Hurtling at breakneck speed through the open door came David Garson, his fair hair flopping untidily over his thin face.

'Made it!' he gasped. 'Thank God for that.' Then he fastened his seat belt, leaned back and closed his eyes as the bright orange plane taxied to the runway, ready for take-off.

Rosie found she was fighting off a pricking of tears as the huge plane gathered speed, to rise like a cumbersome great bird into the sky, leaving the vast plains of Texas spread out beneath them. Suddenly the whole world was falling away, wreathed in clouds ringed with haloes of gold.

'Took some doing,' he told her, opening his eyes for a moment and smiling at her. 'But I managed to book this seat when we landed a couple of weeks ago. Do you mind?'

He was watching her carefully, waiting for her reply . . .

And Rosie was above all an honest girl: a

serene, rather plumpish girl with an ingrained habit of telling the truth. Leaning her own head back, she closed her eyes and said: 'I am glad you managed it, so very glad.'

She did not see his expression; but as they flew into the clouds, higher and higher, seeking the bright blue above, his arm came quite naturally to draw her to him. Her head eased itself comfortably into the indentation of his shoulder, and together they drifted off into a relaxed and loving kind of sleep.

Tea at Three

When Don told me one evening that his Sales Director's wife was lonely, having just moved house into our corner of Surrey, and suggested that I asked her round for a cup of tea, I could only conclude that he was making some kind of sick joke, and told him so.

I had met Lisa Leyton at the firm's Annual Dinner and Dance the week before, and had summed her up in one minute flat. She was childless and elegant, with a devotion to detail in her appearance that told me she had spent at least five hours getting ready. Every flick of her fair hair was in place, tan make-up covered every inch of her that showed (and that was plenty), and she had a toothy smile that had half the room trying to get a word with her — the male half, naturally!

'And,' I asked Don, 'what would I do with the children whilst she's here sipping tea? Lock them in the attic, or sound-proof a room or something?'

He stared at me in honest bewilderment.

'But she'd *love* to meet them. She adores children. She told me so. When I told her we had three-year-old twin boys, and a fourteen-month-old baby girl, guess what she said?'

"How cute'?' I suggested.

'She said she just loved babies. Anyway,' he added, 'I did sort of mention to her about coming round, and she was delighted.' He paused. 'So really I think it would be a good idea if you give her a ring, love.'

I sighed. Although no one could, in any circumstances, describe my husband as a promotion-pusher, I knew that he was worried half frantic by the renewed spate of redundancies in his firm, and I also knew that getting to know the Sales Director's wife could be a step in the right direction. For his sake then, I rang Lisa Leyton the next day.

When I tell you that to spend a mere five minutes telephoning meant that I had to choose a time when the twins were out in the garden, doing God knows what, and the baby was rattling the bars of her cot upstairs in demented fury at having been put down for her afternoon sleep, you will understand what I mean.

For twins, Benjie and Sam are quite dissimilar. Benjie is good with his hands, meaning that he can dismantle the vacuum cleaner or the knobs on the record player without the aid of a single tool, and Sam can cheerfully eat his soup with his fingers if you take your eyes off him for a second, and still persists in coming out of the lavatory with his trousers round his ankles.

The baby — well, it is a bit early to decide how she is going to turn out, but she is a mother's girl, who is likely to throw a fit of screaming hysterics if a stranger as much as puts out a finger to her.

I love them to distraction, but I often wonder why they are not like other people's children. A friend told me the other day that her little boy had told her she looked just like the Queen when she was all dressed up to go out for the evening.

'Mummy, you look just like the Queen. All sparkly,' she said he had said, and so I tried to make my two sons say something flattering about me.

'Do you like Mummy's new dress?' I asked.

Benjie looked up briefly from prising a tack out of the carpet, and said no, he didn't; Sam went all shy on me, his own mother, and started to suck his thumb. The fact that Cathy, the baby, was sick down the front of the dress seemed to prove my point . . .

However, because I had promised, and because I tell myself every single day that my children are going through a phase, and will improve, and it could be that very day, I rang Lisa Leyton and asked her if she would like to come round the following Wednesday afternoon.

'How kind,' she said quickly, making me think that perhaps Don was right, and she was lonely. 'Yes, I'd love to come. Wednesday at three? That will be lovely.'

That's what you think, I thought as I replaced the receiver, and when I told Don he looked proud of me, and I felt proud of me too.

The first thing I did was to appeal to the twins' better natures. It was, after all, no good talking to the baby. All I could hope for was that Lisa would not speak to her, or even glance in her direction, much less attempt to pick her up.

I soon found that the boys did not have a

better nature between them, and was reduced to bribing them with sweets.

★ ★ ★

That Wednesday I polished the sitting room and tidied it until it looked like one of those rooms at the Ideal Home Exhibition, with a rope across its entrance. I gave the twins a lecture covering, I thought, the most likely eventualities.

'Don't touch the tea-trolley,' I said. 'Don't put fingermarks on the television; don't hide the clock, and don't ride your bikes round the sofa.' Then I went to get ready.

What I had not said was, 'Don't pick the rubber plant,' and when, prompt on the stroke of three, the doorbell rang, and I ushered in an immaculate Lisa, the first thing I saw was a pruned and pathetic plant, standing there in the alcove where the fireplace used to be, with only one leaf adhering to its long bare stalk.

Lisa looked wonderful. She was wearing a linen safari suit in an oatmeal shade, and a large and floppy red hat to tone with her jersey. Her fingernails were the exact shade of scarlet, and my two unnaturally clean sons eyed her with frank admiration.

When Benjie is about to make a personal remark, he puts his head on one side, and I had given him a long lecture only the day before on never, but *never*, talking about a person's physical appearance. This was after he had enquired loudly about the hairy mole

38

on the cheek of the old lady who helps out at the greengrocer's!

Now, with a sink of the heart, I saw that his bullet-shaped head was on one side, whilst his brown eyes were narrowing into ruminative slits.

'*Some* ladies,' he said conversationally, 'have big teeth, haven't they?'

Lisa looked startled, and I had to admit that the way Benjie had coined his phrase made it a general remark, *not* personal — not bad logic for a three-year-old . . .

I got up quickly, said I would go through and put the kettle on. I left the boys standing together staring at Lisa as if they had never seen anything remotely resembling her.

The baby was screaming for attention upstairs, and when I went into the sitting room with the teapot, I thought Lisa seemed a trifle flushed and glazed of eye.

'They have probably been telling you all the intimate details of our family life,' I laughed, and, from the embarrassed way Lisa denied anything of the sort, I could only guess what revelations had been made.

The baby, by now, was rattling the bars of her cot so loudly that we could hear it skidding and bumping on the parquet floor above. Leaving Lisa once again I ran upstairs.

Just as I feared, the minute I got back downstairs, Lisa held out her arms for the baby. Cathy, however, delighted me by condescending to be lowered on to the oatmeal knees. For a minute she stared unblinking into Lisa's face then, as if she had suddenly seen a two-headed monster, she arched her back and screamed a scream of undiluted horror.

I will not dwell on the way Benjie opened his sandwich, licked the salmon filling, and put the bread back on the plate when he thought no one was looking; I will only gloss over the way Sam spilled his milk on the carpet, then went to the lavatory and came back with his pants at half-mast.

I still blush at the way the baby moaned and whined until I gave her orange juice in a bottle, then sat there in a corner of the sofa, big and triumphant, holding the bottle like a hardened meths drinker, and making slurping noises as she drained it to the last dregs.

The room, meanwhile, began to take on the appearance of a hovel, with me as a deprived and under-privileged mother who had given up trying to cope with life, there in the middle. I didn't have a chance to talk to Lisa about the latest biography I was reading, or give her my views on the Common Market negotiations.

It was raining too heavily for me to send the boys out into the garden, and when it was time for *Play School* I switched it on in desperation, and tried to carry on some kind of conversation to the background of a nice young man who was jumping up and down pretending to be a kangaroo.

When at last Lisa stood up and said she must go, every single nerve in my body was alive and twitching. I followed her into the hall and handed her the lovely scarlet hat.

'It's been such fun,' she said, adjusting a curve of the droopy brim, then, to my surprise, she blushed rosily, the colour creeping up through her perfect tan make-up.

'I wasn't going to say anything,' she whispered, 'because we've been disappointed twice before — but the first three months is up today and, well, being with your gorgeous children . . . I'm pregnant . . . and I only hope I cope as well as you, I really do.'

And so we went back into the sitting room and, sitting there amongst the crumbs, talked for twenty minutes about layettes; what the clinic doctor had said; morning sickness; the advisability of going into hospital for the birth; husbands being present; the price of knitting wool and where to buy the trendiest smocks.

I ran upstairs and came down with two smocks I had hardly worn, plus a be-ribboned christening bonnet, and a pair of yellow bootees. Lisa made me promise to take the children over to see her the very next week.

As we stood at the door saying goodbye, Benjie came up and, looking at Lisa, put his head on one side again.

I actually closed my eyes and sent up a silent prayer, then opened them again to hear him saying: 'You look like the Queen. She has a hat like that to wear on television.'

The minute Lisa had driven away, smiling and blowing kisses at the children, Benjie and Sam went and sat together on the sofa, sharing a book about Dougal, with the baby. For one moment, it really was a delightful picture of blissful family life. Then: 'When are we going to have our tea, Mummy? Our *proper* tea?' demanded Benjie, just as the baby sicked up her orange juice — all over poor old Dougal!

The Chameleon

Eighteen-year-old Dina is my cousin so far removed as to be hardly noticeable, but when her mother wrote to me from Harrogate suggesting that she share my flat in Chelsea, I found myself appointed guardian, chaperone and protector, all rolled into one, and at twenty-two, that's quite an assignment.

During the two months she had been with me, we had jogged along, playing at being happy and contented bachelor girls; or at least Dina was playing, I was just doing what comes naturally. When you are taller than most of your men friends, and your nose is too small, and your mouth too big, you don't expect too much from life, you take it as it comes.

My cousin was different. I first noticed her chameleon-like qualities when she started going out with Paul.

'Anne. Guess what?' she said one evening, coming into the flat and flopping down on the rug by the electric fire.

Dina is one of those girls who can flop gracefully, all in one fluid movement. She is a golden-brown girl, with long straight hair the shade of an autumn leaf, eyes the colour of cooking sherry, and a heart-shaped face.

'I'm not in the mood for guessing games,' I said. 'You tell me.'

She looked as smug as a kitten who'd just

finished lapping up the last drop of cream. 'Paul Marston,' she said. 'Paul Marston has asked me to go out with him.'

I sat up straight. Paul lives in the flat directly above ours. He is the only man I have ever met who makes me feel small and daintily precious. Six feet three inches without his socks, or is it within? I'm never sure. He is a kindly, amiable giant of a man, devoting his life, after his day's work quantity surveying, to the pursuit of sport.

Come summer, he throws his cricket togs into the back of his ancient car and goes off to captain his old school team, and I'm sure he usually leads them to victory. Come winter, he throws his rugger togs into the back of his ancient car, and goes off to dash frantically round some muddy field or other. Summer or winter, he runs a couple of miles in a string vest and a brief pair of running shorts, before breakfast. And most evenings our light fitting sways rhythmically as he skips or maybe enthusiastically bashes a punchball about.

For some reason I felt unaccountably depressed. It had been one of those days. Being private secretary to a publisher with two ulcers and a habit of starting to dictate long letters at four thirty can be very trying, but Dina was waiting to hear my reaction to her news.

'Where is he taking you?' I asked, feeling a surge of what I didn't recognize at the time as primitive jealousy.

'To watch the All Blacks,' she breathed, and if she'd said that he'd got front stall tickets for

44

the Royal Command Variety Show she couldn't have sounded more enchanted.

Dina is the fragile, diminutive type. About the only exercise she ever takes is to walk to the nearest Tube station in the mornings, and fresh air is something that she vaguely knows you ought to get plenty of.

Her mother sends her a monthly cheque to augment the quarterly allowance allotted by her father. Dina won't earn anything until she has finished her course at a very exclusive modelling school, and yet her clothes are out of this world — wispy nylons, pastel-coloured patent shoes costing the earth, soft, clinging jersey dresses and trailing housecoats.

'What on earth will you wear?' I asked, getting up and going into the cupboard we call a kitchen to make coffee.

The smug look took over again.

'You'll see,' she said.

And see I did! It took her all that Saturday morning to work the transformation, and when a noise like the head-long charge of elephants told us that Paul was on his way down she shot across the room with the impetus of a gold-medal sprinter coming up to the last hurdle, and flung wide the door.

From my position on the floor, where I was sorting through a pile of long-playing records in preparation for a solitary musical afternoon, I stared at her in horror.

Gone were the high heels, the wispy nylons, the clinging dress. The girl who opened the door to Paul was a jolly-hockey-sticks girl, from the knitted woollen cap on her head to the thick crêpe soles of her sturdy shoes. A blanket-like duffel coat enveloped her from throat to knee, and her stockings were ribbed and black, making her slim legs look like liquorice sticks.

'Well then! You're ready!' said Paul, stepping back a pace.

'Off we go then, righty-ho!' said this new Dina, and down the corridor they went, Dina's athletic strides more than keeping up with Paul's long, loping walk.

'Don't let's wait for the lift. I'll race you down the stairs,' I heard her shout, and away she bounded, leaving a bewildered-looking Paul to follow on.

Thoughtfully I shut the door, and slid the first record from its jacket. But I was in no mood for music, especially not the liquid voice of Frank Sinatra singing of love — unrequited love.

And that was only the beginning. As Paul became a frequent visitor to the flat, Dina threw herself with added vigour into her self-appointed role of sportswoman of the year.

She joined a keep-fit class on Mondays, and spent a lot of time with the radio full on, pretending to be a tree waving its branches in the wind. She joined Paul's badminton class on Wednesdays, and through sheer determination managed to get herself into the team.

When she told Paul that she was thinking of joining him on his early morning runs, I could hardly believe my ears. Dina was always a late riser, lying curled up in bed until the very last moment, then crawling from beneath her eiderdown, and moving very slowly round the flat as though she were a sleepwalker.

'You'll never do it, and besides, it's so unfeminine,' I told her afterwards, but Dina gave me one of her long, level looks. There were times when she made me feel years younger than she was, and this was one of them.

'You have to be interested in what *they* are interested in,' she informed me patiently, and went into the bedroom to do her exercises.

On Fridays she went with Paul to the rugger club, and once when Paul had insisted on taking me along with them I wasn't in the least surprised to see her standing at the bar with the husky rugger types, swigging beer down in great masculine gulps.

Saturday of course was the highlight of each week. That was the afternoon when Paul played rugger, and Dina accompanied him, wearing the hideous woollen cap and a scarf at least ten yards long. And yet, in spite of it all, managing to look beautiful and young, touchingly young.

They made a wonderful pair, I told myself. Paul was all that was gentle, all that was kind, he would make a perfect husband, and Dina, well, if she didn't make the perfect wife, she would make a most enchanting one.

On Sundays she usually lounged about the flat all day, too exhausted, I suspected, to do anything else.

And it was, ironically enough, on a Sunday, the only day when she wore a skirt and resembled a girl, that she met Mark. He shared the flat across the corridor with an art student from India and a dental student from Birmingham.

All that we knew about him was that he wrote. Not very successfully we gathered, because on one or two occasions we had seen his mail in the rack downstairs — buff envelopes all in the same handwriting — his own, I guessed. I could almost see the rejection slips pinned to the quarto-sized sheets of manuscript, and I felt vaguely sorry for him.

Mark was thin, painfully thin, with dark hair which fell in a neglected wave over his high forehead and a little-boy-lost appeal.

When he knocked timidly at the door that Sunday morning and asked for just enough milk for three cups of tea Dina grew motherly before my very eyes. Guiding him gently into the living room, she ensconced him in the armchair, despatched me to make some tea, and sitting on the footstool with her light brown eyes limpid with understanding encouraged him to talk about his writing.

It was like opening the floodgates of a dam. Once started he went on, and on, and on.

'I never write fiction as such,' he told us. 'All my work has the basis of truth. I never believe in anything that I can't see or touch, and in my study of human nature I have come to the definite conclusion that loneliness is the greatest problem of our day and age.'

And Dina, who had probably never felt lonely in the whole of her eighteen years, sighed deeply. 'Oh, how I do agree,' she said. Coming back with the tea I saw her staring straight ahead into

48

a positive vista of loneliness.

'Tell us all about your work,' she said, and so for two and a half hours he did just that.

Before he went, forgetting to take the milk, he left a list of books which he told Dina she must read. 'Every page of every book is quotable,' he said, and she nodded. I knew that in her imagination she was already browsing round the bookshops in the Charing Cross Road, and bringing home profound-looking volumes, and making intelligent little notes in their margins.

Paul didn't say much when she told him that she was dropping her Monday keep fit class to join a writers' circle. 'Mark thinks that it is more important to exercise the mind than the body,' she told us quite seriously.

We waited for her together, Paul and I, drinking coffee and smoking cigarettes that we had quite decided to give up. Paul talked about his work, not in the annoying, self-opinionated way that Mark had, but humorously, making light of his responsibilities.

I told him about some of the difficulties of dealing with temperamental writers, especially the ones who were quite sure that they were second Shakespeares, and I made him laugh, and in time he stopped glancing over his shoulder at the door and relaxed.

When at about eleven o'clock Dina came back, Mark was with her, and the two men shook hands warily, obviously hating each other on sight. Dina wore tight trews and a sloppy sweater hanging in folds round her slim hips, and she carried a blue notebook, already half full of earnest little jottings.

They sat down on the floor as befitted their bohemian status, and I made more coffee. I noticed Mark's hands as he held his cup. They were slender, with tapering fingers and oval well-manicured nails. Paul's were large, square-tipped, the sort of hands that would be warm over yours, the sort of hands to cling on to.

And there watching them I faced up to the truth.

I was in love with Paul, lost in love for ever. I had loved him from the very first moment, and I also faced up to another truth — as far as he was concerned, I didn't exist. The only girl who existed for him was Dina, and she was sitting, hands clasped round her knees, listening enchanted to every word that Mark said.

'You do understand about the badminton class on Wednesday, don't you, Paul?' she said after Mark had gone, leaving the scent of after-shave lotion, and an uneasy silence behind him. 'I've promised Mark that I'll do some typing for him.'

I knew that Dina's typing was strictly of the one-finger variety, with every other word rubbed out, but I was tactful and said nothing.

'Saturday then?' Paul said humbly, and my heart ached for him. Why, I wondered, are big men so much more vulnerable when they're hurt? I could hardly bear to see the disappointment in his eyes.

'Well, actually,' said Dina, managing to sound

like Charlotte Brontë and Jane Austen rolled into one, 'I'm going to devote my weekends to my own writing. Mark thinks that I have a promising literary style, and I have an idea for an historical novel, bringing in the Plague as a background, and perhaps the Great Fire.' And she swept into the bedroom with her blue notebook tucked underneath her arm and a ballpoint pen clicked at the ready.

I clattered the coffee cups together, not wanting to see Paul's face. 'Are *you* free on Saturday, Anne?' he asked tactlessly, and I shook my head.

'Sorry, Paul. Standing in a wet and windy field when I could be at home nice and cosy round the fire just isn't me. I'm not the sporty type, I'm afraid.'

He smiled and shrugged his shoulders, and I shut the door behind him, only just restraining the impulse to dash after him and tell him that I had changed my mind. That I would stand knee-deep in mud in the teeth of a howling gale just to be near him.

But a girl has her pride, and feeling acutely depressed I took myself and my stupid pride to bed.

I thought that would be the end of Paul, but he kept on dropping in, trying not to ask where Dina was, but bringing her name into the conversation, obviously gathering little crumbs of comfort by talking about her.

'I suppose she's out with that Lord Byron type?' he asked one evening as we sat together watching *Sportsview* on the veteran one-channel television set bequeathed to me by the last occupant of the flat.

'Oh, that's all over,' I told him, then not wanting to raise false hopes I went on quickly: 'She's friendly with Tony Blane at the moment.'

Paul grinned, rather bravely I thought. 'Tony Blane the doctor chap from across the square?'

'The very same. She met him last week when he came to minister to Mark's sinuses, and that was that.'

Paul leaned forward and concentrated on watching two heavyweight boxers battering the life out of each other, so feeling sorry for him I went into the kitchen and made him some coffee. When I came back he had switched the television off, and as I passed him his cup he stared straight into my eyes with a long and questioning look.

Feeling flustered I put an LP on the gramophone, a recording of the music from *Oliver!*

Too late I remembered that once they had missed a badminton match to see that show, and had come back at midnight hand in hand.

So cursing my stupidity I sat quietly, sipping my coffee and willing the record to come to an end.

But before it finished, Dina came in. She looked as beautiful as ever, serene, with a sort of dedicated air about her. Her long brown hair was parted in the middle and drawn back into a smooth chignon. Her dress was high at her throat, and edged with white, showing off its navy-blue stark simplicity. She carried her handbag carefully in front of her, and seemed to glide along.

For a moment I couldn't think who it was she reminded me of as she passed us palely by, smiling briefly before going into the bedroom.

Then I knew. Florence Nightingale!

She reappeared a moment later, and glanced at our cups of inky coffee.

'Too much of a stimulant at this time,' she told us severely. 'A milky drink is called for before retiring,' and she went into the kitchen, to return with a glass of repulsive-looking hot milk, a leathery white skin already forming on its surface.

'Tony says that I'd have made a perfect nurse. I seem to know about this sort of thing instinctively.'

We stared at her fascinated. Dina has that dramatic way of speaking, holding her listeners in her spell. She sipped heroically at the milk, obviously trying not to pull a face.

'Tony says he may take a post somewhere in Africa.'

'Darkest?' said Paul, and did I only imagine it, or were his lips really twitching?

'Oh, yes. The jungle,' nodded Dina. 'He says that running a practice in London is soul-destroying for the really dedicated medical man.' She gazed at us soulfully. 'What he would like to do is to set out somewhere, anywhere, meet up with a primitive tribe, and cure them of all their ailments . . . you know, leprosy and beriberi,' she added vaguely.

Paul closed his left eye in a wink and this

time I didn't imagine it.

Dina gave an exaggerated sigh. 'Of course he couldn't go alone. He would need a companion — a wife. Someone who wouldn't flinch at the most revolting sights, someone who was willing to dedicate her life to the relief of suffering.'

'Guess who?' mouthed Paul as she turned her back on us and drifted into the bedroom.

She waved an airy good night to us over a shoulder that managed to look brave and resolute at one and the same time. As she closed the door behind her Paul's composure left him.

He laughed silently, in great gasps, he laughed helplessly, as though he were coming apart at the seams, and soon I was laughing too, sitting there on the rug, with my handkerchief stuffed into my mouth, and my face pressed against his knee to smother the sound.

My face pressed against his knee . . . suddenly the laughter died in my throat, and I felt my cheeks grow hot. But before I had time to move away I felt his hand on my hair — his big hand, the hand I had longed to hold.

I held my breath, too startled to move, and now I knew that he had stopped laughing, and his touch grew more insistent, gently caressing the back of my neck, underneath my hair. Before my senses whirled, I thought, Dina! What of Dina?

Then my heart was still. Paul had been laughing *at* Dina, not *with* her, and that could only mean that he no longer loved her.

But then she floated in, wearing one of her

more flowing housecoats. Her hair had been loosened from its severe chignon, and hung like brown silk round her shoulders.

Quickly I moved away from Paul and stood up. He was staring at her as though mesmerized, and he seemed to have forgotten that I was there.

Smiling sweetly at us, she picked up a magazine from the coffee table. I vaguely noticed that it was some kind of nursing journal before she drifted back again into the bedroom.

Close to unexpected tears, I started to empty ashtrays and fuss with cushions, not daring to look at Paul again.

He stood up, and I felt my heart zoom to zero. Did he have to be quite so tall, quite so dark? Did he have to be everything I'd ever wanted in a man, everything I'd ever hoped for? And did he have to be in love with someone else?

'I'm tired,' I said flatly, and I might have been talking to a stranger. 'Will you excuse me, Paul? I have quite a day tomorrow; a budding author to take to lunch, a disappointed one to pacify . . . '

'Anne . . . ' he interrupted me, but I almost pushed him towards the door. I wanted no apologies, no explanations, for what after all had been nothing, just a fleeting caress.

'Anne . . . ' he said again, but I said a curt good night, and shut the door.

Dina was sitting up in bed reading a chapter on the effects of air pollution, but she put her book down, and stared at me with those expressive brown eyes.

'Well?' she asked.

'Well what?' I said childishly. 'Well nothing.'

'Did he propose?' she insisted.

Angrily I unzipped my dress, and sitting down at the dressing table, started to cream my face. 'Why on earth should he propose to me when he loves you?' I asked my reflection. 'Answer me that, will you?'

Dina threw down her book and stopped being Florence Nightingale.

'How dim can anyone get?' she demanded. 'Why do you think Paul has kept on coming to the flat? Why do you think I have stayed out late, leaving you to your cosy tête-à-tête? Why do you think I've made for the bedroom like a homing pigeon every time I've come back in the evening?'

'Well why?'

'Because he asked me to, that's why. Because he said you were so determined to keep him at arm's length, so unapproachable. Because he said that you were all he ever wanted in a girl — gentle, kind, unselfish, sweet. Oh, he became quite lyrical about you one day at Wembley Stadium.'

'He said all that?'

'And more besides,' said Dina. 'You just don't know the first thing about men, do you now?' and complacently she picked up her book again.

Hardly daring to breathe I began to wipe the cream from my face. If what Dina had said was true . . . if only it could be true . . .

'I expect he'll stop trying now,' she said, with

all the wisdom of her eighteen years throbbing in her hoarse little voice.

For a moment I stared at my shining clean face, then trembling a little I applied fresh lipstick and a dusting of powder. All thumbs I zipped myself into my dress again, then ran out of the flat, down the corridor, up one flight of stairs, along another corridor, to Paul's door.

He answered my knock, and stood there, just stood there, not saying a word. Then he walked into the room, and waited for me to speak. His tie was unknotted, and his coat was thrown over a chair, he looked discouraged, unhappy, and I had never loved him so much.

'Well?' he said, just as Dina had, and I took a deep breath and made myself remember her words.

'I didn't know,' I said. 'I didn't realize . . . ' and then the hated tears spilled over, and I was in his arms.

And, oh the relief! Knowing that he wanted me, knowing that his kiss was all I had dreamed it would be, and more, infinitely more.

And Dina, well, she didn't accompany Dr Blane to darkest Africa.

At our wedding she was a bridesmaid to outshine all bridesmaids; moving with studied grace down the aisle, and falling madly in love, right on cue, with the best man.

He happened, by the way, to be a Sanitary Inspector, but that's another story — a rather intriguing one.

Father's Day

This is the day that my wife, Ginny, who is definitely not the conference type, is going to one in London, and this is the day I am going to look after our three children all by myself. Claire is eight, Mandy six and Louise just three. You might be forgiven for thinking that I have coped alone before, but that is not the case.

'I've left a list,' my wife reminds me.

It is no good my saying that she looks guilty at abandoning her family, because she doesn't. She looks, in fact, radiant and I realize just what it must mean for her to get away from us for one whole day! Feeling magnanimous, I kiss her and tell her not to worry about a thing.

'I won't!' she assures me gaily, and leaves.

I go back into the kitchen and consult the list. *Item one:* it says. *Breakfast. Money for school dinners. And make sure Claire drinks her milk.*

So far so good. I pour myself a second cup of tea, open the morning newspaper and settle down to have a quiet read. There is a loud noise from upstairs, followed by a piercing scream. I dash to see what has happened. Mandy tells me Claire has pencilled a moustache on her poster of Donny Osmond.

'Only because she drew whiskers on my *horse*!' yells Claire in retaliation.

I look at the wall and, sure enough, there is

Champion sprouting a nautical beard.

'Get dressed and come downstairs,' I say firmly, and go in to Louise who is sitting up in bed stark naked.

'Wet,' she says smugly, holding out her nightdress.

I investigate and discover that she has chosen to have one of her infrequent 'accidents'.

There isn't time to bath her so I stuff her unceremoniously into her dressing gown.

As we pass the girls' room, they call out that they are waiting for me to do their hair.

'Surely you're big enough to do your own?' I say.

Claire, who I feel is getting into the patronizing-her-parents phase a trifle early, scornfully hands me the brush and two lengths of navy-blue ribbon.

I think I am doing very well until I see that Claire's usual expression of mild disdain has changed to one of startled amazement. Suddenly I realize that I have pulled the hair so tight that her eyebrows are almost touching her hairline!

I move on to Mandy who is busily telling her little sister that she smells.

'Bunches!' says my middle daughter.

I follow her instructions only to end up with her looking like a lady Viking with horns pointing in the wrong direction.

Down in the kitchen I inform the three of them, in tones which brook no argument, that burned toast is good for them. Claire sighs at me through a milk moustache and says she has a pain, but I send her off to school anyway.

Next on the list: *Take Louise to nursery school.*

I manhandle Louise into the bath. She sucks the flannel with evident enjoyment while I soap her lovely straight back, thinking lovely fatherly thoughts. Suddenly she flops over for a 'swim' and soaks the front of my trousers. Time is getting on, so I stuff her into dungarees and yellow sweater, and pack an apron, apple and beaker of orange juice into her satchel, then whisk her out to the car.

I leave her at the door of the nursery school, in the charge of a lady with infinite patience writ large upon her features, and try not to notice her staring at the wet patch on my trousers.

Back at the house I see that I am free until I pick Louise up again at twelve thirty, and decide to give my wife a nice surprise by doing the washing.

Feeling virtuous, I strip Louise's bed, gather a multitude of things from the linen basket and, for good measure, pick up the bath mat which seems stiff with talcum powder.

I bung the lot into the washer, set the dials to hot because any fool knows that things come cleaner in hot water, and start on the washing-up.

Then I run the vacuum cleaner over the sitting-room carpet, decide that the machine is making a funny noise and strip it down on the kitchen floor. When I put the lot back, there is a screw missing and, what is worse, it won't start up again. I leave it where it is and go to take the washing from the machine.

It occurs to me as I drag it into the plastic thingummy that the things that were white when I put them in are now a bright and blushing pink. The culprit seems to be the red cover off Mandy's dolls' cot.

'Now how did *you* get in there?' I ask it, wondering what the chaps at the office will think when I turn up in bright pink shirt with vest and underpants to match. The yellow bath mat has turned a sort of khaki shade, and Claire's white sweater would just about fit a doll who fancied itself in pink.

I find a big white bottle of bleach at the back of the cupboard underneath the sink and, putting the pinkest clothes into water, tip the bleach over them and leave them to soak.

I blow the dust off the mantelpiece, stuff a few assorted things behind sofa cushions, and view the room with pride. Then I notice the time, which startles me somewhat. I get out the car and go and fetch Louise from nursery school.

Too late I remember that I should have taken the fishfingers from the freezer. Reaching home again I get the fish out, rock hard and coated with a layer of snow, and place them hopefully under the grill.

'Mummy makes chips. Curly chips,' Louise tells me, standing by the table, head on one side.

I tell her that we are going to open a nice tin of baked beans instead, and she bursts into tears.

I feel I deserve an aperitif before lunch, so I go to pour myself one. When I come back, the fishfingers have turned black on one side. I am

61

turning them over when I look round and see that Louise has downed my sherry.

As I start to dish up, she gives a loud hiccough, puts her head down on her arms and winks at me through her fingers. She is obviously drunk.

If fine take Louise to the park, the next item on the list says. Leaving the dishes on the table, there not being room for them in the sink full of pink washing, I wipe the tomato sauce from her chin and button her into her anorak.

I am conscious of a dragging sensation in my legs, and an urge to lie on the pavement, but tell myself that the unaccustomed exercise is probably doing me good. We arrive at the swings and I sit down on a bench next to three pregnant women. They look at me as if I ought not to be there, then continue extolling the wisdom of one Doctor Spock as against one Doctor Jolly. Fearful of any more intimate revelations, I walk over to the slide just in time to catch Louise, who is coming down backwards on her stomach.

Honey sandwiches and bananas and yoghurt, the list tells me. *Then drop Mandy at Brownies and Claire at ballet class.*

I remove the tomato sauce from the kitchen table, replace it with a bottle of milk, and the two girls come in and tell me that they have had fish pie and horrible pink custard for lunch.

They eat half a sliced loaf between them and Louise drinks her yoghurt instead of spooning it up from its carton. I am sponging most of it from her hair when Claire comes downstairs

62

dressed like an embryo Margot Fonteyn in white practice tunic, holding out a piece of pink net to which she assures me her hair must go.

'Like a chignon,' she tells me.

I am doing my best when Mandy appears in her Brownie uniform, telling me in a light conversational tone that Louise is pushing her teddy bear down the lavatory. As I am racing upstairs, I tell myself that the Management/Workers' conference at work, tomorrow, is going to seem like a pleasant chat between friends who love each other dearly. I rescue Teddy from a watery grave, yank Louise out to the car, and yell to the other two to follow.

We have gone about half a mile when Claire passes on an urgent message from Louise.

'She'll have to wait!' I say over my shoulder, then glancing in the driving mirror see the familiar dreamy expression on Louise's round face and do a U-turn back to the house.

Bath Louise and take her in dressing gown to pick up M. and C., the list tells me.

Enough, however, is enough and I tell my youngest that, just for once, she is going to have a lick and a promise.

'I want Mummy,' she yells — loudly.

'You're not the only one,' I yell back.

The Brownie and the ballerina, flushed with triumph — the former because she has passed her skipping, and the latter because she has mastered a perfect *sauté* — sit at opposite ends of the bath performing their own ablutions. I tuck Louise up in her nice clean bed and read her a gruesome story about a little boy who somehow gets flattened and is rescued in the nick of time by his brother who pumps him up again. I am so tired I identify with the flattened one.

Three drinks of water and one trip to the lavatory later, I stagger downstairs to a kitchen which looks as if a typhoon has just ripped through it. I just about manage to make myself a bacon sandwich.

I eat in the sitting room, watching television, open a can of beer, then decide to put my head back and have a short nap before giving the place a tidy-up before Ginny comes back.

I congratulate myself that I have done well . . .

* * *

I wake up stiff, with cramp in my leg, to find that I have slept for two hours and that there is someone standing over me with an expression of disbelief on her lovely face.

'I came in the back way,' says my wife, 'through the *kitchen*.'

I get up to kiss her and collapse in agony on account of cramp in my leg.

From the expression in her eyes it seems a good idea to groan more than is strictly necessary and, love that she is, my wife kneels down in her conference suit and rubs my knotted calf until the agony begins to recede a little.

'I did it all,' I tell her with pride, 'ticking off as I went along. How did your day go?'

'First,' she says, 'we'll have a cup of tea.'

I sit back, with my eyes closed, and hear her making soothing wifely noises in the kitchen.

We go to bed early that night, and I tell her I don't mind wearing pink shorts, or even pink underpants and vests.

'Not even if they're *shredded*?' she asks me.

Her shoulders are heaving and for a startled moment I think that she is crying. Then, with relief, I see that it is laughter making her shake like that.

'The bleach?' I ask her, and she nods.

I pull her close to me and am kissing her tenderly when she winces and asks me why I haven't found the time to shave.

'A good question,' I say. And, not quite so tenderly, reach for her again.

Moment of Joy

Marty lay on her back, heavily uncomfortable, and stared at the high expanse of white ceiling.

A solitary tear escaped and ran down her cheek into the pillow, as Staff Nurse Jones, her thick arms marbled in red, swished away the screens.

'And what is there to cry about, I'd like someone to tell me?' she asked over a busy disappearing shoulder. 'Asleep you'll be in next to no time, and when you wake up, you'll have had your baby and never known a thing about it.'

She slid the last screen into position, and came and stood by Marty's bed, lowering her voice to what she obviously considered was a whisper. 'If ever I have any babies that would be the way I'd choose to have them. I can tell you that much for nothing . . . '

Marty closed her eyes and willed Staff Nurse Jones to go away. She heard a loud sniff, then the slap of her feet on the bare linoleum as she walked down the ward.

What did Staff Nurse Jones know about having babies? she thought fiercely. Delivering babies wasn't the same as having them. Delivering babies hadn't told her anything about the first butterfly flick of movement underneath the heart, the feeling of fulfilment, the looking forward, the counting the days.

Marty raised herself awkwardly on to her elbow and groped for a tissue in the large box on her locker, and the lady in the next bed, a proud but rather surprised mother of forty-six, leaned across and spoke to her in her loud, cheerful voice.

'Try not to cry, dearie. A lot of the 'best' people have their babies by Caesarean operation — film stars and royalty — and the scar will hardly show. You'll be able to wear your bikini again. It's surprising what they can do nowadays. Nine and a half pounds my baby weighed, and I can vouch for every ounce. You're saving yourself a lot of trouble, you mark my words . . . '

Complacently she untied then retied the pink satin bow on the front of her quilted nylon bed jacket, and Marty smiled politely at her, then turned away.

Nobody understood how she felt. Not one single person. Not even David . . .

That day, three weeks ago, coming home from the antenatal clinic, she had willed the bus to go faster, anticipating the moment when she could let herself into the flat, and abandon herself to tears.

Then later, sobbing out her disappointment in David's arms, she had felt the familiar caress of his hand underneath the soft weight of her hair.

She had listened to his soothing, loving words. 'They know best, Marty. And what does it matter, anyway? In a way it's a kind of relief to me . . . '

She'd tried to move away, but he'd held her closer.

'I might as well tell you now, love. I was scared stiff in case we didn't get to the hospital in time when the baby started, and scared stiff in case you were on your own and frightened . . . '

Marty glared up at him with red-rimmed eyes.

'I wouldn't have been frightened. I knew exactly what to do.' A left-over sob crept up and threatened to choke her. 'All those classes, exercises.' She dared him to laugh at her. 'I could relax every single part of me quicker than anyone else . . . '

She sniffed, and David groped in his pocket and passed her his handkerchief. It was far from clean, and smelled of tobacco and gear-oil.

'And you'll expect me to get this clean,' said Marty. David laughed and ruffled her hair, and after they'd eaten and put the dishes away in the cupboard they called a kitchen, they'd sat and talked.

It was something they'd always been able to do, and Marty knew how lucky they were. So many of her friends, marrying as they had almost straight from school, had soon found out that once the wedding was over and the novelty of escaping from their parents' vigilance had worn off, they had, almost literally, nothing at all to say to each other.

But with them it was different — so now Marty tried to explain, leaning forward in her eagerness, so that her long straight hair fell forward like a curtain, almost hiding her face.

'I just wanted to be *there* when my baby is born,' she said at last. 'Do you understand? To experience the very moment when it is born. To hear its first cry . . . You know?' she said again, pleading with him to understand.

David's eyes grew cloudy with not understanding, but he nodded, his thin face serious and intent.

Marty bit her lip and tried again.

'Say you built a car, right from scratch, from nothing. You watched it grow, you felt it throb underneath your hands when you ran the engine. Then, at the last minute, when it was finished, you had to hand it over to someone else to make the first run . . . '

'It wouldn't matter so long as they brought it back safe and sound,' David said, obviously weighing every word. 'It would still be mine, wouldn't it? I'd have made it . . . '

He had come across to her then, kneeling on the rug by her side, removing her fur-trimmed bedroom slipper, and tickling the high arch of her instep.

'I feel *cheated*,' she said, jerking her foot away from him, and holding out against laughter until the very last minute.

It was impossible to make David understand, she had realized that, and so she'd simply stopped trying to.

Now the preoperative injection was beginning to take effect, and she opened her eyes and stared at the ceiling again, then blinked as it dipped and swung crazily towards her.

Staff Nurse Jones padded heavily towards her

69

bed, and raising lead-weighted eyelids, Marty stared up at her.

'Could you tell me the time, please?' she asked childishly, to prove that she wasn't asleep, and had no intention of going to sleep.

Staff Nurse Jones consulted the fob-watch pinned to the front of her one-piece bosom, and told her the time, but her voice sounded woolly and far away.

'Thank you very much,' said Marty with dignity, and crossed her hands on her chest.

Staff Nurse Jones put her face close to Marty's. 'Your husband's just been on the telephone, although we told him not to ring for another two hours. He sends you his love.'

Marty tried to thank her again, but something had happened to her mouth. It didn't seem capable of stretching itself round the words . . .

She wondered if David would have remembered to put the casserole she'd prepared for his supper in the oven. She wondered if he'd remember where she'd put the money for the milkman.

She could feel his love for her, warm and real. Almost she could tuck it round her, like a blanket.

'David,' she whispered, and smiled, and didn't feel a thing when Staff Nurse Jones tucked her in.

At first she thought that she had only closed her eyes for a minute, then she saw that the ward lights were dimmed, and a nurse with red hair and a dusting of freckles on her nose was sitting by her bed, smiling at her.

'Well!' she said. 'And are you properly awake

this time? You've got a beautiful little girl, and your husband's been and gone away again. I expect you'd like to see your baby, wouldn't you?'

Marty nodded, feeling nothing except a terrible thirst. Feeling nothing, exactly as she had known it would be . . .

She watched the nurse walk quickly down the ward in a crackle of starched apron and disappear through the swing doors. The lady in the pink bed jacket snored gently in her sleep, and out in the ward kitchen someone dropped a cup.

The nurse was a long time in coming back, and Marty felt mild irritation, that was all.

Even when she heard the footsteps coming down the long corridor, her heartbeats didn't quicken at all. But the baby was quite beautiful, there was no doubt about that. Her head was perfectly formed and round, with a dark Friar Tuck fringe of hair.

The baby belonging to the lady in the next bed had a decidedly pointed head and ears that stuck out, and Marty spared a minute to feel vaguely sorry for her. Gently, with an exploring finger, she touched the baby's petal-soft pale, pale skin.

Bending her head she kissed with careful tenderness the blue-veined eyelids, and traced the outline of the pink pucker of a little mouth.

'She looks so peaceful,' she said wonderingly.

'That's because she hasn't had to struggle to be born,' the nurse said, smiling.

'Has my husband seen her?' Marty asked, and the nurse shook her head.

'He was quite firm about that. He said that you must see her first, and he wouldn't change his mind, even though her cot is right by the door. And now you must sleep again,' she said firmly.

But Marty didn't hear her . . .

'Oh, David,' she breathed softly. 'So you did understand after all . . . '

And then and there, as she stared down at the baby's sleeping face, suddenly, blindingly, in all its splendour, came her moment of joy.

The Gift of Love

David, Isobel's godfather, one of nature's born bachelors, made a beautiful speech at the party given to celebrate her silver wedding anniversary. Just as she always knew he would. '*Twenty-five years,*' he was saying, '*linked together with silver chains of devotion.*'

Behind her paper serviette, bordered with silver bells, she hid a smile. Underneath the table she trod gently on her husband's foot. Sam had drunk too freely of the predinner sherry and the table wine; by his flushed cheeks and the heavy drooping of his eyelids, she suspected that he could be on the point of dropping off to sleep. And when Sam slept after he'd been drinking, he always snored.

Isobel felt that a snore, even of the gentle variety, would not add in any way to the dignity of David's carefully prepared speech. '*Honour thy father and thy mother, and that is what you do this day,*' said David, and Isobel concealed another smile as she saw that tears swam in the pale blue eyes of her daughter, Jean.

Jean's dull, successful young husband sat by her side, and her baby was asleep in a carrying cot in one of the upstairs bedrooms — her first grandchild . . .

David was coming to that, exactly as Isobel had known he would.

'*Four generations, gathered together under*

73

one roof,' he said, his prominent Adam's apple working convulsively as he paused, and beamed over his spectacles at Isobel's mother-in-law, resplendent in a lurex-threaded cocktail dress, her grey hair tinted, her nails a gentle coral.

'*This happy octopus — our family*.'

Isobel felt that was definitely overdoing it. Two of the aunts had not spoken for years, and she and her mother-in-law had never seen eye to eye. Yet now Mother-in-law was touching her eyes with a lace-edged handkerchief, as if she agreed with David's speech.

Across the table, Bill, Isobel's twenty-two-year-old son, closed one eye in a deliberate wink, and Isobel fluttered her own left eyelid up and down to signify that she understood and was equally amused.

How different they were, Jean and Bill. So different in temperament that it was impossible to believe that they were brother and sister, brought up in the same house, and attending the same local grammar school together.

Bill, she knew with a slight pang of guilt, was the child of her heart. When he was hurt, then she was hurt also. When he failed an exam, or when one of his girlfriends jilted him, then she suffered with him. She glanced with distaste at the sophisticated young girl sitting on his right, and tried with all her heart to like her.

In Isobel's opinion, an opinion she kept to herself, Dee, short for Delysia, was not Bill's type at all.

As the speech flowed on, she went off into a daydream about the type of girl she would have chosen if she had had any say in the matter.

A homely kind of girl. Pretty, of course, but well endowed with all the domestic virtues. An imaginative cook, clever with her needle, thrifty — Bill's salary as a primary school teacher made that virtue a necessity — with a bubbling sense of humour to match her husband's; warm, thoughtful, fond of animals, a born mother, a gracious hostess, intelligent, an avid reader with an aptitude for discussing what she had read afterwards, gentle, soft-voiced, and above all, kind. Kindness being the quality that mattered to Isobel more than any other.

Narrowing her eyes, she took another long, cool, appraising look at what she feared was to be her future daughter-in-law. Despairingly she shook her head. It was no good. She couldn't find one single required feature of her dream daughter-in-law, and that was that.

Dee was young of course, barely nineteen. Sam thought she was all right. He'd said so often, pretending to smack his lips, and telling Isobel she was behaving like a fussy mother hen. But all the same . . .

David was glancing at the neat headings on the postcard in his hand, and she made herself pay attention.

'*This happy association began during the war, when as one of the gallant 'Few', our bridegroom played a valiant part.*'

By her side Sam shuffled on his chair, trying to hide an agony of embarrassment. Any reference to his wartime exploits made him squirm.

He had been called up right at the beginning,

and after one frustrating year of 'sitting on his backside', as he'd put it, on an aerodrome 'somewhere in England', he'd volunteered for air-crew, and sailed to Canada, squashed like a sardine in the heavily camouflaged *Queen Mary*, to do his flying training.

They'd married before he went, and when he returned with wings on his blue uniform and a Pilot Officer's stripe on his sleeve Isobel's pride in him knew no bounds.

On the sideboard, directly in her line of vision, was their wedding photograph, resurrected from the oak chest on the landing by a sentimental Jean, and placed with much giggling beside the silver-wedding cake.

How serious they looked. Isobel in her white dress, bought with clothing coupons begged or borrowed from her friends, a flowing white veil covering her shoulder-length, too curly hair, and Sam, tall and straight by her side, very handsome in his uniform, gazing with fixed intensity at the camera.

He'd got a bad cold that day, and his eyes looked watery even on the glossy photograph. Isobel smiled as she remembered the way they'd laughed when they found the bottle of gargle mixture his mother had placed in his suitcase.

'*Returning as a conquering hero to make a home in this very house with his wife,*' said David, and Isobel bit her lip, and crumpled the paper serviette in her lap into a tight ball.

After six long years, when Sam finally was demobbed and came back to her wearing his awful brown demob suit, it was certainly not as a conquering hero . . .

Three tours of operations over Germany had taken their toll on his nerves, and she would never forget the nightmares, and the shouting horror in his voice when, half-asleep and half-awake, he relived the agony of the anti-aircraft guns, the twisting searchlights, and the burning cities far below the plane.

Those were the years that Isobel privately called the testing time.

In every marriage, she believed, there came such a testing time, when love could be sorely tried, so that it either broke under the strain, or endured for ever.

'*Twenty-five years of loving and giving,*' said David, and Sam reached out and gave her a reassuring pat.

To get his degree and continue his interrupted studies, Sam had gone back to college, and to supplement their income and be able to stay at home and look after their babies, Isobel had put a card in the local newsagent's window, and done what she described as 'plain sewing'.

Those were the years when the cheap carpet in the living room seemed to be perpetually strewn with pins, the picture rail permanently hung with other people's dresses; when she seamed and tucked, basted and hemmed, sometimes far into the night, to finish an order, working in the kitchen so that the whirring of the old-fashioned second-hand sewing machine wouldn't disturb Sam.

'*Working together through difficult times,*'

77

said David, and Sam chuckled so softly that only she heard.

In those years, the years following the war, Isobel had thought that she would never hear him laugh again. She played thoughtfully with her silver earring (a silver wedding present from Sam) as she recalled the times when his temper, for no apparent reason, would suddenly explode; when his language would terrify her, when the crying of the children stretched his nerves to screaming point, and when on 5 November, even the letting off of a few harmless fireworks in the back garden could set him trembling with fear.

'That's enough, David,' she told her godfather silently, but he was really getting into his stride by now. His voice came hushed for the next few words, and everyone stared down in fixed concentration at the starched white tablecloth.

'*There are, as we all know, a few empty chairs round this table, speaking metaphorically, of course*,' he was saying, and Isobel bent her head.

She knew that, with his usual complete lack of tact, David was referring to her parents, killed in a train crash in France on their first holiday abroad; to her father-in-law, that quiet, inoffensive little man, beloved by everyone who knew him, dying as unobtrusively as he had lived. She saw, without surprise, that her mother-in-law was making good use of the lace-edged handkerchief again, and wished that she had been able to comfort her.

'How *could* you, David?' she asked him

silently, and the familiar ache of grief whenever she was reminded of Jonathan, their third child, swamped her once more, almost overwhelming in its intensity.

Jonathan would have been eighteen now. In his last year at school, perhaps going on to university.

He had been a beautiful baby, as dark as the other two were fair. He had been an unplanned baby, born when they could ill afford to have him, but he was a delightful little boy, talking at three with a precocity that endeared him to everyone.

Right from the beginning Isobel's mother-in-law had told her that he would be 'difficult to rear'. He was a delicate child, given to inexplicable bouts of sickness, when for days on end he would lie in his cot, burning with fever, his mouth parched and dry. Then only his mother could comfort him.

She would miss nights of sleep to sit by his side and cool his aching forehead with cloths wrung out in vinegar and water. She would listen to his fevered ramblings, and talk softly to him, until the first beads of sweat on his short upper lip told her all she needed to know — that the next day he would be better again.

Would it have made any difference that last time if they had called the doctor earlier? But then how many times had they sent for him, only to find that by the time he arrived, the energetic little boy was sitting up against his pillows laughing at him?

Would it have made any difference if they had

taken him to hospital any earlier? Would they have been able to save him? Would they?

The questions, Isobel knew, would torment her for the rest of her days. She swallowed to hide a rush of tears, and tried to pick up the threads of the speech again.

David had stopped sentimentalizing, and was smiling again, stroking his moustache and swaying gently on his heels.

'Why can't he sit down?' Sam's eyebrows asked her, and she sighed an exaggerated sigh to show that she agreed. Then immediately felt rather ashamed of herself.

He beamed on them all with genuine affection, and Isobel thought he was going to finish at last, but he was enjoying himself far too much. A red flag of excitement burned on each cobblestone cheek.

'*Our own Darby and Joan,*' he said, and Sam nudged her softly, and when she turned and met his eyes, gave her an audacious wink.

In the last few years, secure in his job, freed at last from too-pressing money worries, Sam looked more like the young man in the wedding photograph than he had looked when he came back from the war.

When Jean had announced triumphantly that she was going to have a baby, Sam had teased her unmercifully. 'I don't mind in the least being a grandfather,' he'd said, his blue eyes twinkling at her. 'What I *do* object to is being married to a grandmother!'

Isobel smiled. The tag of Darby and Joan wouldn't impress Sam at all. In his new dark grey suit — all his suits were dark grey, she grumbled when he'd brought it home — he looked much younger than fifty-one.

As they'd dressed for the party together in the big front bedroom, he'd come over to her, and with his arms round her shoulders grinned at her through the dressing-table mirror.

'You've got a smashing figure for your age, Grannie,' he said, and she laughed and pushed him away.

'Too big a bottom,' she said, and he gave the offending part of her anatomy a resounding slap.

'I like my women to have plenty of meat on their bones,' he said, and then turned her round and kissed her, in a far from middle-aged way, and she chided him half-heartedly for disturbing her lipstick and the new and flattering bouffant hair-do.

But their relationship hadn't always been on such a carefree basis, and David's next words echoed her thoughts . . . '*A shining example to us all, in these days of easy virtue, of the holy sanctity of marriage.*'

Isobel dropped her eyes, and felt her cheeks grow hot.

Hugh, oh my darling Hugh. This is no time to be reminded of you. It's all wrong that I should be reminded of you today.

She could see him as clearly as if he'd stood before her. Tall, taller than Sam. Painfully thin, with his dark hair brushed straight back, and his long, sensitive mouth that seemed always to be smiling, even when he was unhappy. His eyes, mirroring his every thought, dark grey with little flecks of green in them, and the way he would smile at her, a smile of such tenderness and sweetness that it seemed at the time that she would die of love for him.

His halting declaration of love had come at a time when, worried by her husband's black moods and uncontrollable temper, and worried almost out of her mind by Jonathan's repeated illnesses, she had willingly surrendered to the arms that offered her solace and consolation.

But that was all it had been. A few kisses, a week or more of anguished tears, then no more.

Infidelity, even so short a time ago, for a woman of her temperament and upbringing was unthinkable. For a man to be unfaithful, well, that was for his wife to tolerate, if not exactly condone. But in her well-taught code of ethics a woman was expected to remain faithful in the face of overwhelming odds.

Isobel twisted her wedding ring round and round.

There had been one perfect day, and she had never wanted to forget it — nor even tried to. There had been blue skies, sunshine sparkling on the still waters of a lake and a warm, gentle breeze.

She had worn a flowered 'New Look' dress, belted tightly round her slim waist with a white belt, cheap pretty shoes with an ankle strap, and huge daisy-shaped earrings accentuating the darkness of her hair.

Hugh had pleaded with her to leave Sam

for good, and take the children and go away somewhere with him.

That was the day she had flung herself out of the house after one of Sam's shouting, terrifying scenes, and Hugh had kissed away her tears, murmuring broken words of love.

There had been soft grasses, and the hot sunshine, and the feel of Hugh's mouth on her own, the young strength of his arms, and the pleading, aching tenderness of his voice.

'*Living together in devoted harmony*,' said David dramatically, and she took a gulp of champagne.

Where were the children that day? she wondered. And how, dear God, had she found the willpower to send Hugh away for ever?

Was it because of Hugh that two years afterwards she had tried to understand about Claire?

Oh, yes. That had been their real testing time. Claire, the vivacious estranged wife of one of Sam's business colleagues, had, right from the start, flirted with Sam, making it obvious that she found him attractive.

Isobel could see her now, with her copper-coloured hair, worn short and curly, with a Claudette Colbert fringe, smiling at Sam, sitting on the arm of his chair, teasing him, flattering him, boosting his deflated ego, at a time when, even after he had attained his degree, he was finding the managerial jobs were not to be his for the asking.

'If I'd sat out the war on my backside in some industrial firm, I'd have been okay now,' he said bitterly. 'The fact that I was six years away from my studies, and six years out of the promotion racket, actually goes against me. A land fit for heroes to live in! Don't make me laugh. What do they care whether I have a bloody DFC tucked away in the top drawer? What do they care about who won the bloody war for them? Answer me that.'

But she hadn't tried to answer him. Still nursing her grief about Jonathan, still weaving daydreams about Hugh, and about what might have been, she had failed to see that they were becoming strangers to each other.

Nowadays the Marriage Guidance Counsellors would call it 'lack of communication', but how was it possible to communicate with someone with a chip on his shoulder? No, not a chip, a whole forest of trees.

Claire, with her easy laugh, her open admiration of Sam, had found him easy prey. As was usual in such cases, Isobel had been the last to hear about it. When she taxed him, Sam had made no attempt to deny it. It was, he said, quite possible to love two women at once and the same time, but for the sake of the children and what they had been to each other, he would stay with her.

That was the time when Isobel would lie in bed, waiting for him to come home, pretending sleep, lying there on her side of the big double bed, knowing that he had come straight from Claire, and praying that he wouldn't try to touch her. That was the time she had taken their wedding photograph down from the mantelpiece, and pushed it away deep down in the chest on the landing.

One day, when she felt she could live with the situation no longer, she had decided to leave Sam. She had got as far as getting the cases down from the fitted cupboards over the wardrobes and started to pack the children's things.

But then the common sense, inherited from her Yorkshire parents, the common sense that had helped her to send Hugh away, had come to her rescue just in time.

If she left Sam, where would she go? How long could she hope to manage on what she earned from her sewing? Claire was just a passing phase, she knew that when she thought about it dispassionately; and what would happen to Sam if she left him to fend for himself?

Love and marriage, she was discovering, weren't things to be shrugged aside as easily as that. And she loved Sam, and always had. She knew that now.

'*And in conclusion*,' said David, and Isobel saw Dee raise her pencilled-in eyebrows ceilingwards in open relief.

'*Before we drink a loving toast*,' said David, and Jean smiled at her mother and glanced in comic dismay at her empty glass.

'*May we wish them years of happiness ahead, surrounded by their loving family and friends, and moving into the autumn of their lives — together.*'

And well satisfied with himself, David sat down, wiping his brow with a huge handkerchief, waiting for the generous applause he obviously felt was his due.

Then they were all standing up, raising their glasses, and David was putting his notes away in his pocket.

'*To Mother and Dad. Isobel and Sam*,' they said.

Smiling, Isobel acknowledged the toast. Smiling, she moved over to the sideboard, and cut the iced cake with its silver bells and white fluted roses, feeling Sam's hand firm on her own.

It was as they were getting ready for bed, later, much later, when she was so tired that even the effort of raising her arms to slip her nightdress over her head was almost too much for her, that Sam spoke.

'Old David fairly enjoyed his speech-making,' he said.

Isobel decided she was too tired to bother about her nightly coat of hormone cream, 'I'm glad we asked him all the same,' she said.

She was always in bed first. Sam had a special routine that had never varied from the first night of their honeymoon twenty-five years ago.

First he would take a clean handkerchief from his drawer, fold it carefully and place it in the top pocket of his pyjama jacket. Then he would go over to the mirror and comb his dark hair, finishing off the ritual by placing one cough lozenge at the ready on his bedside table. Sam smoked too much, and always had.

Isobel lay and watched him. Once it had irritated her, but now she found the familiar, rather ridiculous pantomime vaguely soothing.

He climbed in beside her, and leaned over her, smiling. 'Reading tonight, love?' he asked, and she shook her head.

'Too tired,' and she watched as she always did while he stretched up and switched off the overhead light.

'Really too tired?' he whispered, taking her into his arms. For the first time that day, she relaxed.

'Not as tired as all that,' she said, just as she knew he wanted her to say . . .

Then at last, when she thought he was asleep, Sam spoke again. 'About David's awful speech. He didn't know what he was talking about, did he? I'm afraid it wasn't quite like that, was it, love?'

Isobel burrowed her head deep into his shoulder. She knew exactly what he meant, but she chose her words with care.

'Not quite. But then, if people are really honest, do you think it ever is?' Then she sighed. 'We came through it all right, that's all that matters in the long run.'

'Glad?' he whispered.

'Very, very glad,' she said.

Sam's voice was blurred at the edges with sleep, but he persisted. 'No regrets. Not a single one?'

'Not a single one,' she answered. They solemnly kissed good night before he turned over and she fitted herself spoon-shaped into the familiar warmth of his broad back.

As usual, Sam slept straight away, and again, as she always did, she lay awake, listening to the soft sound of his breathing, and the house they had lived in all their married life settling down around them.

She went over in her mind the busy, happy, hectic day, smiling at the remembrance of David and his pompous, rather silly speech; trying to recall if she had really put the remnants of the cake away in the tin; listening for sounds of the baby still asleep in the spare room; reminding herself to send a piece of cake to a distant cousin who she feared would take umbrage at not having been invited to the party; worrying a little about Bill and the girl she knew he was destined to marry . . .

A breeze had sprung up from nowhere, and the long blue curtains billowed out into the room. Carefully, so as not to disturb Sam, she slipped out of bed and closed the window.

Outside in the avenue, the houses slept, and a pale moon, a *silver* moon, she thought romantically, bathed the gardens in mysterious light.

Thoughts in her overtired brain were still going round and round, like a moth caught in a light fitting. Figures from the past seemed to hover in front of her, hanging motionless like ectoplasm, then darting away.

For a long moment Hugh was there, tall and painfully thin, smiling at her in the way she would never forget. Then Claire was there, still wearing her hair in the curly fringe, laughing and teasing Sam, and before she disappeared into the shadows Isobel silently wished her well and hoped sincerely that somewhere she, too, had found contentment.

This Time Must Be
For Ever . . .

One of my biggest faults is that I fall in love too easily, and this time he wasn't even my kind of man. This one was the square-shouldered, tweed-jacketed, uninhibited type, with a healthy glow in his cheeks and a tang of the open air about him. I knew this instinctively, even though he was soberly attired in his well-fitting dinner jacket.

He studied the menu, printed as usual on thick white cardboard in discreet black letters. Then he turned to me and spoke the immortal words: 'Do you come here often?'

Here was the Annual Dinner held at one of Brighton's lushest hotels by our Veteran Car Club.

'I come every year,' I told him, 'with my father.' I inclined my head to my left.

He peered round my back at my father's pinkly bald head engaged in animated conversation with a handlebar moustache.

'Ah,' he said.

The 'Ah', I felt, could have conveyed many things. It could have conveyed the fact that he liked the look of my father, or it could have meant that he was thinking, What is a lovely girl like you doing wasting a weekend in Brighton with your father?

He went back to reading the menu, and I studied the rugged contours of his profile, and the endearing way his black hair went into a point in the nape of his neck.

'What have you got?' he asked.

I knew immediately what he meant. 'A Lanchester,' I told him.

'Utilizing an epicyclic gearbox, controlled by a preselector mechanism?'

I confirmed this. 'And you?'

'An Oldsmobile, roughly nineteen hundred and four.'

I knew my veteran cars. 'A Curved Dash Runabout?'

Admiration sparkled in his eyes. Deep blue eyes they were, the colour of rain-washed bluebells in spring.

'Super,' he said.

The *truite fumée au citron* was served, and he raised a succulent forkful to his mouth, but for me, and I hope for him too, it could have been battered cod served in yesterday's newspaper.

'Round about what time did you breast Brixton Hill?'

'Roughly half past eight,' I told him.

'Me too,' he said, and I marvelled at the fact that we might have been chugging along almost side by side.

All through the superlatively cooked fish course we talked about the time, money and love lavished on our respective horseless carriages, and during the *médaillon de veau cordon bleu*, we went over the course inch by inch.

Then with the *melon en surprise* he told me that his name was Geoffrey, and I told him mine was Harriet.

'A good, unusual, old-fashioned name,' he said.

Then an over-spangled lady on his right claimed him, and was obviously loath to let him go, and before we spoke again the Loyal Toast was being proposed and it was all over.

It couldn't be all over, I told myself. I couldn't face the usual after-dinner get-together in the lounge with my father and his buddies, each and every one of them retravelling the Brighton Road yard by uneventful yard.

I'd been doing it for three years now, ever since my twenty-first birthday in fact, the year that my mother craftily decided that her sinews couldn't stand up to the strain of being co-driver for another single year.

'It's been nice meeting you, Geoffrey,' I said brazenly.

'I have to change,' he said. 'I'm taking her back tonight; I always do.'

'We always stay the night,' I said.

And so we stood there, not saying anything, and I swear I felt a shiver run down my spine. It was one of those moments when time ceases to exist, when there should have been violins soaring away in the background. No, not violins, a full symphony orchestra swelling into glorious sound.

'I'll ring if I may,' he said at last. 'Where do you live?'

'Clapham. Near the Common.' Then I told

92

him my telephone number and he wrote it down on a menu card.

'Coming, Harriet?' my father said, and all unsuspecting led me away.

Gathered round a little table in the lounge we talked until one, with a De Dion Bouton, nineteen hundred and two, a Humberette, nineteen hundred and four, and a Cadillac of the same year.

In my little gold dress I sat there, sipping my gin and tonic, and thinking about Geoffrey in his Oldsmobile with its Curved Dash, jogging along the winding road back to London.

Would Geoffrey phone? I wondered. And if he did, would the magic still be there? I sighed. This was how it always began with me. Three times I'd fallen in love, and where had it got me? Nowhere. Nowhere at all.

He phoned the very next evening — a Monday it happened to be — and at the sound of his voice the orchestra swelled, and underneath my hand-knitted sweater my heart did its familiar little dance. Its too familiar little dance, I told it sternly.

'Have a good run back?' he asked.

'Yes, and you?' I said, all the gay remarks I'd planned gone from my mind.

'Very good. Smooth as silk. How about a theatre and dinner on Thursday?'

'Marvellous,' I wittily said.

'Pick you up around seven?'

'Fine, Geoffrey,' I managed, hoping it was true that my voice on the phone is supposed to sound like Raquel Welch's. It needed something

93

to make up for my complete lack of repartee.

'I can't wait to see you again,' he said.

'Me too,' I said, being sure that it should have been 'me neither'. Then I went back upstairs to my flat.

I have my own tiny flat on the top floor of my parents' house. I find that the perfect compromise between living with them and existing in a bedsit in town.

I'd tried that for three years, during which I'd fallen in and out of love as easily as a child falls off a swing. First there was Peter, then there was Mark, and latterly there had been James . . . James was solid, dependable, and the answer to my mother's prayers for me, but he'd bored me stiff after six months' engagement. And for each of them, at the beginning, the violins had soared.

Now it was happening all over again, and I couldn't bear it, not this time. Geoffrey was special. He had to be.

For our date I wore the cream corded silk dress and coat I'd bought for a song at work because a customer had smeared orange lipstick round the neck. She was an American, and American lipsticks must be made of sterner stuff than ours, because it had taken me a whole week to get it off.

I have my hair done twice a week as part of my job as Buyer of Evening Gowns in a big store, and I persuaded Henri to streak in subtle highlights of gold.

I took half an hour to do my face, brushing in interesting hollows in my cheeks, and when I

94

was ready I stared at myself in the mirror and knew that I was looking as elegant as anyone who is only five feet one can.

I realized why Geoffrey had been able to get seats at such short notice, because the play was in its last two dying weeks, and it showed. Almost a quarter of the seats were empty. But Geoffrey held my hand, and later, sitting opposite me at a small table tucked away in a discreet corner of an Italian restaurant, told me that when the lights shone on my hair he could swear that it was flecked with gold.

'You could?' I said, like the hypocrite I am, and he nodded seriously.

'Like little gilded feathers,' he said, and reached across the tablecloth for my hand.

He told me that he was a Chartered Automobile Engineer with British Rail, and I thought what a lovely thing that must be to be, and told him so. I told him about my job, and he said that accounted for my wonderful taste in clothes.

'That dress is beautiful,' he said, and mentally I blessed the American lady and her orange lipstick.

Everything was perfect. He made me laugh and I made him laugh, and when he stopped his car outside my house, I knew that he was going to kiss me.

And what was meant I'm sure to be an ordinary run-of-the-mill good night kiss turned out to be a soul-shattering breathless happening, and I let myself into the house and went straight upstairs to my room bathed in the rosiest of glows.

What with the wine and the kiss and everything I went off to sleep at once, but woke up around five o'clock out of a dream in which I was floating down an aisle towards Geoffrey, ethereal in a white lace gown patterned with markings of tangerine lipstick. This was it, I told myself. And then honesty prevailed . . .

This was the fourth time I had woken up feeling just like this, and how soon afterwards had the rot set in? Perhaps I was one of nature's butterflies, destined to wing my way from man to man, and never to know the security of a relationship that endured for ever and ever amen.

I began to feel less and less like a butterfly as the days passed and I heard nothing more from Geoffrey. Often I'd had a foreboding that one day I would meet a gorgeous man who would turn out to be capricious, too.

But, oh, please, don't let it be Geoffrey, I prayed as I hailed a taxi to a fashion show, and tried to look as though the yo-yoing length of the hemline mattered more to me than anything else.

Then one night as I lay moping on my bed listening to Debussy on the radio, the telephone rang downstairs in the hall. It was Geoffrey.

'Hello, Harriet,' he said.

'Hello, Geoffrey,' I said back.

'A friend of mine has this house on the Downs, and I'd like to take you down for the weekend. Near Rottingdean,' he said.

'I love Rottingdean,' I shamelessly said, 'and this Saturday is my Saturday off; I have one off in three.'

'Splendid, so I'll pick you up at nine.'

'Marvellous,' I said, as the orchestra swelled into glorious sound.

I started straight away planning my wardrobe. What did one wear for a weekend in Rottingdean? Then it occurred to me that Geoffrey hadn't mentioned whether or not his friend would be there. Was he planning an illicit weekend, and would my prompt acceptance make him think that I was that kind of girl? Then I thought of Geoffrey and his clear blue gaze, and his Oldsmobile that he cherished like a loved and only child, and I went on with my packing.

Saturday was a day of shifting clouds and sunshine slanting through budding trees. I was ashamed of my ignoble thoughts when Geoffrey's friend turned out to be an accountant who had been married for ten years to a pretty woman called Caroline, with a husky laugh and a sense of humour exactly akin to my own.

'We adore Geoffrey,' she told me as we shared a mirror in the chintzy front bedroom that same evening. 'But he needs a wife. Living alone and fending for himself is no life for a man like Geoffrey.'

Quite shamelessly I fished. 'I suppose he's had lots of girlfriends?'

Caroline was concentrating on outlining her left eye. 'Hundreds. You're about the fifth he's brought down here.'

I went downstairs in a thoughtful mood.

Then in the garden, in the darkness, he took me in his arms. 'I'm thinking that I love you, Harriet,' he said.

I nearly said, 'I love you, too,' then I remembered that with Peter, Mark and James it had been a case of confessed and mutual love on roughly our second dates. So I compromised by giving a noncommittal sigh.

Then as he kissed me again, or at least *after* he had kissed me again — there was no room for coherent thought when his lips were on mine — I remembered the hordes of girls Caroline had told me about in the chintzy bedroom upstairs.

Had he confessed his love with such premature and indecent haste to the five he'd brought to the cottage? Perhaps here on this very spot?

Maybe Geoffrey and I were destined to be *two* of life's butterflies, only lingering long enough on our frivolous ways to take tentative sips of life's honey.

I knew I was mixing the butterflies with the bees, but it didn't matter. 'This is fun,' I said, and wound my arms more tightly round his neck.

He stiffened. 'I wasn't talking in terms of fun, Harriet,' he said, every syllable chock-a-block with rebuke.

'I'm wondering how many other girls you've kissed by this very bush,' I gaily said.

He let me go so abruptly that I all but fell backwards on to the gravel path. 'It's too soon,' I wanted to say. 'Don't spoil things by saying them too soon.'

'Let's join the others,' he said, just as they

do in an old-fashioned film, and in a silence so huffy it hurt to listen to it, he followed me back indoors.

For the rest of the weekend he treated me with indifferent charm, and charm when it's indifferent can be a very damaging thing, and when he took me home, he wouldn't come in for a coffee, and he didn't ask to see me again.

'Oh, Geoffrey,' I sobbed into my pillow that night; I who normally cry only at weddings and children's Nativity plays. 'Why couldn't you have understood?'

During the next week I was beastly to the young sales assistant in Gowns, and when one day I saw her watching me with apprehensive eyes, I hated myself for taking out my feelings on her.

By the time three weeks had gone by, I had lost half a stone and developed purple bags under my eyes.

Then one day I picked up the telephone directory, looked up his number and dialled it.

'I'm having a little party on Saturday. Wine and cheese. Would you like to come?'

'Love to, Harriet,' he said, as though the last three weeks had never been.

'Eightish?'

'Splendid. I've missed you, Harriet.'

'Me too,' I said.

'It's been a long time.'

'Three weeks and two whole days,' I silently said, then spent the rest of the evening ringing up surprised friends who hadn't heard from me in years, and persuading them to come to my party. Many were married, and there was the added complication of baby-sitters, but after an hour of frantic phoning around, ten had promised to come.

Geoffrey got on very well with my friends, and when I discovered that his favourite cheese was Caerphilly too, it seemed symbolic somehow. The party was a huge success, and at nearly midnight my father waylaid him and they sat on the stairs together and talked veteran cars.

They were still talking when my guests started to leave, and I was wrapping the Camembert in foil when Geoffrey came up behind me.

'It was great fun tonight, Harriet,' he said sadly.

I started on the Stilton. 'Great fun,' I echoed, trying hard to keep the misery out of my voice.

He speared a piece of Gorgonzola and passed it to me. 'For three weeks I've been thinking about the golden lights in your hair,' he said.

'They're not real. They won't last,' I said.

He turned me round and kissed me. 'This is real. This will last,' he said.

'How can we know, Geoffrey?' I whispered, and as his hand caressed my neck underneath my hair, my very bones started to liquefy.

'We can't know, we can only hope, but we can live on hope for a long, long time,' he said.

And I believed him, and made a secret vow that I would put much more than hope into it this time.

'For ever and ever, Geoffrey,' I said.

Waiting for Love

The queue for Madame Tussaud's Wax Exhibition went on and on and on. Along Baker Street, past the Planetarium, round the corner, then on for a hundred yards or so down a side street.

Holding tightly to her six-year-old nephew's hand, Melissa followed the closely packed tributary from its source to the end, her heart sinking lower with every step.

'At this rate we'll have at least an hour's wait before we even get to the doors,' she told Daniel of the curly hair and large green eyes.

But in case his aunt did the unthinkable and suggested they gave up and caught the Tube train home, he pretended not to hear.

Though the tourist season wasn't in full swing yet, London seemed to have been taken over by every colour, race and creed. A source of income for one and a half million Britishers, Melissa reminded herself as they took their places behind a family from Japan.

'What shall we do?' Melissa had asked, picking him up that morning, and waving her sister off to her appointment with the hospital gynaecologist. 'It's not a very nice day, so shall we do a jigsaw, then go out and have lunch at that new place in the High Street?'

Daniel had looked faintly disgusted. 'All my life,' he'd breathed, 'I have wanted to go to Madame Tussaud's.' The green eyes narrowed into glinting slits. 'Where all the murderers are. Andrew has been, so has Simon,' he'd added, bringing up the heavy ammunition to add weight to his case.

Then he'd actually clasped both hands together and closed his eyes as if in prayer.

Melissa had hesitated only for a second. 'So that is where we will go,' she'd said.

'On your own head be it,' her sister, complacent in the eighth month of her pregnancy, said, and Melissa sighed.

'It matters not,' she told herself as they took their places at the end of the long queue, 'if we stand here until we take root in the pavement. If we stand here until we grow as inanimate as the waxworks we are going to see. This is how life is going to be from now on. One long wait . . . waiting for *nothing* to happen.'

That had been the story of her life for the past six months. One long wait for Richard to ring, for Richard to call at her flat, for Richard to ask her to marry him.

She glanced up at the sky and tried to calculate whether they would have moved up underneath the covered part of the pavement before the rain came. Not that it mattered of course. Richard had told her in his beautiful voice that she had brought sunshine into his life; that she had shown him it was worth going on after the awful trauma of his broken marriage.

'I will never forget you,' he had told her when finally he broke the news of his impending transfer to New York. 'You helped me through a terrible time, and there will always be a corner of my heart kept specially for you.'

'You have had a merciful release. I always thought his eyes were set too close together,' Melissa's sister had said. 'But they were lovely eyes,' she'd added, seeing her sister's wounded expression.

An important-looking official moved along the queue, walking in the road because the pavement was choked with humanity. With the expertise of a faithful sheepdog, he manoeuvred them into an even denser mass, so that now they stood six or seven abreast.

Melissa found that they were standing next to a man with the collar of his raincoat turned up round a thin face, bending down to listen to a small girl wearing a red knitted cap who looked so like him she just had to be his daughter.

'At this rate, Patsy, it will be at least another hour before we get in,' he was telling her, but like Daniel before her, the small girl was pretending not to hear.

The man raised eloquent eyebrows and smiled. 'We seem to have picked a time when half the world decides this is the one place they want to be today,' he said.

'And it's going to rain.' Melissa lifted her eyes to the lowering sky and felt the first tentative drops on her face.

'I think we might just reach the sheltered part,' he told her, and even as he spoke the important official worried them even closer.

Now they were flanked by the Japanese family in front and an anoraked foursome behind, who were talking to each other in a language Melissa could not even begin to recognize.

'Finnish,' the man whispered as if he had read her thoughts. 'And no, I don't speak it, but I used to go there on business and I can decipher a few words here and there. They're saying rude things about our weather,' he added with a smile.

Suddenly the queue moved forward a few paces, bringing them directly opposite a hot-dog stand.

'I'm hungry,' said Daniel, right on cue.

'So am I,' said the little girl in the red cap, and they nodded to each other, united in their common need.

Melissa glanced at the price and winced, then watched as the three Japanese children moved out of their places, returning with bread-enclosed pink sausages, dotted lavishly with bright yellow mustard.

'There's an ice-cream van a bit farther along,' she told Daniel as they shuffled a few paces, stopped, then slowly started again.

Five minutes later Daniel and his new-found friend, each clutching an outsized ice-cream cone dripping with chocolate sauce, were carrying on an earnest, in-between-licks conversation.

'I'm glad Patsy has found someone to talk to,' the man said. 'Is your little boy an 'only one' too?'

Melissa hesitated. Talking to strangers, especially in London, was not and never had been her way, brain-washed as she had been by a country-bred mother and an early-Victorian-type father.

But this man looked harmless enough. There was nothing but a rather resigned sadness in his expression, an expression that changed completely to one of boyish mischief when he smiled.

'Daniel is my nephew,' she told him. 'My sister is keeping an appointment, and because I have leave this week I volunteered to take him out for the day. Is that what you're doing, helping your wife out by looking after your little girl?'

He lowered his voice. 'My wife died a year ago, and I must admit school holidays *are* a bit of a problem. I have today and tomorrow off, that's all, but I manage with the help of two friends for the rest of the time.'

Melissa nodded, feeling that a conventional remark about his wife would have been unforgivable.

This man was not looking for sympathy; she knew that instinctively.

'They have murderers,' Daniel was telling Patsy, 'and the gallows, the *very* gallows where they used to hang people in the olden days.'

Patsy gave the cornet a satisfied lick. 'And the very knife they chopped heads off with in France,' she said with relish.

The queue moved up another foot and the awkward moment was gone.

'You mentioned 'leave',' he said. 'That sounds like Civil Service jargon to me.'

'Ministry of Pensions,' Melissa admitted. 'I wanted to go to art college, but because my parents are as orthodox in their reasoning as roast beef and two vegetables, I ended up working with figures.'

'And you hate your job?'

'I love it. They were right, you see. The art thing was just a wanting to rebel. I have a logical mind, it seems. Anyway, I was appointed to a London office and moved into a flat of my own.' She laughed. 'They still tell me to be careful crossing the road, and warn me about talking to strangers.'

'So they would be shocked if they could see us now?'

'To the core.'

They laughed together, then Melissa looked up with surprise as she found they had turned the corner. Now they could actually see the sign way ahead that proclaimed that the entrance to the exhibition was coming up over the horizon . . .

Half an hour of shuffling progress later, she had found out that he worked for a British-based American engineering firm; that he had once, when his wife was alive, been their European sales representative, but that now, due to his managing director's kindness, he worked in their London office.

'I am determined to look after Patsy myself,' he whispered, but the whisper was unnecessary as Daniel had spotted a van selling cans of Coke, and was gleefully pointing it out.

'We're thirsty,' the two children declared in unison, turning round with eyes pleading as if they had just trudged through the Sahara Desert with empty water bottles and swollen tongues.

This time the man insisted on paying, waving Melissa's offer away. 'I agree that the cost could almost have bought me a share in the company, but it's marvellous that the two kids have found each other to talk to,' he said.

Melissa waited for him to add how marvellous it was that he had found *her* to talk to as well, but he didn't. He just stared straight ahead for the next few minutes, busy with thoughts of his own.

Richard would have said it, she thought, remembering how they had met as they both tried to flag down the same cab one windy day in Regent Street in the grey aftermath of Christmas.

As they had argued politely, a stout, parcel-strewn woman, waving a long umbrella, had commandeered the cab for herself, leaving them standing open-mouthed on the pavement.

A 'pick-up', as Melissa's mother would have said.

'Meant to be,' Richard had said, and as they waited in vain for another unclaimed cab, he had persuaded her to delay wherever it was she was going to join him in a much-needed drink.

'I'll show you my cheque card if you want proof of my identity,' he had grinned, and because she was lonely at that time she had gone with him.

'You're looking very pensive,' the man at her side was saying. 'Look — we're almost there. Another twenty minutes or so and we'll be in.'

'You look quite excited,' she teased.

He smiled at her. 'To tell you the truth, I

107

am quite looking forward to this. The last time I came here I was ten years old, and the thing I remember best was seeing Charlie Peace, the portico burglar, sitting on the gallows with his executioner down in the Chamber of Horrors, with a look of patient resignation on his face as he waited to be hanged.'

'I remember best Marat murdered in his bath, with a blood-fringed hole in his chest, and his eyes wide open,' said Melissa.

'So it's no wonder, then, is it?' He nodded at the children with a mock serious expression.

'No wonder at all,' she agreed.

At long last they were shepherded through the entrance and up a curved flight of stairs to the lifts.

Then, following the crowd, they moved on into the Conservatory, a palm-strewn hall dotted with waxen contemporary figures. Cricketers, singers, show business personalities, and stern oil magnates.

While the two children darted from one figure to another, with Patsy reading out the names to a not-very-interested Daniel, he stared at Paul Getty sitting sadly on a white wrought-iron chair, and told her that he had never believed money was conducive to happiness.

'The years when I was studying, and my wife and I lived in a bedsit in Balham were some of the happiest I remember,' he said. 'We had a good marriage. I'll always be thankful for that.'

Melissa nodded sympathetically, then, pointing to Glenda Jackson, wondered aloud how the film

108

star managed to stay so slim.

'I wouldn't say you were in the least fat, just pleasantly rounded,' he told her, blushing slightly, and she realized that he was *shy*. Shy and unaccustomed to talking to women.

'Chatting them up,' as Richard would have said.

Passing through into a darkened room with music blaring at them from every side, Patsy dragged Daniel over to where Kojak leaned against a lamp, kind eyes hidden behind dark glasses, a lollipop in his hand.

'Love ya, baby,' Patsy said, showing off.

'Television,' her father told Melissa with a rueful grin. 'I'm afraid I have tended to sit her down and switch it on while I got on with the chores. Sometimes she stays up far too late.'

Melissa stretched out a comforting hand, then drew it back.

Seeing an effigy of an actress, she mentioned that sometimes she watched the late-night horror film, then had to look inside her wardrobe before she found the courage to get into bed.

'You live alone?' he asked, and in the Grand Hall, while the two children reached out exploring fingers and touched the jewelled gowns of Henry the Eighth's wives, they found a red velvet sofa, sat down, and went on talking.

Hemmed in by pushing tourists clutching programmes, they talked as if they were isolated on a small island of their own. When Patsy came back and reported that Princess Anne's likeness was super, Melissa looked up with a start.

'Where's Daniel?' she wanted to know, panic gripping her.

'He's okay,' Patsy said with laconic indifference. 'He's trying to get the King of Sweden's sword out of its sheath to see if it's real.' Then as Melissa dashed off she turned to her father.

'Daddy. Can we go and see the Baddies now? Please?'

By a life-like figure of Crippen leaning with crossed hands on the dock to hear his sentence, the man with the gentle voice told Melissa that the house they lived in at Finchley was too big really.

'But I love the back garden with my greenhouse at the far end. I grow tomatoes in summer, and chrysanthemums in winter. In that small way I'm able to pay back the friends who help out with Patsy,' he explained.

As they stared at Christie in the shoddy kitchen of number ten, Rillington Place, Melissa confided that what she missed most in her fifth-floor flat was a garden, and a place to sit, if and when the sun shone at weekends and holiday times.

'Is it *real* blood?' Daniel asked hopefully, as he stared with morbid fascination at the guillotine.

Not wishing to disappoint, Melissa said that she would not be surprised, and the green eyes grew round with wonder.

And after that, the Battle of Trafalgar was tame indeed, in spite of the authentic smoke and smell of cannon-fire, with Nelson dying victoriously of his wound.

110

The Sleeping Beauty's chest moving up and down as she breathed held the two children spellbound for the time it took Melissa to explain her reasons for preferring the poets of the nineteenth century to their modern counterparts.

'You're a romantic,' he teased, and this time it was her turn to blush.

* * *

It was raining in earnest as they walked out into the busy street, and rushing, hurrying, home-going crowds of commuters jostled each other as they ran for the Tube trains.

'I don't suppose you have time to come for a light meal?' he suggested. 'There's a pizza place just round the corner. It would end a happy day properly, don't you think?'

Melissa glanced at her watch in amazement. 'Oh, goodness me, I'd no idea it was so late,' she said, grabbing Daniel's hand. 'I hadn't realized . . . it must have been the time we spent queuing to get in.' She tried to pull the hood of Daniel's plastic anorak up round his face. 'My sister will be worried sick. She's over-anxious about everything at the moment.'

With dismay she thought about the jam-packed rush-hour Underground platform, followed by the fairly long walk from the station. 'We really must go,' she said, and even as she spoke a cab drew into the pavement directly in front of them.

'We'll take that,' she said quickly on impulse,

and in a flurry of goodbyes, and directions to the driver, she pushed Daniel into the cab and slammed the door. As they pulled away from the kerb, she turned and saw him standing there in the rain, holding his little girl by the hand, their faces a study of shocked surprise.

It had all happened so quickly there had been no time to think, no time for anything. No exchange of telephone numbers, nothing, even though he had talked as if they would surely meet again. All she knew was he lived in North London.

'He wouldn't hear the address I gave to the driver. He was bending down and telling Patsy to button up her coat,' she told Daniel, as he gleefully discovered the let-down seat opposite her.

'Patsy said I could go and see the sunflowers in her garden,' he told her as he bounced up and down on the tiny flap of a seat.

'You don't know where she lives,' Melissa said, her voice so sharp that he glanced at her in surprise.

'Are you cross?' he wanted to know and, because he was tired, his voice wobbled a little.

'Of course not, lovey,' Melissa told him, leaning forward and patting a bony knee. 'It's been a smashing day, hasn't it? Think of all the things you have to tell Mummy.'

She did not tell her sister about the man she had met, nor about the little girl who for the space of a few hours had been inseparable from Daniel.

112

But she told herself she was being quite ridiculous as she sat that evening, staring at the telephone and willing it to ring.

'And how *can* it ring,' she asked herself aloud, 'when he doesn't even know my surname or where I live? And if he did, there's no guarantee that he will want to see me again, is there?'

But the memory of his thin, sensitive face stayed with her as she prepared for bed. So did the sound of his quiet voice, and the twinkle in his eyes when he smiled or teased. She remembered the sadness, and the shyness, and the way they had talked as if it had been important to get to know each other as quickly as possible.

'It's as though I know everything about him, and yet I know nothing,' she told herself, as she lay awake, unable to sleep. 'I have known him for ever, and yet not at all. How can that be?'

He had told her he lived at Finchley, but where in Finchley? Which of all the lovely old Victorian houses, terraced, with big bay windows and glass panels let in to their front doors, was his?

For a wild moment she saw herself walking first up one road, then another, searching for a front garden growing sunflowers at least a mile high.

Then she turned over and buried her face in the pillow and told herself that she must forget him.

Love at first sight was romantic make-believe.

She had thought it had happened that way with Richard until the disillusionment set in.

She had promised herself that next time, if there was to be a next time, she would meet a man and love him for the man he was, not the man she supposed him to be.

With her logical mind she went over and over what had happened that day, and came to the conclusion that from the very moment the man had spoken to her in the queue, their deep attraction for each other had been entirely real, and not just a figment of her imagination. There was no disputing that.

He had not even touched her hand, yet before the afternoon was over it was as though they had known each other for ever, and that last look as the cab had borne her away into the stream of traffic had shown her that he felt the same.

He had been bereft, as she was now . . .

This was not a young girl's fantasy. She was twenty-four years old, and even if she never saw him again the memory of him would always be there, tormenting her with its unfinished promise.

She stared into the darkness. He had said he was at home for two days, and would be working in his garden and his beloved greenhouse the next day, as Patsy was being taken out by a friend.

She had told *him* she was on leave for the whole of the week . . . so that left tomorrow. Suddenly she sat up, hugging her knees, knowing there was a chance that she might sleep, now that she knew what she had to do.

She took a long time getting ready the next morning, brushing her shoulder-length brown hair into a shining curtain round her face.

She told herself that she was all kinds of fool, but her resolution did not waver. What she was about to do was a gamble . . .

If he felt the same . . . and oh, dear heaven, she could not have imagined that look on his face as he stood there in the rain watching her going away from him . . . he would be there.

So she took the Tube train to Baker Street, and if anything the queue for the waxworks exhibition was even longer than it had been the day before.

Melissa walked its length to the entrance, turned and slowly followed it to its source.

They were all there, the American blue-rinsed matrons in their vivid trouser suits, the blonde and beautiful Swedes, the French and the Germans and the Italians, all immediately recognizable. But there was no man with a thin and haunting sadness in his expression, bending down to hear what a small girl in a red cap was saying.

She walked along the edge of the pavement, her heart thudding, part of her wanting to run away, and part of her knowing this was something she had to do. Perhaps the most important thing she would ever do . . .

There was a pushing crowd of children round the ice-cream van, holding up coins in their hands, small pink tongues licking at the pyramid of ice-cream even before they regained their places in the queue.

Today, the sun was struggling to appear from behind grey misty clouds, and as she turned the corner, the hot-dog stall was doing a roaring trade, and surely the sausages were even pinker than they had been the day before?

On she went, past the sheltered part of the pavement to where the same important official chivvied the crowd into a more acceptable shape.

Melissa glanced at her watch, and saw that the time was right. If the queue was moving at roughly the same rate, and if he had arrived at the same time, he should be about here . . .

She stopped, and her head drooped as she realized he had not come. The telepathy, the intuition, the surmising, the feeling of empathy had all led her to this, to a disappointment so great it was a pain in her heart and a heavy certainty that she would never see him again.

She was turning away when she heard his voice, and then suddenly, for a brief moment, he was holding her close, his quiet voice stuttering its relief.

'Never tell me that prayers aren't answered,' he whispered, then heedless of the grinning crowd he held her away from him. 'I thought that if you felt the same way, you would take a chance and come.' He threw his head back and almost shouted his gladness to the grey skies. 'Oh, to think I might have spent the rest of my life looking for you, wanting you and never finding you . . . '

With his arm holding her close to his side, they crossed the busy street, a street filled with red buses, taxicabs and people.

They walked away as isolated, as alone as if they trod some distant deserted shore, with nothing but the waves and the sound of the gulls in their ears.

As alone as only two lovers can be.

The Two of Us

My mother said, 'We'll go on our own, by coach to Southwold. After all, the cottage is booked as usual.' She made a brave attempt at a smile. 'We'll have a lovely time, just the two of us. You'll see.'

So I told my best friend, Laura, that as my parents were splitting up there was no way I could go with her and her parents to Spain. I said I was sure she would make the same sacrifice for her own mother, given similar tragic circumstances, of course.

Laura's parents are devoted to each other. They even look alike. They never have a cross word, according to Laura, which seems a bit much to believe, I must say.

The cottage we rent each August is in Southwold, Suffolk. It's a terraced house with a red front door, and the sea is just around the corner. Across the sea is Holland, and my father once tried to make me believe that if you stood on my bed in the attic and stuck your head through the window you could see whirling windmill sails all along the Dutch coast. He tells some terrible corny jokes, does my father.

One of the best things about going to Southwold year after year was the sameness of everything; the way we did the same things in a repeating pattern that never varied as each year came round.

Like going to the hotel overlooking the market place for dinner on our first evening. It was the one and only time we dressed up. 'We might as well see how the other half lives,' my father said every year.

So this time I went *with* my mother and *without* my father to Southwold in August and on our first evening we sat opposite each other at a window table in the hotel's newly decorated dining room. We decided on fried king prawns, followed by grilled whole plaice, with a choice from the sweet trolley to follow.

'I wonder if they'll have that heavenly creamy walnut gâteau this year?' My mother was wearing a Liberty-printed, Laura-Ashley-kind-of-dress, with her dark hair swept up on top of her head. I thought how pretty she was looking and how young, considering she will never see thirty again and considering that her face was also set in deep lines of suffering.

'We're going to have a fabulous time.' I was desperate to cheer her up. 'One-parent families are all the fashion nowadays. You don't even have to get married to be one.'

A 'proper' family walked past us to get to their table — a mother, a father and two young boys. I saw the way my mother's eyes followed them, so I told her that she never need be lonely with me around, that even if my father married again it needn't be the end of the world.

For a moment her eyes flashed fire, as they say in books, then she got on with nipping the heads and tails off her king-sized prawns. Viciously.

I finished mine first, so I stared silently round

the beige and red dining room and saw exactly how life was going to be from now on . . .

An old lady — well into her sixties — tottered in and sat at the adjoining table, first passing her stick to her daughter and asking her to make sure they weren't sitting in a draught. The daughter had her hair done bouffant-style and wore a dress which looked as if it might once have been the lining of a raincoat. I knew they were mother and daughter because they had identical Pekinese dog profiles and because the old lady was looking as cross with her daughter as my mother was with me.

The shape of things to come . . . I wasn't bitter. I looked down the future to nice ladylike holidays here year after passing year. We would shop sedately in the High Street and buy our thermal vests for the coming winter at the shop I could see through the window. We would walk down to the harbour to watch the yachts and fishing boats at anchor there. It was quite a walk, so mentally I transferred my mother into a wheelchair, with a tartan rug round her arthritic knees.

I was just tying a scarf in a double bow underneath her chin when she said, 'I know you're worrying yourself sick about your O level results, and I *understand*. But you did your best, and that is all that matters.'

I came down to earth with a nasty jolt. I knew I couldn't possibly have done my best with what was going on at home. All the slamming of doors, and scorching rows conducted in whispers to help them believe I couldn't hear.

Both of them working all the hours that God sent them to pay off the mortgage and bills and the instalments on the fitted furniture in the bedrooms which my father said we hadn't needed anyway.

My mother often came home from work so tired she forgot to take the cheese from the fridge in time for it to warm up, infuriating my father, who would prefer her to be there all the time simmering rice puddings in the new split-level cooker we haven't yet paid for.

A waitress with a tuft of fair curls on top of her head came up to our table and slid an enormous plaice on to my plate.

'So fresh its fins have only just stopped flapping,' she told us, and I stared down at my fish and imagined it swimming happily about in the cold North Sea.

I deeply considered becoming vegetarian.

'Go then!' I'd heard my mother shout one evening when she thought I was upstairs in my room. 'I know we can't go on like this.'

'I can't *afford* to go!' I heard my father say, then the door was slammed and I didn't hear any more.

I sat my Biology exam the day after, so was it any wonder I couldn't remember how many legs a frog had when I came to do the paper?

I knew it was my fault, in a way, that my parents were splitting up. I'd got myself into a bit of a state about my exams. I knew how much they both wanted me to do well, and I admit I was foul to both of them.

In fact, if we'd been a family in a film, any

one of us would have won an Oscar for all the drama going on. I remembered one day when my mother rushed in from work and said she thought that at the very least I would have set the table.

Did she *want* me to fail my exams? I thought that it was a reasonable enough question, but when she served the supper the potatoes were like bullets. My father made one of his jokes about this and she snatched his plate and hurled it into the pedal bin. I remembered the lid slamming back like a pistol shot.

'Laura told me she intends to go topless in Spain this year,' I said. 'If I'd gone with her I would have done the same.'

'What with?'

Because it was the first joke I'd heard my mother make for a long time, I laughed. Even though being so flatchested and late in developing is a great trouble to me.

'I think I'll skip the creamy walnut gâteau,' she said, so I sacrificed mine, too, and followed her into the lounge filled with old ladies sipping coffee.

We walked back to the cottage by the East Cliff, past the Sailors' Reading Room. I remembered going in there with my father and looking at the portraits of ancient mariners lining the walls. They all looked much alike to me, with the piercing eyes sailors have, and tufts of hair sprouting from their manly chins.

My father told me that during the Dutch wars the bay was used as an anchorage for the whole of the British Fleet. He told me this with pride, as if he'd been born in Southwold and not in Clapham.

Oh yes, my father really loved Southwold. He said that going there was like stepping back to a time when the good things in life meant a roof over your head and one proper meal a day. He swam in the sea every day, whatever the weather, and he borrowed bikes for us and we rode all the way to Dunwich with its ruins and narrow leafy lanes. He told me that the lanes had once been streets in a town that was the capital of East Anglia.

He loved the Southwold sky, too. He said it must be the biggest sky in the world and I knew exactly what he meant. In the fading light it seemed to stretch into infinity.

I wanted to cry but knew I mustn't, for my mother's sake. She was trudging along the narrow cliff path with her hands deep in the pockets of her long cardi. When we turned away from the sea and saw the white tower of the lighthouse rising above the clustered cottages I told her that when I was a little girl I used to think there was a man sitting up there shining two lamps, one red and one white, turning them round and round to guide the fishing boats safely in from the North Sea.

I turned and looked at her, but I don't think she even heard me.

It rained the next day, but we decided to go out and get wet on purpose, so we walked across the marshes to Walberswick, getting so sodden that even our eyelashes squelched when we blinked. And the next day was sunny but breezy, so we carried a picnic down to the beach and sat behind a wind break watching a man struggling to keep his balance on a sailboard.

In the evening we ate fish and chips straight out of the paper, because that was part of the repeating pattern, too. Then we watched the same old television that made familiar faces seem fatter, and gave everyone appearing on it a bronzed and healthy tan.

The next morning the postman delivered a letter. It lay there on the flowered carpet, a square of white. I was coming down the stairs when I saw my mother run down the narrow hall to pick it up before throwing it down on the table in disgust. It was then she turned on me.

'You don't *have* to be my shadow, you know! You don't have to follow me everywhere.' She marched back into the kitchen. 'The Bartons have rented the pink corner house again. I saw Jonathan ride past the window yesterday. Why don't you go round and say hello? You and he were the best of chums last year.'

Chums? Oh blimey, my dear little innocent mother! Last year Jonathan Barton practically ravished me coming back across the Common one night. Well, not ravished exactly, just kissed me passionately until I shoved him over and he got mud all over his white designer jeans. I'd seen him too, as a matter of fact, cycling along the road with his feet up on the crossbar, showing off. He was wearing his hair this year, I noticed, almost shaved round the back and sticking straight up on top. Upended he would make a good lavatory brush, I'd decided.

124

My mother was pouring a bottle of milk into a jug, so I sat down at the table and waited, as I always did, for her to put my bowl of cereal in front of me. I was feeling terrible. I hadn't slept much and when I did it was to dream I'd failed all my seven O levels, and that two-legged frogs were croaking at me. I dreamed I was down on the beach going topless with nothing to show for it, while out at sea a smiling Jonathan Barton balanced his bicycle on a sail-board, and laughed out loud at me.

'Will you be getting a divorce?' The words burst out of me. 'Will I have to choose which one of you I live with?'

My mother whipped round, the jug in her hand. She looked as terrible as I felt, with her hair flopping into her eyes and her face as white as the milk. I was feeling very frightened, but by now I'd gone too far to be able to stop.

'Is my father having an affair?' I said 'affair' in capital letters. 'Is he living with another woman?'

For a moment I thought she was going to hit me, then she buried her face in her hands and began to cry. The ends of her hair trailed into my bowl of cornflakes and the noise she was making scared me halfway to death. I'd never seen her cry before and I didn't know what to do.

I grabbed a wodge of tissues from the box on the dresser and pushed them into her hand. I kneeled down on the floor by the side of her chair and promised that I would never leave her; that I would stay an old maid for the rest of my life, in order to look after her. I told her that even if a miracle happened and my O level results were good enough to make it worth my while trying for a university place in two years' time, I wouldn't dream of being a burden to her. I would get a job and give her every penny of my wages. I swore I would never look at or speak to my father again.

At last she dried her eyes and told me there would be no need for any of that. She assured me I wasn't to blame, which made me feel a lot better so that I managed to eat my breakfast without it choking me.

Things improved a lot after that little drama, though I still didn't know the cause of the problem. I went around a bit with Jonathan Barton's sister and she said that perhaps my parents had just drifted apart through the stresses of modern living. She agreed with me that her brother was very immature for his age.

'But then, boys are,' I said, and we shaved our legs with her father's razor, and deeply considered piercing each other's ears.

The day before we were to go home was the day my exam results were due to arrive at our house in Maida Vale, so to take my mind off it my mother took me to the Summer Theatre in St Edmund's Hall to see a thirties comedy.

The women in the play all wore satin dresses cut on the cross, while the men lounged about in baggy flannel trousers, with cravats tucked into the open necks of their sport shirts. Throughout the three acts they all smoked furiously, the women puffing on cigarettes in long holders, and

126

the men clenching pipes between their teeth, and talking in clipped accents. All through clouds of smoke.

They all went to bed with each other in a sort of frantic permutation. I hoped the dwelling on infidelity wasn't too upsetting for my mother but when we went into the Shore Bar for coffee after Act One she chatted away quite happily to Jonathan Barton's mother. I asked his sister where he was — not that I was interested — and she said he had just nipped outside for a quick drag on a fag. We said how typical and pathetically juvenile.

My mother and I walked back to the cottage through the little streets of clustered houses with their step-gable roofs, and when we turned into our street we could see the sea glittering as though it had been powdered with moonlight. And somehow the terrible sadness had gripped my mother again.

Our holiday was over, the worst holiday of my life because my father hadn't been there telling his awful jokes and running down the long slope to the beach each morning to swim in a too-cold sea and spot windmills on the horizon.

The key was there as ever, hung from a nail beneath the window ledge, and my mother took it and opened the door. Slowly I followed her inside.

And there was my father, standing in the kitchen looking tired and haggard, holding out an envelope I'd addressed to myself ages ago.

'I thought I'd drive up to save you waiting until tomorrow for your results,' he said, handing the envelope to me. But he was looking at my mother.

'Well?' he said, and they stared at each other for a moment without moving.

'Well?' my mother said back, then my father was holding out his arms and she was going into them, and they were kissing and she was saying she must have been mad, and he was saying they must forget it and start all over again.

The envelope was in my hands. I felt my mouth go dry and my heart began to beat with heavy thuds. I left them kissing and I ran upstairs into my room at the top of the house. I sat on the bed where, if you stood on tiptoe and stuck your head through the window, you could see the sea.

It was such a flimsy envelope. I could feel the slip of paper inside. I laid it down on the bed, squeezed my eyes tight shut and whispered a prayer.

'Dear God. Four out of seven will do. Two would be better than nothing but if by any chance there's been a miracle . . . ' I slit the envelope open quickly, my heart thudding louder than ever, and took out the slip of paper — and there it was. The unbelievable!

'Seven!' I ran downstairs so fast it felt like flying. They held out their arms and we rocked together and laughed together, the way it had always been before this dreadful summer.

And the next morning, before we left for home, I went round to the pink house to say goodbye to Jonathan Barton's sister.

She was out but he was there, on the front

lawn, fixing the chain on his bicycle. His hair looked flatter somehow.

'Will you be coming down next year?' he asked me, and I said I might if I didn't go abroad with my best friend.

'Me too,' he said. 'Bumming it round Europe. You know?' He busied himself with the oily bicycle chain. 'On the other hand it can be good fun down here. What do you think?'

'I'll certainly deeply consider it,' I said, walking away from him down the path to where the cliff fell sharply away to the sparkling sea below.

The Scarlet Glove

Once upon a time there was a young man with the unlikely name of Lancelot.

Now Lancelot grew up to be a practical kind of man, a feet-on-the-ground, looking-things-straight-in-the-eye kind of man, and when he was twenty-three, just after he had taken his degree, he fell in love with a girl named Lucinda.

And there was the problem . . .

It just so happened that Lancelot was also a slow-to-make-up-his-mind kind of man. He kept telling himself that marriage was for ever, and he knew that for ever was a long, long time.

Lucinda was beautiful, in a fairy-tale princess kind of way. Her hair was long and fell to her shoulders. She was small, and her voice was lullaby-soft.

Lancelot's thin young face would be serious and intent as he looked down at her.

'I love you . . . ' he would say, and her lovely mouth would lift at the corner, showing an unexpected dimple, and she would say: 'I love you, too . . . '

And there was the problem. Lancelot couldn't say the words which should have followed. 'Will you marry me?' Just four words, taking less than ten seconds to say.

It wasn't a question of money, because although Lancelot was only at the start of his career, he knew exactly where he was going. In fact, with his gift for self-assessment, he expected a partnership in the family firm by the time he was thirty.

And it wasn't even the housing problem, because Lancelot had looked this firmly in the eye, too. He had gone straight from rooms at university to a bachelor flat in Kensington, and all that would be necessary would be for him to exchange his single bed for a double one, and Lucinda could move in.

Why then, oh, why, couldn't he, or wouldn't he, propose?

After all, he knew that Lucinda's love was without guile, knowing nothing of pride or pretence. She loved with the innocence of a child, and this knowledge of the power he had over her made him at times unreasonably depressed.

He even started to sleep badly, tossing about in his narrow bed, and, as it grew light, counting the triangular motifs on the wallpaper. He evolved their symmetry into complicated equations, and about an hour before it was time to get up he would fall into a deep sleep, and dream of Lucinda.

Now on the second Wednesday of the month, Lancelot always took his mother out to lunch, because, although he would have denied it most vehemently, his heart was large, and of the sentimental kind. So he took her to her favourite restaurant, on the top floor of a large store in Regent Street.

The lights were pink, the tablecloths were

131

pink, and the table napkins were pink. It seemed to Lancelot that all the tables were dotted with middle-aged matrons, all wearing fussy, nodding hats, and eating salads.

Lancelot knew exactly what to order. It was always the same . . . chicken salad, followed by fruit salad and coffee, and one cigarette (tipped and expensively Turkish).

Now on this particular second Wednesday in the month, Lancelot's mother was wearing a hat made of incredibly red feathers, and a pair of long gloves in *exactly* the same shade.

She had bought them, she told her son, just ten minutes ago, from the department on the ground floor.

Delightedly, she waved to an acquaintance wearing a purple velvet toque, while Lancelot moodily chased a forkful of elusive garden peas round his plate.

Totally unaware that his mother was regarding him with anxiety, he sighed heavily. He felt sure that it wasn't usual, or even very manly, for a grown man to ask his mother's advice, but that was exactly what he was going to do.

'How would you feel about it if I told you that I was considering asking Lucinda to marry me?' he said, apropos of exactly nothing.

Beneath the red feathers, his mother's face glowed.

'Dear boy . . . ! I think I'll buy something in a soft caramel shade for the wedding. One gets so tired of blue. Lucinda's a sweet girl. So right in every way . . . '

'I haven't exactly decided . . . ' Lancelot

began, and followed her glance to where the purple-toqued acquaintance was gathering gloves and handbag together in readiness for a visit to the Ladies.

He had no doubt, no doubt at all, that his mother would follow her there, and gleefully impart the good news in two seconds flat.

Left alone, he brooded into his coffee . . .

Lucinda's mother would be just as pleased. There had been a questioning look on her face for months, and all at once Lancelot felt trapped. He hadn't made up his mind, and he liked to consider things carefully; after all, marriage was for ever, and for ever was a long, long time . . .

'It isn't *settled* Mother,' he said desperately, when she came back. 'Lucinda may not want to marry me.'

'She will,' said his mother, smiling.

'Yes, she will,' said he, scowling. 'She'll say yes, straight away, and that will be it.'

His mother's blue eyes gave him a speculative stare as she picked up the long scarlet gloves, but noticing nothing, Lancelot paid the bill, and followed her out.

All that afternoon in the office, he alternated between joy and despair. Then, back in his flat that evening, he telephoned Lucinda.

'I'll call for you early tomorrow,' he said. 'We'll go and see that Polish film — the Academy Award winner . . . '

Then Lucinda was speaking, and her voice breathed gentleness: 'I'm sorry, but I can't see you tomorrow,' she was saying. 'I've made other arrangements.'

133

After a startled silence, Lancelot discovered that he was shouting without having meant to shout.

'What other arrangements? You know we always go to a film on Thursdays.'

'Exactly!' said this new, cool Lucinda. 'That's why I'm going somewhere else, with someone else.'

'Who with? With whom?' he roared.

'There's no need to shout. After all, we aren't engaged or anything, are we?'

Lancelot was standing, stunned into silence, when a clicking noise told him that Lucinda had hung up on him.

He stared into the mirror at his astonished face, and watched a slow tide of emotion creep upwards from his white collar.

Walking over to the nearest chair, he sat down heavily. Then he stared at nothing for a long, long time, his mind blurring into disbelief, and finally, all composure gone, he actually banged his forehead with a clenched fist, and groaned aloud.

Of course they weren't engaged, but that was only because he hadn't got round to it. Surely Lucinda knew that it was only a question of time?

A glass of rather cloudy port, all that he could find, left him feeling more puzzled than ever, and slightly sick.

Lucinda had been as gentle as she always was. Gentle, regretful, but very determined. He stretched out his hand to the telephone. He would ring Lucinda and ask her again.

Then he stopped. He couldn't bear to hear that soft, regretful 'no' again, and the apologetic click as the receiver was replaced. So he went through into the tiny kitchen and made himself a cup of strong coffee, which he promptly forgot to drink.

An hour later, he came to a momentous decision . . .

He had never run after a girl before, but now he would humble himself at the feet of the girl he loved. The only girl he would ever love.

He knew that now.

Scorning his coat, although it was a cold night, a night without stars, he rushed down the stairs, ignoring the lift. He flung himself into his car and switched on the ignition with fingers that shook a little.

Lucinda lived in a select suburb which not so many years ago had been a village. At that late hour, the houses were mostly shrouded in darkness downstairs, with peachshaded lights in the bedrooms showing that their occupants were going sedately to bed.

Lancelot stopped his car outside a house showing no lights at all; not even a glimmer from the dormer window of Lucinda's little room over the garage.

Grimly Lancelot pressed the front doorbell.

Instantly, lights seemed to glow from every part of the house. He heard voices and hurried footsteps. The front door opened a fraction of an inch and showed Lucinda's mother, neatly netted for the night, and wrapped in pale pink quilted satin.

'Come along in, dear. There's a cold wind blowing from the east tonight,' she said calmly, and showed him into the sitting room. There was, Lancelot noticed, not the slightest trace of surprise on her plump face.

Deftly she removed newspapers from the floor, switched on the electric fire and the standard lamp, picked up her knitting from the coffee table and, smiling graciously, excused herself.

Lucinda looked startlingly beautiful in a short filmy négligé tied with floating satin ribbons. Her hair, released for the night from its usual shiny topknot, hung fair and straight, almost to her shoulders.

Lancelot stared at her for a long moment, his heart thudding in his chest.

All the things he had meant to say, all the angry words, the remonstrances, were suddenly unnecessary. He couldn't hurt her. He loved her far too much.

He would accept the fact that she was tired of him. Lancelot had always been a feet-on-the-ground, looking-things-straight-in-the-eye kind of man.

But he stared past her, into a tragic vista of emptiness.

Humbly, he asked her: 'Could I kiss you goodbye?' She nodded and slowly lifted her face to his.

He felt the familiar soft languor of her in his arms, and the kiss that had started off as a friendly farewell left him shaking and out of breath.

The words he had fought against saying for

so long almost said themselves: 'Will you marry me, Lucinda? I love you so much. Marry me soon — now — next week — tomorrow.'

She reached up and traced with her finger the trembling outline of his mouth. Her lovely eyes were all melting tenderness.

'It can't be soon enough for me, darling,' she said against his lips.

Lancelot closed his eyes, and all that was heaven rocked around him as he kissed her again.

And then, when all was said and settled, and they were in the hall saying a lingering good night, he saw the splash of bright colour on the small carved hall table . . .

A long scarlet glove, bought just that day to match a hat of incredibly red feathers . . .

Happiness, light as a bubble, floated inside him.

With a wife like Lucinda, and a mother who knew exactly when to interfere, how could he do anything else but live happily, gloriously happily, ever after?

Love in Disguise

My sister Meg, who's twelve, was leaning against the fridge eating an ice lolly when I got home from school. 'There's a smashing boy moved in next door,' she said in between licks.

I put my satchel down, and rubbed my arm. We had homework in four subjects that evening, and the satchel was heavy.

'He looks like Cliff Richard,' Meg said.

'So what?' I said.

'Try not to be vulgar, dear,' Mother said. She was rolling out pastry, and there was a streak of flour down her nose.

Meg put out her tongue for another lick. 'He has dark curly hair and gorgeous dimples. Not little round holey ones, but long ones that crease his face up when he smiles.'

'Sounds like a soppy date,' I said, and took a banana from the fruit dish.

'Judy dear, I wish you wouldn't . . . ' Mother began, when there was a loud knock at the front door.

'I'll get it,' I said, the way they always do in a television play.

I bounded down the hall just as I was in my school uniform. It consists of a tunic shaped like an ill-fitting Roman toga, the green of a garage door. The head sends you home if you dare to give it a bit of style by wearing a stiff petticoat underneath — she has absolutely no idea. The hat is a green version of the dish Mother bakes her custards in, and the shoes are simply unspeakable. They are flat, brown, and laced with hideous brown laces.

Anyhow, there I was, looking perfectly ghastly, and there he was, looking like Bronco and John Saxon rolled into one. Meg had said he was like Cliff Richard, and I suppose he was a bit, but twenty or thirty times more handsome.

His dark hair fell over his forehead in a sort of neglected wave, and he was tall, and his eyes were a dark mysterious blue, with long spiky eyelashes.

I might as well tell you, I nearly dropped my banana, I was so overcome.

'We're your new neighbours,' he said in a deep, thrilling voice. 'Could you possibly lend us such a thing as a drop of milk?' and he held out a white jug with a red rose printed on its fat side.

My love is like a red red rose, I thought tenderly as I took it from him.

Just then my mother came bustling down the hall. She had floury streaks in her hair now, and a tea towel in her wet hands, but in less time than it takes to tell she had made the vision promise to bring his mother and father round straight away to have cup of tea with us.

'How could you?' I wailed. 'When I look like this?' and I dashed upstairs.

I was looking at my new white and blue party dress, and wondering if it would look a bit much if I went downstairs in it, when they came in. I heard them trooping down the hall, and a woman's voice saying: 'You really are too kind, you know' . . . so all I had time to do was to flick a comb through my hair and squirt myself with my mother's eau-de-cologne, and put some lipstick on.

When I went into the kitchen, they were sitting round the table drinking tea out of the best china cups. I'd heard Meg nipping them out of the dining-room cupboard quickly as they were coming up the path.

'And this is Judy, my *big* girl,' my mother said proudly as I came in, and my cheeks burned.

I hoped they hadn't heard her, and held out my hand and said: 'How d'you do?' in the voice I keep for speaking to the head, or answering the phone.

'Still at school, dear?' his mother said, and I treated that remark with the scorn it deserved and said: 'I'm leaving at the end of this term and going to the Commercial College.'

'That will be nice,' she said.

I accepted a cup of tea from my mother, and politely took the smallest and plainest biscuit from the plate on the table. Then I sat down on the red kitchen stool, curling my feet up underneath, and praying he wouldn't notice those beastly shoes.

In ten minutes flat, my mother had discovered that their name was Stevens; that Mr Stevens worked in a bank and had had his gall bladder removed the previous summer; that Mrs Stevens did all her own washing; and that *his* name was Gavin, and he was at the Technical College where he was learning to be a draughtsman.

140

When they got up to go, Mother insisted on filling the white jug full of milk, and I passed it to Gavin with a burning look, which he didn't see.

'Oh Meg,' I breathed when they'd gone. 'Isn't he the most terrific, gorgeous boy you ever saw?' And I put my arms round her, and gave her a big hug.

Her ponytail swung out as I lifted her clean off the floor.

'Who's a soppy date?' she said.

★ ★ ★

I told all the girls about him at school the next day. 'Fancy having someone like that living right next door,' Annette Coles said. 'I hope I see him the next time I come visiting you.'

And she did too.

I was furious when he came past as we were standing at the gate talking. There was just no alternative but to introduce him to Annette. She was wearing stiletto heels at fourteen, and lipstick at thirteen, and she has hair the colour of a copper chrysanthemum, and eyes the green of a glass bottle, so I don't need to say any more, do I?

Annette is in the Church Youth Club, and she collects boyfriends as a squirrel collects nuts. That day she was wearing a smashing new raincoat with a flowered lining. It was the same limpid green as her eyes. She smiled her wide smile, which shows her back molars, at Gavin, and he stepped back a pace. He looked,

141

I noticed with disgust, positively stunned.

Why I have Annette for my best friend I really don't know.

The next day at school she said, sort of casual like: 'Why don't you ask Gavin to come to the Youth Club Fancy Dress Dance?'

'I might,' I said vaguely. 'If I remember.'

But Annette didn't know that the only way it was possible for me even to catch a glimpse of Gavin was by studying his reading habits, and stalking him to the public library.

'Why do you change your library book so often?' Mother asked as I set off for the library for the fourth time that week.

'Reading improves your mind,' I said.

Mother glanced at the title of my book, and raised her eyebrows clean over her reading glasses: *Love Knocks But Once.*

'She never reads them,' Meg said from the floor where she was sprawled out.

'Well, why on earth . . . ' Mother began, but I was off.

'I'll be back in plenty of time to finish my homework,' I said soothingly as I went out.

I was lucky that evening, because there he was, deep in thought amongst the Science Section A-O. I kept my eye on him by browsing among the light romances, which is directly opposite the Science Section A-O. I'd just decided to drop my book and make him turn round, when an awful thing happened.

Jimmy Grimshaw, one of the Youth Club crowd, came up behind me and hissed in my ear: 'Read any good books lately, Judy?'

I jumped a mile and uttered a gurgly sort of shriek.

That made Gavin look up all right, and he grinned at me with a grin that seemed to say: 'Having fun, children?' Then he went out with a dry-as-dust-looking book underneath his arm.

'Oh, you!' I said to Jimmy Grimshaw. 'Oh, you!' And I went off in a real tizz to have my book stamped.

Jimmy caught me up outside.

'Going to the Fancy Dress Dance, Judy?' he asked.

'I expect so,' I said in a bored voice, although my costume was all ready and I wouldn't have missed it for worlds.

'You wouldn't consider going with me, would you?' he said, and even though it was quite dark I could see a blush sort of creeping over his freckles.

'I'm afraid I'm already going with someone,' I surprised myself by saying.

'Anyone I know?' Jimmy said, and I could see he was struggling against overwhelming jealousy.

'I don't think you do know him,' I said, making it up as I went along. 'He's a newcomer to the district.'

'Oh, I see,' Jimmy Grimshaw said slowly. 'Well, so long, Judy. I'll be seeing you.' And he swung himself on to his bicycle and rode away into the night.

I watched the red winking tail light of his bicycle disappear down the road. I felt a bit mean. Jimmy Grimshaw is one of the nicest

143

boys in the Youth Club, and quite handsome if you like red hair and freckles. Before Gavin moved in next door I'd have been quite pleased to go with Jimmy to the Fancy Dress Dance.

What had made me tell that whopping lie? I wondered, as I walked slowly home. Now I'd have to tell another one about old 'newcomer to the district' being struck low with some dreadful disease just on the very night of the dance.

I was so engrossed in my bitter thoughts, as they say, that I nearly bumped into someone walking along the road just in front of me.

'Hello, Judy,' a voice said, and I came out of my bitter thoughts to find I'd been walking behind Gavin without even knowing it.

'You're looking very grown-up tonight,' he said, looking down at me through those spiky eyelashes. 'I like you with your hair like that.'

'Oh, it just goes that way when I comb it,' I said, and thought how glad I was I'd slept in fourteen rollers the night before.

We walked along, and I thought how beautiful everything looked. The trees in the avenue were black against a navy-blue sky, and just at that moment I wouldn't have changed places with anyone else in the world.

When we came to our house, Gavin leaned against the gate.

'It's funny how I seem to see you at the library most nights, Judy,' he said.

'Life's full of coincidences,' I replied innocently.

'I suppose it is,' he smiled, and those gorgeous dimples of his creased his face up as he spoke.

'You're a nice kid,' he said.

I swallowed hard. It was now or never.

'We're having a Fancy Dress Dance at the Youth Club. Would you like to come, being new to the district and everything? You'd have to dress up,' I warned him.

Gavin rubbed his chin for a moment, then grinned. 'That's all right; the sixth form gave a Shakespeare play the term before I left. *Romeo and Juliet* it was, and I think I still have my Romeo costume. Thanks, Judy, I'd love to come.'

I told him more details, then we said good night. I went inside feeling as if a bubble had burst inside me. I kissed my father on the bare patch on top of his head.

'I've got the most wonderful unexpected news for you,' I said to him.

'You've come top of the class in physics,' he said.

'Even more wonderful and unexpected than that,' I laughed. 'Gavin is coming to the Fancy Dress Dance.'

They weren't all that impressed. Parents never are when you most expect them to be, but Mother did say: 'Thank goodness we've finished your costume, Judy.'

That did it.

'As if I'd go in that now,' I said, shuddering.

Mother put her knitting down. 'But we've spent nearly three weeks making it,' she said.

I picked my library book up and turned to go upstairs.

'I'd rather die than go in that dreadful old thing now,' I said.

My father swivelled his eyes reluctantly away from the boxing match on television. 'What was she going as?' he asked.

'A skeleton,' I said indignantly.

I must admit, though, that before things turned out the way they had, I had been absolutely thrilled about my costume. Bones, made out of stiff white paper, dangled loosely from a black sweater and a borrowed pair of black ballet tights. A realistically grinning mask was to cover my face.

Well, I ask you. How many girls do you know who would go out on their first real date with a marvellous boy wearing a realistically grinning mask?

When I told Annette Coles that I was actually bringing Gavin dressed as Romeo, she said nothing. I think she was too surprised to say a word.

I daren't mention the word 'costume' to my mother for a few days. She'd worked her fingers to the bone, as you might say, on that skeleton. But even she had to admit I looked pretty good when the great day came and I was ready.

I wore a last summer's full skirt of vivid blue, padded with three stiff petticoats. Laced tightly round my waist was a black waistcoat, and I'd borrowed a beautiful white Swiss blouse from my Auntie May, who goes abroad every year. Meg had grudgingly lent me a pair of her white nylon knee-length socks, and I'd made a wreath of artificial flowers for my hair, and sewn on bunches of coloured ribbons.

'You make a very sweet Austrian peasant,

146

dear,' Mother said. 'It really is more *you* than the skeleton outfit.'

I was just giving her a quick hug and kiss when Gavin knocked at the door.

His tall, dark good looks were shown off to advantage by the Romeo costume, although the grey gaberdine raincoat he wore over it spoiled the effect a bit. As we walked down to the hall, I breathed a sigh of relief that I had been ruthless about the skeleton.

I rushed to the cloakroom, wanting to hurry on the moment when we would make our entrance. I wanted to see Annette Coles's face when she saw us together.

I took off my coat and hung it up, and turned to the mirror to fix my headdress.

Then I nearly died.

Craning their necks, pushing like mad round the mirror, were no fewer than nine Austrian peasants! They were complete with black waistcoats, white blouses, coloured skirts, and what seemed like hundreds of coloured ribbons dangled gaily from their flowered headdresses.

Too late I remembered that the Art School had recently held a folk dancing contest. Nine Austrian peasants had obviously decided to give their costumes another ariring.

But worse was still to come.

Gavin was waiting for me outside the cloakroom, and his mouth dropped open when ten Austrian peasants trooped out.

'Just like the opening scene of a musical comedy,' he grinned.

As we went in, jiving had just stopped and the

147

lights were lowered for an old-fashioned crumby waltz. Suddenly the spotlight flickered, wavered, and was still.

Annette Coles stood there, halfway down the stairs. Her white dress, gleaming silver, fell in draped folds to her feet. On her shining red-gold hair she wore a small cap of pearls. She leaned gracefully over the banisters.

'Juliet,' I heard Gavin say in a funny breathless voice, and he went up to her and took her hand. They started to dance, and I knew that I was forgotten.

'Hi, Heidi! How about a dance?' someone called, and there in front of me stood Jimmy Grimshaw, alias Guy Fawkes, complete with beard, drooping moustache and voluminous cloak and large-brimmed black hat.

For the rest of the evening Romeo sat out at a little table with his Juliet, drinking Cokes and gazing into her green eyes. He did tear himself away to ask me about going home.

'Guy Fawkes will see me home,' I said with dignity, and he dashed back to hold his Juliet's hand.

'Did you ever see anything so soppy?' I asked Jimmy on the way home. 'And to think I thought that he was so . . .'

'That he was so what, Judy?' Jimmy said, and he stopped suddenly and tilted my chin with his finger. I looked up at him from underneath my eyelashes, but the moment was spoiled by his beard falling off, and we giggled all the rest of the way home.

My mother made no comment when she saw

that Jimmy, instead of Gavin, had brought me home. She can be very understanding at times. But I distinctly heard my father whisper, 'Romeo, Romeo, wherefore art *thou*, Romeo?' and I think Jimmy heard him because I saw them exchange a wink.

Outside at the door, Jimmy tilted my chin and kissed me.

I thought how beautiful everything looked. The trees in the avenue were black against a navy-blue sky, and just at that moment I wouldn't have changed places with anyone else in the world.

This Year — Next Year

Some people dedicate themselves to the pursuit of love from around the age of fourteen. Some people discard four or five marriages with the same practised ease.

It is all supposed to be indicative of the uncertain world we live in; a natural defence put up against the ever-constant threat of total annihilation.

But according to all this I must be a biological phenomenon. Because right up to the age of twenty-three, I have loved only one man — and he is Jonathan . . .

Sometimes I wonder if it is hereditary, this single-mindedness?

My father had died when I was a baby. He had disappeared on one of his flights halfway across the Atlantic, on a U-boat patrol. All I knew of him was a posed studio portrait of a young man in a peaked cap, with wings on his tunic, and the self-conscious beginnings of a fair moustache on his upper lip.

My mother is still slim, with only a few threads of silver in her dark brown hair, and yet when he died, something in her died, too. Friends will ask her quite openly why she hasn't married again, and her answer is to smile gently and to say nothing.

I knew that she worried about me, especially around Christmas and New Year. It was a bad time for both of us. For Mother because the telegram telling her that my father was missing had been delivered just as she was wrapping up his present — a massive sweater in navy-blue oiled wool, knitted laboriously by her on the long blacked-out winter evenings.

'He was so cold up there, stationed on the island of Benbecula,' she had often told me. 'He used to say that the wind never stopped howling. It was like a wild animal screaming to be set free.'

And Christmas for me . . . well, unrequited love is bad enough for most of the year, though teaching ten-year-olds in the year preceding their eleven-plus examination can be a pretty absorbing business. But at Christmas, when the last carol has been sung and the last hand-painted Christmas card taken home, the loneliness is far worse.

Jonathan's mother — I had known her all my life as Aunt Margaret — and my mother were childhood friends. The rambling stone house, seemingly held together by trailing ivy, and with countless children running up and down the wide and winding staircases, had been a haven of delight for my mother, an only child. Now Jonathan's grandparents, Grannie and Grandpa Mack, as they were known to almost everyone in the village, lived on there alone. An apple-cheeked Darby and Joan, they ate in the big warm kitchen, and in the evenings sat round a fire in the small breakfast room, leaving most of the rooms unoccupied. Except at New Year.

Then the ivy-covered house came to life again. From the large square hall, with a log fire blazing in the brick fire-place, to the attic with its sloping roof, every corner bulged with aunts and uncles, grandchildren and even a sprinkling of great-grandchildren, almost a clan gathering.

And every year, on New Year's Eve, around six o'clock in the evening, Mother and I walked down the lane to the big house, and became part of the large and boisterous family.

Jonathan, now fully chartered as an accountant and living a bachelor existence in London, would arrive in his battered old car, trying to appear detached from it all, but invariably being drawn into the warmth of a united family. Eventually he would unbend and join in the games, and then he would tease me and ask me about my little 'horrors'.

Through a combination of naïveté and wishful thinking, I had begun to believe that every New Year would be the same, until one year, I hoped in the not too distant future, Jonathan would, as they say in all the best love stories, take one look at me and know. I had planned exactly how it would happen . . .

We would be walking together, hand in hand, through crunchy snow. A pale sun would touch the frosty trees to glittering glory. There would even be a robin somewhere around, and suddenly Jonathan would stop.

'Cathy,' he would say, and there would be newly awakened wonder in his deep voice, and his dark eyes would glow with tenderness. 'Cathy, I love you. Why haven't I realized it before? I must have been blind all these years . . . ' and he'd kiss me, and somewhere in the distance the bells would start to ring out.

Perhaps this year it would happen, and if not this year, well the next, or the next. I was prepared to wait. I would wait for ever for Jonathan.

'Margaret feels it's all too much for the old couple this year,' my mother said one dismal afternoon as she sat at her desk searching frantically for last year's Christmas card list. 'But they won't have it. They keep saying wistfully that it may be the last time the whole family are gathered together.'

'I wonder if Jonathan will come as usual this year?' I said, carefully making it sound as though I couldn't care less one way or the other.

Mother had found her precious list, and began to tick off names with almost hysterical haste.

'I wonder if Jonathan will come this year?' I said again.

She selected a card festooned with holly and dripping with tinsel, and without looking at me said, 'Yes, Margaret says that Jonathan is coming, and this year he's bringing a friend with him, a girlfriend.' She slipped the card into an envelope, and made a great show of tucking in the flap. 'Her name is Madeleine.'

'That's a pretty name,' I said quickly, proud of the fact that my voice gave nothing away. 'Is he bringing her from London?'

'No,' said my mother, still without looking at me, 'she's at RADA, but her family live about fifteen miles away from here, and apparently

153

Jonathan is bringing her over just for the day . . . '

Then she stuck a stamp in the corner of the envelope, banged it down with her fist, and declared that she must catch the next post.

Left alone, tears started to my eyes, surprising me . . . So it had happened, the thing I had known in my secret heart was bound to happen. I stared at myself in the gilt-framed mirror.

Madeleine, I told myself, and an actress. And who do you think you are to compete with that? She's sure to be beautiful, and you aren't beautiful, not in the least. I stared with distaste at my hair, short, brown and curly; at my eyes, the same ordinary brown colour, and my nose, not Grecian or even straight, but decidedly turned up at the tip. I stared at my mouth, too big, far too big for beauty, and I was just wishing that my complexion could have been described as anything but 'fresh', when my mother came back.

On New Year's Eve everything at the big house was the same, everything just like every other year, and yet nothing was really the same . . .

Logs crackled in the brick fireplace. The tree was brilliant with candleshine, and cousins of every shape and size dashed about, shrieking, pulling crackers, and being tickled by uncles wearing ridiculous fancy paper hats.

And in the sitting room a place was found for me on the sofa, between Jonathan's brother, Roger, a cynical twenty-year-old in his second year at Oxford, and a hearty uncle from

Birmingham, wearing a policeman's miniature helmet on top of his shiny bald head.

Someone passed me a glass of sherry, and I smiled at Roger, and told the uncle that I was feeling very well thank you, and sipped the sherry, and all the time I was looking round for Jonathan.

When I saw him I knew that nothing had changed. Not for me anyway. Just to look at him made my heart stand still, and because he hadn't seen me I could stare at him, and love him without anyone knowing . . .

He was as dark as I remembered, but his hair had been clipped close around his head. He sat there on a too-low pouffe, his long fingers curled round a glass of sherry . . . But Jonathan didn't drink sherry, he always said that it was a woman's drink. Jonathan drank beer . . .

And then I realized. The drink he was holding belonged to Madeleine, and she was sitting on the floor by his side, her arm draped over his leg and her hands clasped possessively on his knee.

I had been quite wrong. She wasn't beautiful at all, at least not in an orthodox kind of way. Her hair, the colour of ripe corn, swung as straight as rain round her small pointed face. She looked about seventeen years old, and her big blue eyes were made up as expertly as a ballerina's, but her pale skin was clear and shiny as a child's. She wore black stretch slacks, which accentuated the length of her slim legs, and a black polo-necked sweater clung to her lovely figure.

In my cherry-red woollen dress, and my sling-back high-heeled shoes, I felt suddenly over-dressed and countrified. I would never have dreamed of going to a party wearing slacks and a black sweater, but then I was Cathy Blane, teacher of the fourth-year juniors at a village school, and she was Madeleine, an aspiring actress from London . . . She was all that I could never be, or even hope to be: smart, sophisticated, and as modern as tomorrow.

A wild-eyed aunt wheeled a trolley loaded with turkey sandwiches, jellies, cream, mince pies and slices of rich moist Christmas cake through from the kitchen.

'Food, glorious food,' said Roger on my right, and gratefully accepted a plate, a paper napkin, a turkey sandwich and two mince pies. Madeleine, I noticed, refused everything politely, but over a slice of Christmas cake, Jonathan's eyes met mine . . .

'Hello, Cathy,' his lips said, then he bent his dark head down to Madeleine. 'That's Cathy,' I saw him tell her, and with one look from the exotically made-up eyes I saw her dismiss me and my red dress as negligible.

'Don't say Aunt Dora's going to sing? Surely the old dear's past it?' said the incorrigible Roger, not quite underneath his breath. From across the room Jonathan closed one eye in a deliberate, but kindly wink.

For many years now Aunt Dora had been singing her piece at the New Year party. I remembered Jonathan and me sitting on the floor, stuffing handkerchiefs into our mouths to stop giggling.

And then my mother was moving over to the piano and playing a few chords. Aunt Dora, her usually fluttering hands clasped together underneath her shelving bosom, cleared her throat ready to begin. The applause afterwards was deafening, and Aunt Dora, pink with pleasure, her long nose quivering with delight, accepted the ovation along with a glass of home-made ginger wine.

An uncle with a flourishing moustache and a yellow waistcoat made a penny appear from the top of Madeleine's blonde head, and another from behind her ear. Then, prodded by a proud parent, a small cousin with a thatch of red hair and a lisp gave a spirited rendering of 'Sea Fever', rather spoiling the effect by bursting into tears when he forgot the last verse.

The dear familiarity of it all seeped into my heart. This was what being in a family really meant . . .

And then it was time for the organized games, the bobbing for the apple, charades, and a boisterous version of hunt-the-thimble, with the adults cheating madly and leaving the thimble for the children to find.

Obediently we were all shooed into the hall by an officious little nephew smartly dressed in a grey flannel suit, topped by a Beatle hair-do. Now perhaps there would be the opportunity for a word with Jonathan, and, as I knew he would, he came over to me, and stood looking down at me with his endearing wide grin.

'Same old mixture as before,' he laughed, but all the time he was looking round for Madeleine, and he pulled me with him over to the staircase, where she was sharing the bottom step with Roger.

'Move up one,' he commanded, and we watched an orderly queue forming up by the Christmas tree.

One by one the family disappeared into the sitting room to be greeted by hilarious shouts of laughter.

'What on earth are they doing now?' asked Roger. 'If I'd known what I was letting myself in for, I'd have been conspicuous by my absence.'

Madeleine giggled. 'Can't say that I blame you,' she said. 'I'd thought parties like this went out with the Ark.'

I hoped that Jonathan hadn't heard the remark, but I saw by the way his mouth tightened that he had.

'Last year I refused to come,' Roger went on. 'I went to stay with old Phil. He's an absolute pro when it comes to playing the clarinet, and we had the most marvellous jazz sessions. As a matter of fact he wanted me to go this year, but the parents talked me into putting in an appearance at this orgy.'

Madeleine giggled again, which was all Roger needed. 'As a matter of fact,' he said again, 'old Phil lives only a mile or so away from here. We could be there in a flash in my car. Did you see it as you came in, by the way? Goes like a bomb . . . how about the four of us piling into it, and making a quick getaway?'

I held my breath as Madeleine jumped to her feet, her eyes sparkling. 'Oh yes, let's, Jonathan. I've never been so beastly bored in my whole life, and when that old dame started to sing I thought I'd die!'

'Me too,' said Roger. 'Come on, if we slip upstairs for our coats, and nip down the back stairs, they'll never miss us.'

Jonathan put a restraining hand on Madeleine's arm. 'You go by all means, Roger,' he said quietly, 'but we'll be staying. There are the presents to be given out yet, and the old couple haven't forgotten anyone.'

I had seen that look on Jonathan's face before, and that glint of determination in his dark eyes.

'Don't be so sensitive, darling,' Madeleine said lightly. 'What difference can it possibly make if we slip away?'

Roger was halfway upstairs and she shook off Jonathan's hand and started to follow. 'Come *on*, darling,' she said over a disappearing black woollen shoulder. 'Another minute and they'll call us in for that ghastly game, whatever it is.'

Jonathan stood at the bottom of the stairs, looking gravely up at her. 'We're not going, Madeleine,' he repeated. 'We came here, and here we stay.'

'Big brother has spoken,' said Roger from the curve of the stairs, but Madeleine's blue eyes flashed diamond bright, and a deep flush stained her pale cheeks.

'*You* may be staying, but I'm not,' she said, 'and don't worry about how I'm going to get home, because Roger will see to that, won't you, Roger?'

He came down a step and had the grace to look ashamed. 'Look here, sweetie,' he blustered, 'don't get me involved or anything. I didn't mean to start a sordid row between you two.'

Madeleine gave him a radiant smile. 'There's no row, darling, but Jonathan knows that I will not be told what I must do, and what I must not do,' and she leaned forward and touched him lightly on his cheek. 'So goodbye, darling.'

For an incredulous second Jonathan stared after her. Then she was gone, and they were calling us in to carry on with the game.

I was almost glad that the first thing they did when we went in was to put a blindfold round Jonathan's eyes. They looked haunted, and his voice stumbled as he repeated the meaningless jingle of the game. Desperately I wanted to comfort him, perhaps just to touch his hand as we stood round the piano a few minutes later joining in a singsong. But after a rousing chorus of 'Nellie Dean', I saw Jonathan suddenly stride out of the room.

Even above the singing I heard the slamming of the big front door, and in my mind's eye I saw Jonathan tearing down the lane without his hat or coat, his head bent against the cold wind. Whenever he was very hurt or angry he did what he called 'walking it off'. Later someone — I think it was Margaret — said, 'Where's Jonathan?' and I realized that he had been out for almost an hour.

160

'He'll be back,' laughed the uncle with the moustache. 'Probably taken his girlfriend for a stroll, and I can't say that I blame him, either. She's a stunner!' And the uncle, happily married and the contented father of twin sons, put his arm round his wife and gave her an affectionate and husbandly kiss.

I glanced at my watch. Suppose, just suppose, that he had gone after Madeleine? She had hurt him deeply by her contrariness, and Jonathan could be very impulsive in the way that sensitive people often are.

As unobtrusively as I could, I edged my way out of the room and into the hall. My high heels forced me to run in tiny steps down the curve of the long drive. The cold wind tore at my hair and whipped my breath away, then I stopped. Jonathan's ancient car was parked by the iron gates, and in the driving seat, leaning on the wheel, was Jonathan.

I wrenched open the door, and without stopping to think for a minute about what was right and proper, climbed in to sit beside him. He was staring straight ahead, drumming his fingers on the wheel, and his thin shoulders were hunched forward in utter and hopeless despair.

'We missed you, Jonathan,' I said softly.

He turned to face me then, and as if speaking to himself he said, 'It's funny, isn't it, the way you can love someone terribly, so much that a day without them is wasted? So much that you're nearly driven mad by their moods and wondering if they care, and then they do

161

something, or say something, and you stare at them, and they're another person, and all that love, all that anguish, is gone as though it had never been — just like that . . . '

I felt my throat tighten against the threat of tears. Jonathan's face was so close to my own I could see the long curve of his sensitive mouth, and the pain reflected in his dark eyes.

'But that isn't love,' I said slowly, the words almost saying themselves. 'Real love doesn't die as quickly as that. Real love accepts the loved ones as they really are, and nothing they say or do can make the slightest difference.'

'That's infatuation, Cathy, not love.'

'But infatuation doesn't last for eight, nine, ten years, does it?' I said, almost dazed by his nearness and my aching love for him.

And then, surprising me, a tear spilled over and ran down my cheek. I tasted the sad saltiness of it as it passed my mouth, and Jonathan took out his handkerchief and wiped it gently away.

'Cathy?' he said, and my name was a question that I could only answer by lifting my mouth to his . . .

His kiss was all that I had dreamed it would be, and it left us both shaken. Then we sat there in a sort of wondering silence, holding each other tight until the door of the big house opened and light shone out into the drive.

And it was all as I had planned it would be. There was no snow, no robin anywhere about, and no New Year bells. But when we went together hand in hand into the hall, I could see by the smiling faces turned towards us that everyone knew.

'We've been waiting for you, Jonathan,' Grannie Mack gently reproved him, and my heart echoed her words. But now my waiting time was over, and the happiness could really begin.

Memories of Melanie

All kinds and sorts of people rented the house next door, and our mother would have been horrified if she'd known how much time my twin brother, Jason, and I spent in peering though the hedge at them. But, by the time we were nine years old, she was spending longer and longer each day in her bedroom.

Our father seemed hardly to know that we existed and, thinking back, now that he has been dead for so long, there is hardly anything that I can remember about him.

He was tall and thin and dark-haired — like Jason — and he would catch the train each day to his office in the city, returning in the evening to eat his dinner in silence. Then he would go upstairs and sit with our mother, leaving us to the slap-happy ministrations of Mrs Brown, our so-called housekeeper.

Mrs Brown was so fat that when she sat on one of the round kitchen stools, folds of tweed-skirted flesh would hang over the sides. It was from her that we gleaned our information about the tenants of the ivy-covered house next door . . .

She never failed us and, when the house was to be reoccupied, we would reconnoitre for days, lying flat, watching as avidly as seasoned bird-watchers the comings and goings of the new occupants of the house.

There was the actress of thirty or so — middle-aged, we decided — 'resting' the summer away, lying near-naked in the sun on a tartan rug. Her hair, overbleached to the texture of candy floss, her eyebrows shaved off then drawn on again — we thought she was beautiful and told her so.

When she left, she gave me a half-empty jar of wrinkle cream and Jason a cigarette lighter which didn't work. We felt ourselves to be in her everlasting debt . . .

It must have been the summer after that when the French family came. There was Mama and Papa and two little girls with black hair scraped back so tightly that they wore expressions of perpetual surprise at everything.

We played polite, dull games with them on the terrace in front of the French windows, until they were replaced by a writer, who, according to Mrs Brown, couldn't write a word unless he was well and truly 'the worse for drink'.

We wasted no time in introducing ourselves to him, only to find that apart from a slightly fishy gaze, he was, to all intents and purposes, a perfectly respectable human being.

'People who write books should *look* as if they write books,' Jason told me in disgust.

Then, after our twelfth birthday, our mother's health deteriorated and we were judged too much for her and sent away to school. The next summer the Americans came to live in the ivy-covered house . . .

They were Texans, the husband an officer in the American Air Force, and they had a daughter, a girl one year younger than Jason and me.

Her name was Melanie.

'She's prettier than me,' I told Jason, longing to be contradicted, but he merely grunted, being busy at the time with a mysterious black box, and a collection of wires.

About that time he steadfastly refused to have normal conversation with me, insisting that I communicate with him by speaking down a tube.

'She has fabulous clothes,' I told the tube. 'She doesn't have to wear uniform for school and today she showed me how to pop corn.'

'Receiving you loud and clear,' said Jason. 'Over!'

'My brother is brilliant,' I told Melanie, and she threw back her head and laughed out loud. She had the merriest, most infectious laugh I'd ever heard. Then, when she saw my hurt face, she wound a strand of her long fair hair round and round her finger.

'Well, what d'you know?' she said.

We didn't hear Jason coming towards us across the lawn. He wore a grass-stained pair of khaki shorts and there was an ink stain on the end of his nose. I felt he did himself less than justice, but Melanie didn't seem to mind.

From the very beginning they adopted a teasing attitude towards each other and Jason would gently mock her accent.

'Hi!' he'd say when he met her and, although he was at an age when to be seen out with a girl was definitely shame-making, he took her for long bicycle rides, borrowing my bicycle for her, without telling me.

We'd meet every morning in Melanie's yard — we never did get her to call it a garden — and sometimes, when Mother was unwell, we'd stay to dinner.

Melanie's mother fed us on golden fried chicken and buttery corn on the cob and called me 'Honey', in a warm voice that made me want to cry.

They were in the house next door for three years, and then, in the summer of our sixteenth year, our mother died.

I remember the awful finality of it all: the way I cried and the way, on the day of the funeral, Melanie came into the darkened house and talked non-stop to Jason.

The stiff mask that was Jason's face had relaxed by the time she'd gone back through the hole in the hedge, and he was able to talk to our father in the evening and make brave and manly plans for the future.

Somehow, that seemed to be the end of our childhood, and when, soon afterwards, Melanie came round and told us that her father had a posting back to America, her news fitted in perfectly with the general gloomy pattern of things that year.

Jason shook hands with her formally, made promises about writing, then spent the rest of the day in his room, whistling tunelessly underneath his breath, a sure sign that he was upset.

Our father died before Christmas, suddenly and needlessly, swerving his car to avoid a stray dog, and as there was money enough, we were able to stay at our respective schools and spent the next few years living with a succession of aunts and uncles, until Jason went up to university to read English and history for a degree.

I managed to scrape a place at a domestic science college in London and it was there I met Andrew.

We were married as soon as my training was completed, with Jason giving me away. He looked unfamiliar in a dark suit, instead of the inevitable jeans, and had submitted to a badly needed haircut the day before the wedding ceremony.

'I'm worried about Jason,' I told my new husband. He was to become used to hearing me say just that . . .

By now Jason had a post, teaching English and history in a large school.

'Ninety-eight per cent of my pupils are unfeeling, uncaring, semi-illiterate morons,' he would say in a sarcastic, cynical voice. It was obvious to anyone who loved him as much as I did that Jason was far from happy.

He refused to live with us and took a room in the house of a motherly widow who fed him on pies and suet puddings, without managing to increase his weight by a single ounce.

Jason, at twenty-five, was as thin and tall as our father had been, with the same expressive dark eyes. He had a succession of girlfriends and, after my first baby was born, I became accustomed to bathing her, watched by the girl of the moment.

'Well, what's the verdict this time?' Andrew would say, and I'd shake my head sorrowfully.

Andrew would tease: 'Well, I thought she was a stunner. What do you want for Jason? Cleopatra and Miss World rolled into one?'

Around that time my second child, a boy, was born and around that time, there was Serena.

Serena was as gentle as the sound of her name, and for a time, I thought she was the one. We became firm friends and she would sit on the bathroom stool as the others had done, talking to me about Jason.

'He's asked me to marry him, but I haven't said yes,' she confided one day, turning a tin of baby powder round and round in her hands. 'There's something stopping me . . . I love *him*, but deep down I know that he doesn't love me. He's fond of me and I know I could make him happy, but I get the strange feeling sometimes that he's waiting for something to happen and that he's asked me to marry him because he's given up hope of this other thing coming true.'

I saw, with dismay, that tears glistened in her eyes.

After that day I never saw her again and, for the next few months, Jason came alone to visit us.

He was, he told us, writing a book. One evening, he read a chapter aloud to us. I thought it was wonderful, but terribly, achingly sad. I told him so.

169

'*C'est la vie!*' he said and I wanted to tell him that it wasn't, not always, but he pushed the manuscript into a tattered envelope and ruffled my hair.

'I'm worried about Jason,' I told Andrew that night, as we lay in bed together, lovingly entwined. 'He should be married by now, living happily ever after like us, not spending his time pounding away at a typewriter in that terrible dingy room of his.'

'Forget Jason,' said Andrew, as he pulled me closer, and so, obligingly, for the time being, I did.

Jason's book was rejected by at least seven publishers and his visits to us grew farther and farther apart, until one day, in early summer, the telephone rang imperiously.

His voice at the other end was alive with a singing, incredulous joy. He was bringing someone rather special to see us, he said, and did I mind?

The babies were put to bed with indecent haste and I fed the long-suffering Andrew on cold lamb and biscuits and cheese, then I peeped through the curtains as Jason's ancient car drew up at the gate.

I saw him rush round and open the door for a girl who vaguely reminded me of someone . . .

She was tall and slim and had golden hair. She was laughing at something Jason had said. She was laughing with her head thrown back . . . Then I was running down the stairs, flinging the door open and still I couldn't be sure . . . Who was she?

'Bumped into her, quite literally, outside Swan and Edgar's,' Jason was saying, holding tightly to her hand. And their blazing joy in each other was so complete that I had to turn away and wipe a stupid tear from my cheek.

'Over here for a month,' Jason said, and now I saw that the waiting look had gone from his face. 'Long enough for me to persuade her to marry me.'

Andrew came out then and I introduced them to each other.

'How d'you do?' said my husband, taking her hand.

'Hi!' said Melanie.

When the Blow Falls

I was cleaning the lounge window that Friday afternoon when John came home from work to tell me he'd been made redundant. At first I couldn't take it in, even though we'd known for a long time that the firm he worked for was in financial difficulties.

'Rumours,' we'd said.

'And even if it did happen,' I'd said glibly, 'so what? You're a skilled draughtsman. You'd get another job easily. But it won't happen, so we're not going to worry about it. Okay?'

I suppose I'm a born optimist, always have been. I know I wake up each morning being quite sure that this is the day something wonderful is going to happen. We're going to win the pools; a distant relative we hardly knew has died and left us a fortune; that slogan I wrote for a breakfast cereal competition has won us a holiday for four in the Bahamas . . . At least, that was the way it used to be.

A believer in rainbows, the shimmering kind, with something good always waiting for us at the end of it.

So, as John stood before me, his shoulders bowed, I remember I went to him and put my arms round him.

'We weren't going to let it get us down. It is a challenge,' I said. We'd face it together, and it might even turn out for the best. He would get another job with a firm who recognized his true potential, and the day might come when we'd look back and bless the day his old firm had the lack of foresight to hand him his redundancy papers.

Oh yes, I said all that, and more. I made John a cup of tea, and we sat there in the kitchen and John clasped his fingers round his cup as if he were cold, although outside the sun still shone, and the room was baking hot from the heat of the oven.

'I'm glad the girls are out,' he said, still holding his cup in that peculiar way. 'What time will they be back?'

I glanced at the round clock on the wall.

'Well, Janice will be back from her Brownie meeting around eight o'clock, but Susan may be a bit later. They're practising hard for the dancing display at the end of next week. I've two costumes to make before then. Any ideas about the way an elderly gnome ought to be dressed?'

I was trying so hard to cheer John up, trying so hard to make him see that what had happened to us was happening to families all over the country every day. I wasn't going to be the kind of wife who made her man feel that he'd been dealt a mortal blow just because he'd lost his job.

I was trying too hard, I can see that now, because John's next words didn't even make sense to me.

'What am I going to tell them, love? How can you explain to a child that before long ballet lessons will be out of the question?

That a week's summer camp with the Brownies is more than her parents can afford? Kids nowadays take things like that for granted. I'll tell you something, Meg, something I was thinking about as I drove home. Once when I was a kid — about eight I'd be, the year after my dad died — we were told at school to write a composition about our holidays. My holiday. And, you know, I wrote those two words at the top of my paper, and I sat there staring at it as all the other kids in my class scribbled away. I couldn't write a word, because I hadn't had a holiday, because there wasn't enough money even for a day's outing to the sea. I sat there and sat there, with a dirty great lump in my throat. I thought I'd forgotten all about it, but I hadn't. It's as clear in my mind as if it had happened yesterday.'

I remember I grew angry; getting up from my chair, collecting the cups and rinsing them out furiously.

'For heaven's sake, John Graham. Stop being such a pessimist! For one thing, you won't be out of work for long, and for another, Janice and Susan aren't like that. We haven't spoiled them, and if they have to do without things for a while, they'll understand.'

'Let's hope so,' John said, and went upstairs to our room to lie on the bed, staring at the ceiling, leaving me to tell the girls when they came in, still shocked by his defeatism, still unable to grasp the enormity of what had happened to us.

I grasped it all right as the weeks became

months, as John wrote letter after letter applying for a job, attended interviews, and was repeatedly told that thirty-seven was rather older than the age they had in mind.

It wasn't long before the small nest-egg we had in the Post Office had dwindled to nothing, and it wasn't long before the mantelpiece was littered with bills we couldn't pay, and the mortgage repayments on our small semi loomed on each monthly horizon like a waking nightmare.

I'm not the sort of woman who feels a cabbage because she has to stay at home and do housework. I suppose I'm a mum-in-the-kitchen kind of person, but when Susan started at the big comprehensive school and we couldn't find the money for her uniform of navy blue and red, I took a job in the local supermarket, walking round the store, replenishing the shelves with tins and packets, trundling them about in a wire trolley.

'They're not going to suffer,' I told John. '*We'll* do without, but not the children,' and he stared at me as if I were a stranger, as if I were trying to blame him, and before we knew it, we were in the middle of another row.

'Daddy's always picking on me,' Susan said, 'just because he's had a row with you.'

I felt awful because I knew she was right.

We thought we hadn't spoiled our children, but I suppose we had. At least, we'd taken it for granted that we had a family holiday each year, and that the girls had bikes, and although Susan was only eleven, she began to want grown-up clothes and shoes.

'All the girls at school have midi coats and boots,' she wailed, her hair, which she was growing long, wisping untidily round her small, pointed face. 'There are some boots in the shop in the High Street, lace-up, and they're only nine pounds. I'll have them for my birthday,' she said, and, because I was tired, my temper flared.

'Nine pounds!' I exploded. 'Do you realize that's more than I get for a week working mornings? And don't talk about them to your dad. He has enough on his mind.'

And even Janice, my little placid Janice, with her curly hair and rosy cheeks, broke into uncontrollable sobs when her beloved bike, left carelessly on the grass verge, was backed into by a reversing lorry, and damaged beyond repair.

'All my friends have bikes. How can I go out and play with them when I haven't got a bike? I hate being poor,' she sobbed. And that next day, on my way home from work, I stood for a long time outside the shoe shop, staring at the lace-up boots displayed in the window, then moving farther along the street to scan the advertisements in the newsagent's shop, looking for an offer of a second-hand bike.

'How do you explain to a child that her world has suddenly turned topsy-turvy?' I asked John that night. 'Maybe if I worked full time . . . '

Instead of replying, he took me by the shoulders and turned me to face the mirror over the fireplace in the lounge.

'Take a good look at yourself, love,' he said, and there was more than a hint of despair in his voice. 'How do you think I feel, seeing you come home tired out and watching you start to work again? From next week on I'll cook the evening meal. I could, you know. It's only a matter of following a recipe.'

In spite of everything, I had to laugh. A real man, John was completely undomesticated, making even the boiling of an egg into a full-scale manoeuvre. And, thank God, he laughed with me, but when he turned away I did take a good look at myself in the mirror, and my heart sank.

My hair is thick and coarse, as straight as a die, and without its half-yearly perm, without even an occasional visit to a hairdresser for a shampoo and set, it framed my face shapelessly. The constant worry about the mortgage, the rates, the payments on the three-piece suite, the bickering between John and me, the children's requests for money for this, money for that, were taking their toll. The woman staring back at me looked far older than her thirty-two years . . .

'And who says money doesn't count?' I said, half to myself, but John heard, and told me that he had decided to stop looking for a job in his own line, that as from then he would take anything.

'I'll even sweep the streets,' he shouted. 'Anything rather than have you look at me like that.'

'I'm not looking at you like anything,' I said, close to tears, and he got up from his chair and left the room. I watched him go, his shabby cardigan unbuttoned, and his down-at-heel slippers flapping from his heels as he went.

177

What was it my mother had once said? 'When poverty comes in the door, love flies out of the window.' How right she'd been. John and I were beginning to act like strangers to each other. Strangers who didn't even like each other all that much.

John didn't get a job as a road sweeper. There just weren't any jobs going at all. And I hurt my back stretching up to a high shelf with a heavy tin of biscuits in my hand.

The doctor said it was a slipped disc, and the hospital said a badly torn muscle, but either way it meant me giving up my job and lying flat for a week, then moving round the house in constant pain, my lower half encased in a rigid contraption which made every movement a torture.

John applied for Social Security, and we sank what was left of our pride and had the girls put on the free school meals lists.

I think that was when we really touched rock bottom. Almost overnight, it seemed, Susan changed from a loving, obedient little girl, into a sullen, disgruntled stranger.

She was coming up to the age when girls want worn-for-the-minute dresses, gimmicky fashions, and pocket money to spend on magazines, records and tights.

Some days John didn't bother to shave, and once when Janice asked for some money to go out to the ice-cream van, he exploded into uncontrollable rage, pulling out the linings of his pockets to show her there was nothing there.

For myself, it didn't matter. My wardrobe

had been fairly well stocked when the blow fell, and clothes made of man-made fibres last a long time, but the girls were growing, and growing fast.

'I can't go to school with a darn in my sweater,' Janice wailed, and when Susan caught her raincoat on some barbed wire it was a major tragedy.

I had never been good at sewing. I spent one entire evening trying in vain to mend the coat so that the tear wouldn't show, my fingers hot and sticky as the thread caught itself up in knots, with Susan watching me, announcing that she'd rather die than go to school with a mend in her coat that showed.

John was out in the back garden, lighting a bonfire, a form of therapy that he'd indulged in a lot lately. He would stay out there for what seemed hours, prodding the pile of burning rubbish with a long stick, sending up showers of sparks, then watching, seemingly transfixed, as the spiral of smoke rose up into the sky.

With sitting in one position for so long, struggling with the coat, my back had begun to ache again, and when Susan came over to me, examined the tear, and announced that it looked just terrible, and that she'd go to school without a coat rather than wear that old thing, I did an unforgivable thing.

I started to cry, and once I'd started I couldn't stop. It seemed as if all the tears of my life were draining my heart. They rolled down my cheeks, and I buried my face in Susan's torn raincoat, and cried as if my heart were breaking.

179

And suddenly I felt a pair of arms go round me, suddenly Susan was kneeling there, holding me tight, rocking me backwards and forwards, as if I were the child and she the mother giving comfort.

'Mummy,' I heard her say. 'Please don't cry. I don't care about the coat, honestly. I didn't mean that it was horrible. Mummy, please don't cry.'

And Janice, who had come into the room without me seeing her, started to cry with me, and there we all were, clinging to each other, cheeks pressed together, our tears mingling, whilst outside in the garden, oblivious to it all, John stood silently, leaning on a spade, watching the grey smoke swirling up into the sky.

And suddenly, the real me, the believer in rainbows, came to life again. Suddenly everything came into perspective again, and I wiped the tears away and started to talk.

'Look,' I began, 'I think it's time we had a talk — the three of us. We can't go on like this; we're just being silly, all of us.'

They were only children, but they stared at me, trying to comprehend, their faces solemn and earnest, anxious and loving.

'Through no fault of his own, Daddy lost his job. It's far worse for him than it is for us. We have a nice house to live in, we have enough to eat, you're both growing up big and strong, and some day, perhaps next week, Daddy will find a job. And even if it isn't as good a job as the one he had before, it won't matter, because we've still got each other. Do you see?'

Janice nodded, her round face serious.

'Becky's father died, and that was worse, wasn't it?'

'Much worse,' I agreed.

'And there's a girl at school with only one arm,' Janice said, warming to her subject, dramatically.

'Exactly,' I said. 'So what have we to cry about?'

★ ★ ★

There isn't a dramatic end to my story. But bad times don't last for ever, and the tears I'd been trying to hide had brought us closer together. From that day the girls were less demanding and far more understanding of the problems facing their father and me.

Eventually, after being out of work for almost a year, John got a job of sorts, working nights at a nearby factory. We were able to hold up our heads again, and there'll be a pair of kinky lace-up boots for Susan's birthday and a second-hand bike for Janice.

It's love that counts every time, love and sharing, and the other day I swear I saw my rainbow again, a bit tarnished at the edges, but a rainbow just the same.

A Time to Remember

When Jonathan loved her, and there was sunshine everywhere, and life was worth living, he would ring her at six o'clock every evening.

Helen knew that was when the secretaries, and his boss in the next room, had gone their various ways, and he had the office to himself. And as her flat was only round the corner from the school where she taught, she could be home easily by that time.

In the first months of their loving, he rang almost every day. At ten minutes to six, she would feel the first thrill of anticipation, and when the telephone bell rang she had to restrain herself from picking it up straight away.

Even then, she wasn't all that sure of him. Jonathan wasn't the sort of man any woman could be sure of. Tall black-haired, with grey eyes that sometimes took on the look of a dreaming boy, he had a take-me-or-leave-me attitude about him that fascinated her.

'I love him too much,' Helen would tell herself. 'I have been too honest with him, I should have 'played it cool', as they say in the films. It's all wrong that I'm there every time he rings. It would do him good to dial my number, and sit there at his desk listening to the ringing tone, realizing to his astonishment that I'd gone out somewhere.'

But as some people in love have a tune

all their own, they had a *time*, and Helen was always there, waiting, just waiting for the telephone to ring.

In the time of their loving, it was as though she walked alone, untouchable, remote, heedless of staff-room crises at school, the lively bunch of fifteen-year-olds who demanded so much of her energy; forgetful of family loyalties; vulnerable, loving him so much that even the sound of his voice could set her senses whirling.

Tim Mathieson, Headmaster, as fair as Jonathan was dark, and as stockily built as Jonathan was tall and lean, asked her one day to have dinner with him in town, and go on afterwards to see a film.

'We could go straight from school,' he said innocently, and although, of course, that was impossible, she was flattered, because Tim Mathieson was a far from ordinary man. He was young as headmasters go, a mere thirty-two, and he drove a dashing white car, more like an advertising executive's than a headmaster's.

He had a natural, unassuming maturity. His in-born sense of authority was tempered with kindness and perceptive tolerance.

But how could she go anywhere with him straight from school, when that meant she wouldn't be in the flat at six o'clock, when the telephone could ring?

Tim's invitation came at the time when Jonathan's calls were becoming less frequent; when the first niggling doubts that he didn't love her half as much as she loved him were beginning to keep her awake at nights.

183

But Helen wouldn't listen to them, she *dare* not listen to them. She loved him so much, it was impossible to conceive that he didn't feel the same way. Love begat love, and hadn't he told her himself that her utter devotion to him was a boost to his ego?

She could recall the exact time and place he had said that, as indeed she could recall and mull over every word he had said on their evenings out together. They were sitting in a rather dingy café somewhere in the labyrinth of streets behind Baker Street Station. Jonathan had collected two cups of tea, and hers had slopped over into the saucer. The man at the next table drooped over an empty cup, as though he were asleep.

'I can't go on seeing you like this,' Jonathan had said. 'Each time we meet it gets worse. My work is suffering.'

And she had covered his hand with her own, and told him that she agreed it would be better if they only met twice instead of three times a week, and he had squeezed her hand, and nodded, but sadly of course . . .

'Jonathan is writing a book,' Helen told her fellow teachers in the staff room, in answer to their teasing questions. 'In his spare time, and until it sells, he has to keep on with his job in insurance. But some day he's going to write full time, in a cottage in Cornwall.'

That was a dream that stayed with her during term time, when, on difficult days, she wondered if teaching were her vocation after all; when it seemed that the faces at their rows of desks were

184

more than usually expressionless and blank.

The dream was of a rain-swept stone cottage, set into the steep side of a Cornish cliff, with the sea pounding on the rocks below, and Jonathan writing away for dear life. She concocted the meals he liked in the primitive kitchen, not caring a jot one way or the other about such mundane things as electricity, or hot water gushing from a tap.

She would get a job teaching in some village school, perhaps miles away, and she would bicycle there through leafy, winding lanes, and in the evenings she would sit with Jonathan round an open fire, listening to his reading of the chapter he had written that day.

And because she loved him so much, she told him about the dream . . .

They were parked at the time outside her flat, dazed with kissing, just sitting there, staring down the long, deserted avenue, busy with their own thoughts. So, quite naturally, her heart brimming over with love, Helen described the dream.

Without his saying anything she had sensed his lack of sympathy, and when the next day's six o'clock came round, the telephone didn't ring.

Not that it mattered, of course. She couldn't expect him to ring her every day. He was busy. Once he had taken her inside his office, and she had seen the rows of desks, the hooded typewriters, the telephones sprouting from every desk. She had ached at the thought of his having to spend his days cooped up there.

'You're good for me,' he said. 'Me, the

185

impractical one, and you with your feet firmly on the ground.' And she had held him close, and stroked his thick black hair, a Madonna-like smile of contentment curving her wide mouth.

'You appeal to the mother in me,' she said, quite seriously, and he laughed.

'You're adorable. You are the most adorable girl I've ever known.'

And in bed that night she had brooded about the other girls he had known, for Jonathan had made no secret about his fondness for women. That was one of the things she loved him for, his transparent honesty.

At five to six the next evening she actually watched the minute hand of the clock creeping slowly up to the hour. It was as though life itself were suspended; as though what was going on in the world outside had nothing to do with her. All that mattered was that the telephone should ring.

At five past six she lifted the receiver to check that the telephone was in working order, then hastily replaced it again, in case he should be dialling at that very moment.

She could ring him, of course. This thing called pride was overrated, so she dialled his office number, only to hear the ringing tone burring on and on. She could ring him at his digs, but there the telephone was a call-box in the downstairs hall, and his landlady always seemed to be lingering there, ready to put the caller through an inquisition before calling her paying guests from the upper floor.

The last time Helen had rung him at his

digs, after he had been fetched and answered, she sensed the irritation in his beautiful voice.

'I hope it's important,' his tone had implied.

So she waited, and when he didn't ring she told herself that there was always tomorrow, and only twenty-four hours to live through before she could hope again. And if he rang, no, *when* he rang, she would be gay and flippant and pretend he'd been lucky to catch her in. She was foolish to love him so. There was Tim Mathieson, wasn't there, with his steady blue eyes, and his air of knowing her better than she knew herself?

One of the girls in Five B, a mature, sophisticated fifteen-year-old, had written 'Sir fancies Miss' on the blackboard one day, and she'd rubbed it off quickly, without any comment, ignoring the stifled giggles behind her back. She had the feeling that her class were watching her.

Jonathan loved her, and if he hadn't exactly said so, she knew it in her heart. He would ring her that very day. When her clock said six o'clock he would ring, and it would be the time for loving again.

And if it wasn't that day, then it would be the next, or the next . . .

★ ★ ★

There was a staff meeting, and Miss Fish, the needlework mistress, went on bringing up points, making the others groan and exchange anguished glances, but she knew they were only thinking about such mundane things as wives kept waiting, or buses to catch. To them, Miss Fish's delaying tactics were just a nuisance. To Helen they were a matter of life and death.

She actually ran all the way home, taking the stairs up to her flat two at a time, and seeing the telephone squatting there silent on her coffee table, she actually spoke to it, out loud. 'Did you ring? Did you ring ten minutes ago, when I wasn't here?'

There were days when she told herself that it was all over, and there were days when she told herself she didn't care.

Talking to herself had become a habit by now, and she told herself out loud that the day she was somewhere else, by her own choice, at six o'clock, would be the day she had stopped loving Jonathan.

'Love is like a plant,' she'd read somewhere. 'If it isn't cherished and tended, it dies.' This, she knew, was what was happening to their love, and because she was intelligent, and came of practical Northern stock, she accepted this, knowing it to be the truth, but at six o'clock she was there, staring at the telephone.

She grew thin and pale, and Tim Mathieson, in his forthright way, told her that she was growing thin and pale.

He asked her again to come out with him, this time to have a coffee with him, straight after school, at the new place in the High Street, and because Helen could no longer bear the waiting time, she agreed to go, telling herself that if she left at a quarter to, she would be home in time.

They sat opposite each other in the little walled-in booth, and Tim asked questions, and she answered them, telling him about the terraced house in Lancashire, where she had lived with her parents. Yes, she told him, they were still living there, and they were proud of having a teacher in the family. Now her brother was at training college, too. And as she told him all about them she wondered why she had never talked like this to Jonathan. Remembering Jonathan, she glanced at her watch, and making some excuse, left him, and ran all the way back to her flat. He had offered to drive her to her 'next appointment'. How could she explain it was with the telephone?

'Why do you call me Cinderella?' she asked Tim one day as they sat together, sipping their coffee, and he grinned, his blue eyes twinkling at her.

'Because I know that in a few minutes you are going to run away. You've been looking at your watch for the past ten minutes. Why is it that you can always stay with me for so long, and no longer?'

Now their after-school meetings had become a habit, and they had talked so much, she felt she had known him all her life. Sometimes they talked 'shop', and Helen told him about Caroline, the spotty, none-too-clean girl in Five B, who could not spell and hardly managed to make two and two into four.

'She wrote an essay about what Christmas meant to her, and it was so simple, so touchingly beautiful, I cried all over the pile of exercise books,' she confessed.

Tim nodded gravely. 'I know, and next term, at the earliest possible moment, she will have left school and be working in the nearest factory, and in a couple of years, maybe less, she'll be married to a boy in a dead-end job, coping with babies that have arrived too soon. Where will her dreams have gone to then?'

'Dreams are a waste of time, anyway,' she said, but Tim didn't agree. He said that dreams were the stuff that life was made of, and for a while they argued, happily.

Suddenly, with a start, Helen glanced at her watch, saw the time and panicked. If she left now, that very minute, she could get back in time. It would mean running along the avenues like some demented thing, but she could do it . . .

She stretched out her hand for her bag, looked up and saw Tim watching her, one fair eyebrow raised comically.

'The witching hour?' he said, and his voice was light, but there was a bleakness in his eyes.

Helen hesitated. In her mind's eye she could see the telephone; in her imagination she could see Jonathan, deciding to ring her, dialling her number and then waiting, listening to the ringing tone, waiting for her to answer.

'*I'll be in touch*,' he had said, and she had clung to the words, believing them, thrusting him. She half rose from her seat, and she saw Tim sigh in a resigned fashion and reach for the bill.

In the time of their loving there had been sunshine everywhere and life had been worth living, but now it was all over and she would accept. She should have accepted a long time ago.

Slowly she sat down again.

'Would you mind if I had another cup of coffee?' she said quite clearly. 'I'm in no hurry this evening.'

The coffee came, and they talked and laughed, and when six o'clock came she didn't even notice. They were still sitting there, as if there was all the time in the world . . .

The Last Moment

At last the moment has come. We are sitting here together, my daughter and I, alone in the house, waiting for the car which will take us to the church for her wedding ceremony.

My wife has already gone, wearing a hat which could surely launch a thousand ships, and accompanied by the three bridesmaids: one in pink, one in blue, and a tiny one in yellow. And soon, too soon, the wedding car will call for us, its white ribbons fluttering in the summer breeze.

I go over to the drinks trolley and pour myself a large whisky. Then with the glass raised halfway to my lips, I hesitate.

Is it in keeping with the solemnity of the occasion for the father of the bride to take his place at the altar with the smell of alcohol on his breath? I wonder. I stare into the amber liquid, then put the glass down again.

Elaine, my daughter, is sitting on the sofa, her filmy veil billowing around her, her eyes downcast, her mouth curved in a faint, tremulous smile. She's beautiful — so heart-breaking in her beauty.

I know that the time has come for me to say so many things, and yet I cannot form a single sentence in my mind . . .

What *should* a father be feeling at a time like this? Pride? Joy? Or a smug satisfaction that his daughter is marrying a boy he likes — though he's tried hard enough not to!

One thing I know for certain is that I should be thanking my lucky stars that she's marrying in the church where she was confirmed — and not simply moving in with someone without even bothering to get married at all!

I go over to the mirror, adjust my silver-grey tie, and smooth down the sideboards which I consider to be a trifle too long. I call myself all kinds of a fool for pandering to the whims of my wife, and wish now that I'd pleased myself.

'All right, love?' I say, and Elaine nods, but says nothing.

I stare at the glass of whisky, and know a sudden upsurge of anger so strong that it surprises me.

'You're too young!' I want to shout at her. 'Do you realize what it is you're doing? You're only eighteen, and you think you know it all! Have you stopped to think what it will really be like to be moving over two hundred miles away from home, living with a boy who's not yet twenty-one, in a three-roomed flat in a strange town?'

I suppose I've been against this wedding from the start — not like my wife. It's strange how these past weeks have turned her into a virtual stranger. She's been moving around the house with glazed eyes, clutching little lists; bending over that blasted sewing machine, sometimes far into the night; gaily plunging me into the red at the bank — and admitting without a blush that her new suit cost more than the electric lawn mower I've been wanting for months!

I'm not normal — that must be my problem. I should have been able to look at the long list of wedding guests without shuddering as I did little sums in my mind! Eighty guests at what is surely an astronomical amount per head — money just squandered on fiddly bits of nothing on biscuits and what sounds like enough champagne to float a battleship!

I go over to the window. Three women are standing gossiping on the other side of the road, waiting for a glimpse of the bride. Soon the car will be coming back, and then it will be too late to say what I want to. This is my last chance to tell my daughter just how much I love her, how I'll always love her, and always be here if she needs me. But that's just it — she won't be needing *me* any more!

I glare across at Elaine, but she's sitting there so quietly, with her eyelids lowered. She doesn't see the accusation in my eyes.

Does he know, this boy she's marrying, does he realize that she's still a child — that she's even afraid of the dark, still?

He didn't see her at the time she came home from that film on exorcism. He wasn't around then. But *I* saw her. It was me who sat with her for over two hours, holding her hand and promising that if the devil himself turned up, complete with horns and forked tail, I would take him on single-handed. Do *you* know, Keith, how to make her laugh when she's scared?

'All right, love?' I say again, and this time she raises her head and smiles at me.

'Relax, Dad,' she says, and I ask her if she would like a small sherry, just to calm her nerves. But she smiles and shakes her head. And I swear that damned whisky is winking at me, tempting me to swallow it in one soothing gulp.

I tell myself that, come the night, she'll be lying in her husband's arms . . . Oh my God, she's not ready, I tell myself. She's too young!

'Have you talked to her?' I asked my wife only the other day, and she actually laughed out loud.

'Who's an old square?' she teased. 'Elaine could probably teach us a thing or two.'

And I could have hit her, honestly I could. But all I did was turn away . . .

I glanced at my watch. Any minute now, the car will be back. I go and sit beside Elaine on the sofa, and she tells me in a whisper that I'm sitting on her veil.

'Sorry, love,' I say, and I get up quickly and go over to stand by the window again.

They're still there, those three women. What do they think this is, a peepshow or something?

If only I was good at this kind of thing — the sort of chap who could say it all in a few well-chosen flowery words. But I'm hopeless. So hopeless in fact that they decided my brother, Ted, should be the one to make the speech to the bride . . .

And there's another thing. I'm not unsentimental or insensitive, although I've been called both at times. I did remember to bring my wife flowers for our anniversary last month, didn't I? It was a pity they came out of my briefcase a trifle squashed, but I couldn't have carried them through the streets, not for all the tea in China.

Yes, that's me: practical enough but always unable to express the way I feel, even though all the lovely singing words are there, locked up tight inside me. Like now . . .

I love you, I want to tell my daughter. I've loved you ever since the day you were born. Your mother had a difficult time, and you were such an ugly baby, with your pointed head and scarlet pressure mark on your blob of a nose. You were a tiny, wizened scrap of a baby, with eyes shut tight in furious slits — a spotty, hiccoughing baby — a skinned rabbit of a baby. But I was so proud of you; and I loved you so much. I thought my heart would burst.

Do you remember how, as a little girl, you were always my girl? Remember how you refused to go to sleep until I'd come in from work and climbed the stairs to read you a story?

Do you remember, Elaine, my daughter, sitting there in your white gown, serene and beautiful with your tiny waist and your hands clasped round the Bible we gave you on your confirmation day?

When was it exactly that you started to grow away from me?

At twelve or thirteen? A little girl who changed overnight into a demanding, cynical teenager, questioning everything we'd ever taught you, growing your hair long and hiding your face behind it when I tried to reason with you.

What a lot of problems you gave us!

Jeans so tight they showed every line of your little round bottom, eyes drawn in with hideous black pencil, arguments about the hours we expected you to keep, homework you skipped — and boys, each one longer-haired and more furtive-looking than the one before.

How many times did you tell me that I didn't understand? Me, your father, who understood only too well!

Then Keith came along. Tall, mumbling, a long-haired cowboy in a red checked shirt and brown boots.

When I saw the way it was between you I wanted to grip him by the lapels of that appalling fringed jacket he wore, and shake him until his teeth rattled.

'Just look after her,' I wanted to shout. 'Hurt her — and, so help me, I'll swing for you! Frighten her, and I'll tear you apart, limb from limb!'

Your mother told me that it was all my fault that Keith turned into a mumbling idiot when I was around — she said he was afraid of me because it was so obvious that I distrusted him.

Oh, Elaine, couldn't you see that I was the one who was afraid? Right from the beginning, I knew that this day would come — the day when he would take you away from us.

Was it because of my attitude, then, that you changed, and stopped confiding in me? Have I hurt you that much, love?

I like your Keith now. I can even see that some day we'll be great buddies. I'll probably learn to look on him as the son I never had. He's kind and gentle, and he loves you so much it shows in everything he says and does.

But can't you understand the way it was then for me?

I want to tell you all this and now it really is too late! The car is here, drawing up to the kerb, white ribbons fluttering in the breeze of this lovely summer's day.

The driver is getting out and giving me the thumbs-up sign through the window; the three women are turning expectant faces towards our front door, and I need that whisky. I need it as a drowning man needs his straw.

'Ready, love?' I say, and I hold out my hand to you, and you stand up and come towards me. You walk slowly, unhurriedly, as if there's all the time in the world.

Now you're standing before me, and I swallow the lump that has suddenly risen in my throat. There are tears pricking away at the back of my eyes. Me, the unfeeling one, the dad you once accused of being so insensitive . . .

I just look at you, and you reach up and lay your hand against my cheek. 'It's okay, Dad,' you say. 'Honestly.'

That's all. Just four words, said so softly, so lovingly, that my heart melts away inside me.

We haven't talked, not in all that time of waiting, and yet your complete understanding is there in your eyes, plain for me to see.

Together, we go out into the sunshine, and carefully — oh, so carefully — I help you into the back of the car, folding your veil in after you, as tenderly as any woman could. Then I take my place beside you for the short ride to the church.

You and me, Elaine. Me and my girl, the way it always has been, and always will be. I know that now.

I'm Going to Tell You the Truth, Amanda

It started so simply. Amanda, aged three and a bit, newly tucked up in bed but playing for time, told her mother what Santa Claus was bringing the other children at nursery school.

Sarah sat down on the bed. Downstairs, she had a magazine illustration to finish, with the deadline only two days away, but she believed in dealing with important matters as they cropped up.

'Darling,' she began gently, 'there is no such person as Santa Claus.'

She groped for an explanation acceptable to the child.

'Christmas is a holiday, a winter holiday. Families give each other presents, as they do on birthdays. That's all.'

Amanda sat up and put her head on one side, a sure sign that she was preparing to be awkward.

'Melanie says that Santa Claus comes down the chimney, dressed in a red coat. And he has a long white beard, and she hangs a pillowcase up, and he fills it . . . with . . . with things.

'Last year she saw him,' she said defiantly. 'She sawed him, with her very own eyes.'

'Saw him,' Sarah said automatically. 'But she can't have, darling. He doesn't exist.'

She almost added that he was a fairy tale, a myth, then stopped herself in time. Fairies, the Sand Man, and storks that brought babies in their beaks were other things that Amanda had talked about recently. She had explained about them, too, in simple language.

Cheerfully she patted the raised mound of bedclothes that was Amanda's bony knees.

'And now, darling, I must go downstairs. There's a lot of work for me to do. If I don't do it, there won't be any money to buy you all the things you want for Christmas.'

Obediently Amanda lay down again. Sarah walked briskly to the door and switched off the light.

Not long ago Amanda had suddenly developed a fear of the dark. Patiently, with the aid of an orange and a ball, Sarah had gone into a lengthy explanation of the movement of the earth and the sun. There had been no further trouble.

But as she closed the door she heard Amanda say fiercely, 'Don't switch the dark on, Mummy, and Melanie sawed him. She did. With her very own eyes.'

Sighing, Sarah left the bedroom door wide open. Much against her principles, she switched on the landing light.

Downstairs, she made straight for her easel, and stared critically at the illustration.

Since Bruce's desertion and the divorce, she was finding the burden of being mother and father to the overimaginative little girl almost overwhelming.

She recognized that her determination to make

Amanda face facts sprang entirely from her own hurt pride.

Life was not fair. If Amanda grew up accepting that, it would be a sure defence against any disappointments that came her way.

Perhaps if she herself had been less vulnerable . . . Perhaps if she hadn't loved so much . . .

But when Bruce had told her that he had fallen in love with someone else, that he couldn't help himself, she had only wanted to die.

What was this thing called love that could make a man give up his wife and the child he adored?

Immediately, trying to make up in some small way to Amanda, she had given up her full-time job as Art Director to a glossy magazine. She switched over to the far less lucrative freelance work she could do at home.

She would devote herself entirely to her small daughter, she'd decided.

If she wanted Amanda to grow up with her mind uncluttered with dreams and half-truths, then surely that was best?

Wearily Sarah stretched out an arm, and manoeuvred a hinged lamp into a better position. The dull threat of an impending headache beat at her forehead.

'Go away!' she told it. She had no time to be ill.

Although Bruce had been generous with an allowance, the money she earned was necessary. This illustration must be finished on time.

But the headache took no notice of her, and

developed into a full-blown hammering at her skull. Wearily Sarah kept at her work.

Next morning she felt like death. She boiled an egg for Amanda, and watched the little girl jab a piece of toast into its gooey centre.

Amanda took a long swig from her beaker of milk before swallowing the toast.

'Don't eat and drink at the same time, darling,' Sarah admonished her. 'And if you don't hurry, Melanie's mother will be phoning to see where we are.'

Amanda smiled at her mother through a milk moustache. 'Melanie's cat has had three kittens. Giblets.'

'Triplets,' Sarah said, smiling, but not really in the mood for anything funny.

Snatching up her car keys, she went out to the garage. Alternate weeks she drove the two little girls to nursery school.

As she drew up at Melanie's gate, the front door opened, and Melanie's mother came down the path. She was still wearing a quilted dressing gown, and the remains of the previous night's mascara ringed her blue eyes.

'I'm dead,' she announced cheerfully, 'and the baby's playing up like mad. Hugh and I went out last night. The Firm's Annual Christmas Dinner and Dance. We didn't get to bed until two.'

'Who on earth did you get to babysit till that time?' Sarah asked.

'Oh, Mother came over. She stayed the night. That's why Melanie's not quite ready. She was in her grannie's bed at seven.'

Sarah thought about her own mother,

widowed and living a life of complete independence in Lancashire.

★ ★ ★

Sarah had written asking her down for Christmas. Her letter had crossed one from her mother, saying she was going to Austria with her friend, Miss Reynolds, another buyer in the big store where they both worked.

Sarah knew that her mother was determinedly living a life of her own. She supposed wryly that was where she herself had inherited her own independence of spirit.

'It's like history repeating itself,' her mother had said at the time of the divorce. 'You were only four when I was left to bring you up alone.'

But Bruce left me, Sarah had cried silently. My father died.

Melanie's mother was saying something. Sarah smiled, hoping that was the right response. Then Melanie hurled herself down the path, coat flying open, her long curly hair tied back in a sketchy topknot.

None too gently, she carried a doll. A round-faced plastic doll, with authentic-looking blond hair, and a rosebud mouth open in perpetual surprise.

'It's Jesus,' she explained, climbing into the back of the car. 'We're doing the 'Tivity play today, and Miss Edwards said I could bring my doll.'

'Jesus was a boy,' Amanda said. There was a

suspicion of scorn in her voice.

Melanie bounced up and down on the back seat, completely undismayed.

'I'm to be Mary,' she announced. 'And sing 'Away in a Manger'. I know three verses. Grannie teached me.'

'Taught you,' Sarah said automatically.

Amanda wriggled round in the front seat, to face Melanie.

'It's all right,' she said. 'When it has its swaddling on, it won't show.'

'What won't show?' asked Melanie.

'That it's a girl,' said Amanda, and sat round again, honour satisfied.

Sarah drove carefully, thinking vaguely about the Nativity play. She wasn't a churchgoer — she couldn't remember when she had had any strong religious beliefs. She had worried a little about how that might affect Amanda.

'I won't influence Amanda in any way,' she had told Bruce, on one of his visits to see his daughter. 'When she's old enough to understand, she can make up her mind. I'll just tell her the truth — that Jesus was a good man who was killed for His beliefs. Then she can judge for herself.'

She wasn't sure what Bruce had said but it had sounded like 'Poor little beggar.' From that time on she had had Amanda ready and waiting for him when he'd called.

She had been very careful not to influence Amanda one way or the other, so why was it that not once had Amanda mentioned the Nativity play?

'Are you in the play?' she asked, as she pulled up at the red-brick building that was a nursery school in the mornings, and a welfare clinic in the afternoons.

Amanda nodded. 'I'm the Third Shepherd, but I don't sing. Only Melanie sings.'

'Because I know the words,' Melanie added smugly, climbing out of the car and swinging the unlikely Jesus by a pink plastic arm.

'I might sing, too,' Amanda said.

Melanie said that she couldn't on account of not knowing the words. Quarrelling happily, the two little girls walked arm in arm up the path.

Sarah waited until they were safely inside, then started the car. She drove for a few moments, then drew up at a newsagent's.

The commercialism of Christmas depressed her. But pushing her scruples to one side, she chose a game in a large cardboard box, swayed by the assurance on the lid that the toy would encourage a child's interest in natural history.

She gave a cursory glance at the display of Christmas cards, shop-soiled now — and no wonder, she thought, remembering that they had been on show since early October.

Harassed women jostled her, their expressions of frantic anxiety mirroring the fact that their purses were smaller than their intentions.

Sarah bought a packet of balloons and a few extra trimmings for the tree.

It was ten o'clock when she arrived back home, so she decided to leave the chores and get on with the illustration before collecting the children again at noon.

She just hadn't time for Christmas, she told herself ruefully.

The phone rang, making her jump, every nerve alive and quivering. The voice at the other end of the wire was faintly apologetic.

'It's Ethel Reynolds, dear. I don't want to alarm you, but it's your mother.'

Sarah's heart dropped like a stone. 'Yes?'

'She's in hospital, dear. She scalded her foot rather badly. It's nothing to worry about, but I thought I ought to let you know. We've had to cancel our holiday, of course. She won't be able to walk for some time.'

'I'll come,' Sarah said. 'I'll come at once. You're sure that it isn't serious? I mean, if they've taken her to hospital . . . '

Even as she begged for reassurance, she was telling herself that her mother was only in her fifties, and as strong as a horse.

Miss Reynolds sounded relieved. 'Well, that would be nice, dear. She'd love to see you, I'm sure.'

'And you're sure it isn't serious?'

'I give you my word,' said Miss Reynolds, with all the assurance of twenty years as Head Buyer behind her.

Sarah thanked her, and said she'd be there that evening. As soon as Miss Reynolds rang off, Sarah phoned Melanie's mother and explained she'd be away the rest of the week at least.

'But must you take Amanda with you?' Melanie's mother said at once. 'You'll be running backwards and forwards to the hospital while you're there, and who would mind Amanda for you?'

'Mother's friends will help out, I'm sure,' Sarah said, 'but it wouldn't be much fun for Amanda, I admit.'

'And she'd miss all the exciting things happening at nursery school,' Melanie's mother said, as if that was unthinkable. 'That's settled then. Amanda can stay here.'

Mentally Sarah counted heads and the number of bedrooms, but as if reading her thoughts Melanie's mother spoke again: 'There's always room for one more,' she said. 'Especially around Christmas.'

In less than an hour, Sarah had packed a couple of suitcases, one for herself and a larger one for Amanda. Leaving Amanda almost paralytic with excitement at Melanie's, she started on the long drive up the M1.

* * *

She switched on the car radio to a programme which told her that now was the time to ice the Christmas cake. Switching over, she got a choir making full use of the descant in 'Silent Night'.

Glancing at her watch, she knew that if she could keep up this speed she would be in time for evening visiting. She tried to anticipate the look on her mother's face when she walked into the ward.

At the awful time of her divorce, Sarah had wished that she was closer to her mother. She loved her and admired her. But in some ways, she suspected, the admiration was stronger than the love.

When her mother had been widowed, she'd quickly taken up her career again. Sarah never remembered a time when she could come home from school to a smell of baking, and a mother waiting in the kitchen with a floury smile.

The cosy image made her almost laugh out loud, as she thought of her tidy, precise mother.

She pressed her foot down on the accelerator. The wind through the quarter-window tore at her hair, almost snatching her thoughts away.

Idly she flicked the switch of the radio again. A disc jockey with a jolly voice told her how very few shopping days were left to Christmas . . .

It was dark when Sarah reached her home town. Letting herself into her mother's house, she smiled at the neat orderliness of the rooms, so typical of her mother.

At half past seven exactly, she was at the hospital, waiting patiently for the summoning bell.

'Well, Mother!' she said, kissing the smooth cheek, and pulling up a chair to the bed.

'What a thing to happen,' her mother said.

She went into a lengthy explanation of how exactly she had come to scald her foot by picking up the overheated handle of a pan, and, in the first moment of startled pain and surprise, dropping the entire contents on her foot.

'What I feel most of all is letting Ethel down about the holiday,' she said. 'But I wouldn't

209

be much good at shinning up snow-covered mountains with a foot like this.'

She pointed to the cradle covering her legs. Then she asked about Amanda and Sarah told her about Melanie, and the doll that was Jesus. Her mother's eyes sparkled with amusement.

'What are you working on at the moment?' she asked.

Sarah told her how she was illustrating summer stories for the magazine she used to work for, and how difficult it was gearing one's thoughts to sea and blue skies when the air around was pervaded with 'Jingle Bells'.

We have no natural affinity, she thought suddenly, surprising herself. We are friends, good friends, and that's all.

Somewhere over the years, while her mother pursued her career, and she was forced by circumstances into a mature independence, the warmth of a loving relationship had been lost.

She looked at her mother's hand on the bedspread, a slim, well-manicured hand, and wondered for an illogical moment what would happen if she covered it with her own.

'I'll be out in a couple of days,' her mother was saying.

Sarah pulled herself together.

'Then I'm going to take you back with me,' she said. 'You can sit in the back of the car with your leg stretched out. Amanda will be thrilled to have you with us for Christmas.'

Her mother smiled. 'No, thank you, dear. Ethel has promised to move in with me as soon as I get home. We'll spend a quiet Christmas together. It's the least I can do for her when I've let her down about the holiday. She's quite alone, you know.'

And so are you, Sarah thought, then smiled to herself. No, her mother would never be quite alone. She was too self-sufficient for that.

As the dismissal bell went, and she gathered her gloves and handbag together, she suddenly remembered something Bruce had said: 'You don't need me, Sarah. Not like Margaret does . . . you don't need anyone, you're too self-sufficient for that.'

With unexpected tears pricking behind her eyes, she walked across the parking ground to her car, and drove the short distance to her mother's house.

The first thing she did was to phone Melanie's mother, to be told that Amanda was fast asleep in bed.

'Melanie let her have the top bunk and Grannie's been in there reading stories and supplying drinks of water and switching on and off lights, but they're fast asleep now.'

Sarah said that she would be home in a couple of days. The friendly voice told her not to hurry back.

Next day was the day for afternoon visiting. Sarah was pleased to see that her mother was out of bed, her injured foot stretched on a leg-rest.

'I've decided to go back to London in the morning,' Sarah said.

Her mother said of course that was what she must do.

'I'm glad you came,' she said, when visiting time was over.

As she walked away, Sarah had an almost irresistible urge to rush back and put her arms round her mother.

But her mother was smiling cheerfully, her arm raised in a farewell wave, and so she walked on.

Her mind a jumble of thoughts too complex to grasp, she missed her turning in the long hospital corridors. Instead of turning right by Pathology, she found herself in the children's wing.

From behind an open door came the sound of childish voices. '*Away in a manger*,' they sang. Like a snippet of sound from a film, she heard Melanie's voice: 'I know three verses. Grannie teached me.' And Melanie's mother's voice, warm with pride: 'She was in her grannie's bed at seven o'clock this morning.'

Turning, Sarah retraced her steps, but not before she had seen a scarlet-robed figure with a cottonwool beard, dark trousers showing incongruously beneath his coat, handing out presents to the children sitting up in their row of beds.

'This is the day the mayor visits the children,' a smiling nurse told her.

Sarah walked back down the corridor and out to her car in the parking ground.

Usually she drove slowly in traffic, but this time she only just stopped herself from jumping the lights in the High Street. Inside her mother's house, not caring a jot that the cheap rate was a whole hour and a half away, she dialled a number.

Her mind was no longer a jumble of chaotic thoughts. She knew exactly what she had to do, what she had wanted to do all the time, if she hadn't been afraid.

Afraid of what?

Of life itself and the hurt it can bring. She knew that now . . .

When Amanda was brought to the phone, and Sarah heard her voice, high-pitched and full of importance, she could hardly speak for the feeling of utter love and tenderness that threatened to choke her.

'Who do you think I saw this afternoon?' Sarah asked. 'You'll never guess!'

Then she took a deep breath.

'Santa Claus,' she said. 'I saw him, darling. I really did. With my very own eyes.'

A Very Special Man

Gareth Jones drove home from town in his shirtsleeves as usual, his dark grey office jacket hanging on its swinging coat-hanger from the side window. There was a sentimental pop song oozing from the car radio, all about forbidden love, and he found that he was identifying with it. Completely.

There was this girl at the office, you see. Tall she was, with long honey-coloured hair, and long slim legs, and grey-green eyes. And her name was Meriel . . .

She was twenty-five — he knew because he'd looked it up in the office records — and *he* was forty-nine, but what did that matter? When he was with her in his dreams, it seemed as if they were much of an age; and he would run with her along some deserted beach, the surf pounding on the rocks, echoing the beating of his heart. And he would lie with her in the sweet meadow grass, raising himself on an elbow and bending over her, whilst above them, in the clear blue sky, a lark would soar, almost bursting its tiny throat with the passion of its song. And he would talk with her, sitting on cushions in front of a log fire, with the flames leaping and throwing shadows on her lovely face.

'I love you so very much,' she would say, in this oft-recurring dream, and he would lift the soft weight of her hair away from her neck and kiss her tenderly.

'I love you too, Meriel,' he would say, and she would sigh, and all the sadness of their love would be contained in that lingering sigh . . .

Without realizing it, he had turned into the avenue, and stopped the car in front of his house. Mock Tudor it was, and as he opened the front door, the grey jacket slung over his shoulder, Meriel was still with him.

My own love, he thought wistfully, then before he stepped into the hall with its walnut panelling and brick fireplace, he heard the baby crying.

Immediately the muscles at the back of his neck hardened into twisted ropes of tension, and he felt the warning stab of yet another headache. He walked through into the kitchen and saw his wife, Rose, trying to spoon gripe water into his grandson's widely protesting mouth.

And the dream dissolved reluctantly, like a wispy cloud drifting away to nothing . . .

At forty-eight, Rose was still a pretty woman, with the soft curly hair and delicate features that even tiredness and a kind of frantic frustration could not eradicate. Her face had a kind of wiped-out exhaustion about it, and when Gareth bent to kiss her, he smelled sickly-sweet baby powder, tinged with a whiff of cod-liver oil.

Meriel smelled of a subtle evocative perfume, he reminded himself disloyally. Once he had caught the scent of her as she passed his desk, and the tan on her slim brown arms had looked so tempting he had felt the need to stretch out a hand and run his finger down it . . .

He held out his finger to the baby, and immediately it was guided into the wailing mouth and clamped upon by all four of his grandson's teeth.

'He's teething,' Rose said unnecessarily. 'He's cried all day on and off, but it's no use trying to put him down in his cot when he's upset, he just wouldn't settle.'

'Tricia working late again?'

Gareth tried to keep his voice noncommittal. The last time he had complained Rose had flown at him in swift and uncharacteristic rage.

'She's secretary to the managing director of a big company. She can't say she isn't able to stay late because it's the baby's bedtime. You said . . .'

Oh, he knew what he'd said all right, but then he had forgotten what it would be like with a baby in the house again. He'd forgotten the crying in the night, the nappies in the airing cupboard when he was in a hurry looking for a clean vest.

'She did ring,' Rose was saying now, pushing a strand of hair away with one hand and patting the baby's back with the other. 'It's quarterly balancing or something.'

'You look worn out, love,' he said, hardening his heart against the baby's burning red cheeks, the eyes narrowed into furious slits, the fat legs kicking wildly inside the fluffy blue sleeping bag. 'I'll go and change and give you a hand.'

'She can't help it,' his wife said again, but he chose to ignore her, and taking the stairs two at a time, he asked her silently why she *always* had

216

to be so much on the defensive.

Then, as he threw his jacket down on the bed and loosened his tie, he closed his eyes, and like a medium calling forth his special guide from the spirit world, he summoned up the powerful vision of Meriel . . .

This time they were having a meal in a restaurant together, and he was plucking a rose from the table centre and passing it over to her, and she was fastening it in the deep curved neckline of her dress, tucking the stem down . . . Thinking of the thorns, he changed the rose quickly to a gardenia, but didn't smile, his sense of humour having deserted him. Completely.

As he changed from his suit into slacks and a roll-neck sweater, he talked to her in nothings cushioned in sweetness, in the make-believe situation of fraught intimacy.

Lovely she was, tall and golden-skinned, with her hair looped back from her face in Madonna-like simplicity. He made the comparison quite seriously.

Meriel making him laugh, analysing his every motivation, with flattering attention to what she would call his endearing characteristics, his lovable idiosyncrasies . . .

Back downstairs, on his way to get a much-needed drink from the sideboard, he tripped in the hall over the wheels of the folding pram; then, before he could sit down in his chair, he removed a pile of folded nappies and a round pink teething ring attached to a length of ribbon.

Next year he would be fifty years old, he told

217

the glass in his hand. A faithful husband and father, with a son, David, away at university, all set to take up a research scholarship in Canada, and a twenty-year-old daughter, Tricia, the unmarried mother of the baby still screaming its head off next door. He frowned at the drink, surprising himself at the speed with which he had apparently downed it.

Fifty next year . . .

A time for closeness with his wife. For coming home to a quiet house. A meal for two, on trays in front of the television if they'd a mind, with the lounge all tidy, and no toys cluttering the carpet. Rose's voluntary work at the hospital had taken up only three mornings before Tricia came back to live at home . . .

'I'm going to live with him, Daddy,' Tricia had said, her voice soft with the ache of love. 'His wife will give him a divorce when he makes the final break. He's told me so.'

And Rose had cried a little, and, God forgive him, he'd shouted more than a little, but Tricia had gone all the same, putting her hand on his arm, trying to make him understand.

'We can't help it, Daddy. We love each other so much, and he is so sad, so very sad. He *deserves* to be happy. He's a very special man.'

Refilling his glass, Gareth took a mouthful, then stared at the carpet. Oh, a very special man all right. Trotting back to his wife once he had found out that Tricia was pregnant, a wife who welcomed him with open arms, even accepting with triumph his Judas kiss, thought

Gareth with bitterness.

And Tricia telling them she could manage, determined to keep her baby, living in one ghastly room and depositing their grandson at a nursery on her way to work each morning. It happened to other people's daughters, not to theirs, dear God. Not to Tricia, with her mother's soft curly hair and gentle ways. Gareth sighed. Never to his dying day would he forget how they went round after a call from her landlady and found Tricia huddled in bed, burning with a bad dose of flu, nappies drying round an electric radiator, half-rinsed bottles in the sink, the pathetic tins of baked beans in the cupboard that was supposed to be a kitchen.

What else was there but to bring her home, snuggled into a blanket on the back seat of the car, the baby on Rose's knee as she made soothing noises into his little sleeping face?

What else *could* they do?

And financial considerations apart, the wisest thing had been for Tricia to take up her well-paid secretarial job again whilst Rose stayed and looked after the baby. No need for two women in one kitchen, a chance for Tricia to save. It had all seemed so right. So sensible . . .

It was quiet now, and going through into the kitchen Gareth found his wife rushing round, frantically tidying away the aftermath of the baby's extended six o'clock feed. Hair flopping into her eyes, pushing the high chair into a corner, dashing with a soiled nappy into the utility room. Washing her hands, rinsing the feeding bottle and slinging it into the sterilizer, apologizing because for the third time that week the evening meal was not even at the planning stage.

'He started to grizzle at four o'clock again. It's his worst time of the day, just like David used to be, remember?'

Apologizing, too tired not to apologize, looking ten years older than she had any right to do. Rose, his wife, who would, he knew, sleep the evening away in front of the television, then fall asleep again the moment her head touched the pillow, too tired some nights to respond even to his good night kiss.

'Tell me what we're having and I'll do it if you tell me what to do. You go up and have a bath and change into something that doesn't smell of baby powder,' he said. 'I can grill chops, for goodness' sake, and open a packet of frozen peas. I'm a clever boyo, remember?'

There wasn't time to think of Meriel as he struggled to have chops, potatoes and peas all miraculously ready at one and the same time. And then Tricia came in, apologizing as her mother had done, running upstairs, coming down again, setting the table in a fever of contrition, pushing her dark hair back from her pale face, telling him she wasn't tired, that the baby had slept till five o'clock that morning. He felt his heart contract with pity and the ache of fatherly love.

Was this what that special man had done to his daughter? Changing her from a laughing girl with merry dark eyes into this always hurrying, always apologizing shadow of the girl she used to be? Had he watched her walking by his desk one day, nut-brown from the sun, shining hair swinging round her pretty face — watched her, dreamed a dream about the way it could be if one day he stopped her and stretched out his hand?

Had he, this oh-so-special man, turned into stark reality that dream of his that should have *remained* a dream?

Gareth turned down the grill, turned up the gas jet under the pan of potatoes, and showered the packet of peas into boiling water, hoping for, but not expecting, the best.

★ ★ ★

No one mentioned the fact that the potatoes were mushy, that the peas were bullet-hard, or that the chops were frilled with black. And Gareth didn't apologize; there'd been enough apologizing in the house for one day, he decided.

They would manage if Tricia worked part time — the mornings, he thought, so that she could put her own baby to bed, leaving Rose free to be herself again. His thoughts clicked into place with computer-like clarity.

She would be able to go out on the odd evening whilst they babysat; she was still so young, her life wasn't spoiled at all. Restricted, oh yes, that young boyo upstairs in his cot would see to that.

But with a bit of planning it could be more like the way he had thought it would be. Gareth and Rose, the two of them, no longer young, but a long way from being old . . .

'Gareth! That's the third time I've spoken to you and you haven't answered. What's got into you lately? You're always far away.'

Rose was smiling at him, scooping up the grey watery pieces of potato on her plate, trying to look as if she were enjoying it. And watching her, Gareth felt his very heart dissolve with love, affection and loyalty.

Now Tricia was teasing him, her head on one side, pointing her fork at him, accusing, laughing . . .

'Yes, five new pence for them, Daddy. Or are they worth more than that?'

Gareth slowly leaned back in his chair and smiled at them.

'Much more than that, lovey. And when we've cleared away we're going to have a little talk. About ways and means,' he added mysteriously.

And they wouldn't let him make the coffee, not even though it was of the instant variety.

'You just don't trust me to make it without lumps in,' he said as they pushed him from the kitchen.

Rose and Tricia, the two girls in his life, the *only* two girls in his life. Gareth stared at himself in the mirror on the wall before settling down in his favourite old chair.

'Be honest, boyo,' he whispered to his reflection. 'The only two that *matter*, that's what you mean.'

He studied his face intently, narrowing his eyes. Yes, his new haircut was a definite improvement. Actually, it had been Rose's idea . . .

This was the right moment in time for him to say a virtuous but rather reluctant farewell to Meriel, the girl of his dreams. But Gareth had always been an honest man.

'There will be days when I'll still run with you along some deserted beach, and lie with you in the long meadow grass,' he told her softly. 'When a man stops thinking and sometimes dreaming of a pretty girl, his days are certainly numbered. Okay, boyo?'

'Daddy's talking to himself now,' Tricia said, coming in with a tray of lumpless coffee. 'I think he fancies himself.'

And before Rose passed his cup over to him, Gareth reached up a hand and gently touched her smiling face.

'It's *you* I fancy, my own love,' he whispered, and the look in her eyes made the breath catch in his throat.

'Now,' he began, 'both of you. Listen to me . . .'

No Choice in the Matter

When they told five-year-old Daniel that he was adopted, he listened, but wasn't all that impressed, being busy at the time in exterminating the entire population of Mars with his new death-ray gun.

'We *chose* you,' his mother said carefully. 'Out of all the other babies, we chose you.'

'Because I was the best,' said Daniel, merely stating a fact.

'Of course you were, old son,' said his father, ruffling his hair. 'One look at you and the rest didn't have a chance.'

They'd laughed together, as though they were in some sort of conspiracy, and wanting to show off as he always did when he felt particularly happy, Daniel raised his death-ray gun and buzzed round the room mowing down a whole crowd of unsuspecting Martians.

Who cared about being adopted anyway? For Daniel there was love in abundance; three meals a day, a new kite hanging in the garage and a couple of white mice in a cage in the garden shed.

School was a bit of a nuisance, it was true, but there were always the holidays to look forward to, and he was quite prepared to take the rough with the smooth.

He never really gave the matter of his adoption another thought until one day, when he was lying in bed recovering from a feverish cold, his parents came into the room, holding hands and smiling at him.

'We've something to tell you,' they said together, then laughed.

'Something very special,' his father said. 'At the end of June you're going to have a baby sister.'

His mother shook her head. 'Or a baby brother.'

'Or both,' his father said, and they leaned against each other and giggled.

Daniel sat up in bed, his snuffles forgotten. 'Can I come with you?' he asked, and their faces went blank.

Patiently he explained.

'To choose the baby. To make sure we choose the best one.'

'Well actually, old son, it's like this,' his father said, coming to sit on the edge of the bed. 'This time your mummy is growing the baby herself, in her tummy.'

'It's just like a seed,' she said, and they nodded.

'Like a seed.'

Daniel lay back on his pillows and meditated. Issues too complex for him to grasp were revolving in his brain. He knew that they were expecting him to say something, so he said it.

'Why didn't you grow me?' he asked.

★ ★ ★

When at last they tucked him in and went back downstairs, he lay in the darkness, chewing the whole thing over in his mind.

Apparently, though he found the idea very hard to credit, *another* lady had grown him, because the doctor had said that his own mother hadn't the right kind of tummy. Daniel put his head underneath the sheet, and started a satisfying sucking of his thumb . . .

But the doctor had been wrong, and now there was a baby inside her, curled up, fast asleep, and waiting to be born . . .

The rhythmic sucking was having its desired effect, but as the familiar sense of languor crept over him, Daniel was sure of one thing.

He didn't like the situation. Not one little bit!

The next day he was allowed up in the afternoon. His legs felt wobbly, he didn't want to read or do a jigsaw, and outside the garden was wet with rain.

Daniel was tired, but determined not to admit to being tired. He went to lean against his mother's knee. She smelled as usual of talcum powder and newly baked scones. If he hadn't been too old to contemplate such an idea, he would have climbed on her knee and snuggled his head into the welcoming warmth of her bosom but, of course, at five and a half years old, such action was unthinkable.

It was a long time, however, since he had climbed on her knee, and there was no one to see . . .

Halfway on, he stopped, appalled. Something

had happened to his mother's lap! It had actually disappeared, or at least dwindled away to nothing.

For an angry, frustrated moment, he butted his head against the bulge that seemed to be getting in his way, but his mother laughed out loud, and held him away from her.

'Don't hurt baby, dear,' she said . . .

Daniel went over to the window, and stared out, pressing his nose against the glass, and counting the raindrops as they ran down the pane. He wouldn't look at his mother, he couldn't, and almost without volition, although he had long since confined his thumb-sucking to bedtime, his thumb crept into his mouth.

From time to time his father would make jokes about what he called 'Jimmy Bump'. Daniel smiled politely, but thought the joke less than funny, and unworthy of his father, who usually told the best jokes he knew.

And as his mother grew bigger, so Daniel's demands on her grew more unreasonable. He demanded to be lifted out of his bath, swore he had forgotten how to tie his shoelaces, and ran on ahead when they were out in the street, urging her to catch him up.

He fought an unadmitted and undeclared battle with 'Jimmy Bump', and at the end of June went sadly off to stay with his grandmother, carrying his precious death-ray gun underneath his arm.

In spite of their preoccupation with the imminent arrival of their second child, his parents found time to worry about the change in Daniel's behaviour.

'Surely he can't be jealous of a baby that isn't even born?' his mother said, then bit her lip, and tried hard to remember all she had been taught at the relaxation classes. Her husband kissed her tenderly, and telling her not to worry, things would sort themselves out, escaped from the room with relief, leaving her in the hands of the midwife.

* * *

Daniel came home at the end of a week, and was taken straight upstairs to greet the new arrival.

His mother was sitting in a chair, with the baby on her lap — a lap restored to its former pleasing proportions, Daniel was glad to note.

'Well, here he is,' she said. 'Your new brother! What do you think about him?'

So obligingly Daniel looked — and looked again. And what he saw boosted his deflated ego in one glorious split of a second . . .

Was this the end product of all his anxiety? All his doubts of the past few months? This red, wrinkled, ugly duckling, with its pointed head and purple pressure mark on its blob of a nose?

'Can it be unwrapped?' he asked, and smilingly his mother loosened the baby's shawl.

Daniel stared at the bandy legs protruding from the towelling nappy, and shook his head in silent disbelief.

So that was what happened when baby

was *born* and not *chosen*! A risky business altogether.

A smug sense of superiority overwhelmed him, and almost choked him with its intensity.

Then the baby opened his eyes and stared at Daniel in what was surely cross-eyed recognition? Then with surprising firmness it grasped his outstretched finger.

And Daniel grinned, first at his mother, and then at his father . . .

Considering they'd had no choice in the matter, just having to accept what came, as it were, things could have been a lot worse, he supposed.

'Hello, Jimmy Bump!' he said.

What a Difference a Day Makes

Usually, when a girl is all alone on her birthday, it is because she is a loner by nature, or an orphan with no one to care, or pathologically shy, or suffering from an infectious cold in the head. But none of these things applied to Jenny MacFarlane. She was a tall, smiling girl, friendly and loving, and the only thing infectious about her was her joyous laugh. She had hair the colour of ripe corn, a figure that was more than passable, and she possessed a complete incapacity for feeling sorry for herself.

She was merely, that particular birthday, an unfortunate victim of circumstances . . .

To begin with, her father, up in Edinburgh, had recently been made redundant, and had decided to spend his golden handshake on a cruise to the Canaries with Jenny's mother.

'We know you won't be on your own down there in London,' Mrs MacFarlane had written. 'You have Patrick, and I know you'll want to celebrate with him; so in a way, dear, we both feel that this letter could be more than slightly welcome.'

Jenny was glad for them — so glad that she had answered the letter straight away, omitting to mention that the easy friendship with Patrick was over, wishing them a happy time, and sending them all her love.

That was circumstance number one, and the second was that her close friend, Margo, had fallen swiftly and passionately in love with a man she had met going down in the office lift.

'We're engaged!' she had cried, waving her left hand about. 'I'm taking him home to meet my family next weekend; but you must come too, Jenny, for your birthday. We have lots of room — really, truly.'

So for the second time, Jenny had evaded the truth.

'There's no need to worry about me, not for a moment,' she said brightly. 'I'll be so busy turning down invitations I won't know which to refuse.'

And the relief in nice, kind Margo's eyes was comical to see.

Oh no, Jenny MacFarlane was not, and never had been, a sorry-for-herself kind of girl. She made up her mind that she was certainly not going to sit around in the lonely emptiness of her flat, dripping tears into a frozen television dinner. She was just not made that way.

So she asked one or two of the girls in the big insurance office where she worked if they would like to spend the day with her, but it seemed that everyone was already busy.

Jenny stopped asking people and resigned herself to the inevitable . . .

Now, the bit of suburbia where she lived was not a very good place in which to be alone. Her own little ground-floor flat was part of a block where the residents were fiercely determined to keep themselves to themselves, not to get involved whatever happened. It was a place where doors opened and closed furtively, and where chance meetings on the way to and from the communal dustbins outside evoked no more than a nod or perhaps a brief and noncommittal good day.

It was a bright little flat, gay with pot plants and cushions; but late on the Saturday afternoon before her birthday, Jenny stared round its comfortable untidiness and knew that something was seriously wrong.

There was, apart from a few cards and presents waiting to be unwrapped, nothing to denote that Sunday would be anything other than an ordinary day.

'I must do something,' Jenny said aloud. 'Buy a bottle of champagne; get something special for dinner . . .'

For Jenny, to think was to act; so right that minute she ran through into her bedroom and snatched up the enormous bright red tote bag she always carried with her on shopping expeditions. Then, without picking up her coat, she banged the door of her flat behind her and rushed down the bleak entrance hall and out into the street.

There wasn't much time, and as she hurried along, the crisp air tangled Jenny's golden hair into a whipped-up froth of curls, and her cheeks glowed as red as her cheerful tote bag.

In spite of the way things were, she couldn't help being glad it was her birthday, what with the sun shining down and the birds singing and all . . .

She swept into the butcher's and bought a duck. It was an extravagance but, after all, it was her birthday. Then she went on from shop to shop, buying champagne, paper napkins, long, slender red candles, a bunch of yellow roses . . . There was only one thing missing — a cake.

As she twirled out of the florist's on the corner, the packages almost knocked over a man she knew as a face on its way to the communal dustbins — a tall, dark and unhandsome man who lived in one of the bachelor flats on the top floor.

'Whoops!' he grinned. 'Whoops-a-daisy!'

'Sorry,' she laughed; then because this was no time for remembering the unwritten rule of no-involvement, she told him what she was looking for.

'Last-minute decision to celebrate my birthday,' she explained, and accepted his offer to hold her parcels, while she dashed to the baker's before it closed. There was one rather battered cream cake left in the window and Jenny found herself explaining to the assistant why she wanted it.

'Happy birthday!' the pewter-grey-rinsed lady on the till said as she handed over the box.

Jenny smiled.

'What I really wanted,' she told the tall, unhandsome man as they walked back to the flats together, 'was a cake with lots of icing and candles. But I suppose twenty-three candles would hardly fit on the cake.'

'I know just what you mean,' he said, steering Jenny and her parcels through the swing door. 'A birthday cake without candles is hardly worth having.'

He was a very friendly sort of man, with horn-rimmed spectacles that he kept putting in and out of his pocket, a lot of black hair, and feet that seemed to be walking in a different direction from the way he was going.

Jenny had often seen girls tripping up the stairs on their way to his flat; and heard bursts of music as he let them in.

She knew what his name was from the card index which was displayed in the hall, so she said politely: 'Thank you for your help, Matt Garland.'

And he raised an imaginary hat to her before taking the stairs two at a time.

★ ★ ★

Coming out of church next day, her birthday, she met Miss Browne from the flat directly above her own: Miss Browne with an 'e', a prim little scribble of a woman, who, it was said, did freelance illustrations for magazines on a drawing-board set up in her bedroom.

They walked back to the flats and Jenny explained about her battered birthday cake.

Miss Browne smiled understandingly, but Jenny was too shy to ask her if she'd like to come in for a drink.

When she turned on the radio, *Family*

Favourites was on, with people sending loving messages round the globe. Jenny promptly turned it off again.

Later, she switched on the television, but there was a war film on one side and football on the other. Jenny switched that off as well. She thought of her two parents sunning themselves in deckchairs as their ship sailed through a blue sea with a blue sky above, and just for a moment — but not very sincerely — she thought about Patrick, and wondered what he was doing.

It wasn't really that she wanted him back. He'd been more desirable in theory than in fact, now she faced up to it. Patrick Miles: with springy dark hair and devastating deep blue eyes; Patrick Miles: salesman superb with his easy charm and bulging bank account.

No, she didn't really want him back. She'd been flattered to be his girl for a year — who wouldn't have been? — but, try though she had, she'd never fallen blissfully in love with him . . . not the way Margo had, not the way her parents had, not the way she'd always dreamed she would . . .

Jenny shook herself. This was her birthday; she should be enjoying herself.

Quickly she set about getting her special dinner ready: succulent duck, delicious orange sauce, sweet green *petit pois* . . . She sighed sadly at the thought of eating it alone.

Just then, the doorbell rang with an apologetic burr; but when she went to open the door, there was no one there.

Lying on the mat was a white box with 'Happy

Birthday' printed on it, and when Jenny took it inside and opened it, her eyes widened in surprised delight.

For there, nestling in tissue paper, was a cake, delicately iced with lily-of-the-valley — and a single birthday candle.

Miss Browne with an 'e', Jenny thought. God bless her clever artistic fingers. And she gently placed the cake in the centre of the table, blinking back what surely couldn't be tears.

Swiftly she raced upstairs and pressed the bell on Miss Browne's door. 'Oh, thank you . . . thank you for the cake,' she said.

Miss Browne blushed crimson and introduced an identical scribbled-out little woman standing just behind her. 'This is my sister from Willesden. I don't quite understand. Did you say a cake, dear?'

'No, yes . . . ' Jenny stammered.

'Happy birthday,' the sisters said together, and Jenny smiled and said thank you; then she flew up the next flight of stairs, blushing even pinker than Miss Browne had done.

When Matt Garland opened his door, she found that suddenly and quite uncharacteristically, she was overcome with shyness.

'Thank you for the cake,' she said softly. 'It was the kindest thought — one of the kindest things that's ever happened to me.'

'You must come in,' he said, and there in the one big room that was everything — living, kitchen and dining room — was a green felt card table covered with icing-bags, blobs of marzipan and cake crumbs.

'I'm not really used to this sort of thing,' he explained; and Jenny stared round at the typically masculine room, and saw on the draining board a packet of chipolata pork sausages and a tin of baked beans.

'Your Sunday dinner?' she asked, appalled. 'I thought you'd be eating with friends today.'

He folded his arms and stared at her through the horn-rimmed spectacles. 'I'm a victim of circumstances,' he announced in mock sepulchral tones. And Jenny clasped her hands together and told him that so was she, and asked would he . . . oh, would he possibly like to come down and share her birthday dinner?

He didn't answer straight away. He just seemed to be swallowing hard as if there was something caught in his throat. Then he grinned happily and opened his arms wide.

'A happy, happy, lovely birthday. I'll come this very minute,' he said, and they ran down the stairs together, past Miss Browne's tightly closed door, and into Jenny's little flat.

And somehow, in the short time she had been away, a miracle had happened. Her tiny flat looked somehow warm and beckoning in the candlelight — a place to come home to.

The whole room seemed to have come alive, and there on the table stood the cake Matt had taken such care over.

They stood together, very close, Matt Garland and Jenny MacFarlane, two people who had each thought that they were alone in the world.

And just for a second, the candlelight touched

237

their heads — one so fair and one so dark — as if in blessing.

They turned and looked at each other, deep into each other's eyes, and they fell instantly in love. Just like that.

238

After the Baby Came

When they told Robert that the baby had arrived, he was not all that impressed.

After all, he was six years old and intelligent, and he had known for a long time that sooner or later the baby would materialize.

His mother had explained it to him very carefully. She had told him that a seed was growing in her tummy, and that she would get fatter and fatter, until at last the seed would develop into a baby who was ready to be born.

Robert found the story quite interesting, but much preferred his friend Nigel's version of the facts of life. Nigel said that Jesus threw babies down from the sky in summer, and during the winter months Father Christmas took over.

All that Robert could see of the baby when they proudly presented it to him was a tuft of black hair and a red, squashed face. The rest of it was parcelled up tightly in a blanket.

'Isn't he beautiful? Say hello to your brother,' his mother said.

And, feeling very foolish, Robert did as he was told, and was not in the least surprised when the bundle made no response whatsoever.

'What's it like?' Nigel asked the next day as they set off down the road together to school.

Robert searched his mind for something complimentary to say. He was experiencing for the very first time the uneasy responsibility of family loyalty.

'He's smashing. About as big as that.' He stretched his arms wide to show Nigel. 'And he knew me straight off.'

Nigel stopped dead in his tracks.

'How did he know you straight off? Babies don't know anything. Babies don't know anything at all,' he stressed.

Robert sniffed in a superior kind of way.

'This one does,' he said. 'It spoke to me.'

Nigel's eyes narrowed to suspicious slits.

'What did it say then?'

'It said Hello! Hello! Hello!' shouted Robert, and ran down the road, the steel tips on his shoes ringing metallically as he went.

'Has it got any teeth?' Nigel asked as they climbed over the school gate in preference to going through it.

Robert sighed. He wished Nigel would let the subject of the baby drop. The only time he had a chance to forget it was when he was out playing, or at school. The whole house revolved round the baby. He could not jump downstairs in case it startled the baby, he could not practise in the garden with his catapult in case a pellet hit the baby's pram, and, worst of all, he had to wait for his tea until the baby had been settled for the night.

But honour was at stake . . .

'It has ten teeth,' he said. 'No, *twelve*. I forgot the two that came yesterday.'

'Does it bite?' asked Nigel.

'He's not a *dog*,' Robert replied scornfully,

240

and ran into line as the assembly bell clanged out.

Before the baby came, Robert always knew that his mother would be waiting for him by the school gate, and sometimes they would go home the long way round by the shops and she would buy him an ice-lolly or, if the weather had turned cold, a packet of fruit pastilles.

But the day after the baby's birth his father had come into his bedroom and sat down on the edge of his bed.

'How would you like to start coming home from school by yourself?' his father had asked. 'You're a big boy now, and it would help Mummy now that the baby's here.'

Robert had considered this for a moment, then said, 'She could bring the baby; lots of people bring babies in prams. There's hundreds of prams outside the gates, every day, every single day.'

His father had removed a death-ray gun from the edge of his pillow.

'I know lots of mothers do,' he had said. 'But you show us how big you are. All right?'

Robert had opened his mouth to protest, but it was too late, his father had switched off the light and closed the door behind him. So, resigned to the inevitable, he had rescued his death-ray gun from the chair by his bed, pulled the sheet up to his chin and composed himself for sleep.

For a while, however, he had stared into the darkness, hating the baby. Nothing would ever be the same, he had decided, and he was right.

Nowadays, the house smelled of wet washing, and his mother smelled of talcum powder and cod-liver oil, and the baby cried all the time. Once, when he had thought that no one was looking, Robert had given the baby's cheek a good poke with his finger, and it had opened its eyes and screamed with startled fury. His mother, realizing what he had done, had given him a hard slap on his leg before snatching the baby up, and crooning to it softly.

'Who's a little darling then?' she had said.

Robert had withdrawn in disgust from this scene and had kicked a ball so hard in the garden that it had landed on one of his father's seed frames and shattered a pane of glass.

It was on the way home from school the very next day that he and Nigel found the puppy. A shivering, bedraggled little creature, it was crouched by a wall, its black and white coat matted with mud, and its heart beating madly beneath their hands.

Regardless of the fact that he was wearing his new grey flannels, Robert kneeled down in the lane and caressed the puppy's rounded head.

Dark brown eyes, liquid with love, gazed up at him, and one black paw reached up and touched his face.

'Who's a little darling then?' Robert whispered, unwittingly using the same crooning tone that his mother used for the baby. The puppy's jaws fastened on his finger, and he felt the sharp prick of the tiny milk teeth.

'It's mine,' said Nigel, scooping the dog up and buttoning it inside his gaberdine raincoat.

'I saw it first, and I'm going to keep it. For ever.'

Robert put his head on one side, and considered the matter. He could, of course, start a fight, for although he was a good three inches shorter than Nigel, he usually managed to emerge triumphant. But he was beaten even before he started, and he knew it.

He had wanted a dog for a long time, or a cat, or a rabbit or even, in desperation, a budgerigar, but his parents had stood firm.

'Once the novelty wears off, I'll be the one who will have all the work and worry of it,' his mother had said firmly.

'Wait until you are eight, and old enough to look after an animal yourself,' his father had said.

Nigel, surprised at Robert's silence, showed a sudden and uncharacteristic generosity of spirit.

'You can come home with me if you like, and watch me feed it,' he said, and Robert forgot himself so far as to say a humble thank you.

Without a single qualm, he set off down the long lane, passing the end of his own avenue, until they came to an estate of new houses that sprawled in uniform precision on the outskirts of the town.

It was the first time he had visited Nigel's house, and he marvelled at the way Nigel kicked the back door open with his muddy shoes, and went straight into the kitchen without bothering to wipe his feet.

'Mum!' Nigel shouted. 'Come and see what I've found.'

And he put the puppy down on the floor where it rolled over, exposing a pinkly spotted belly, and waved its damp paws in the air.

'Well!' said Nigel's mother, coming in from the living room. 'What a bedraggled little creature.' And she tickled the puppy's tummy with the toe of her slipper.

Quick as a flash the puppy snatched the slipper from her foot, and began to chew, its jaws champing rhythmically on the slipper's fur trimming.

'It's mine,' Nigel said proudly. 'I found it, and I'm going to call it Jo.'

'Josephine would be more appropriate,' his mother said, then turning to Nigel, she added: 'Don't set your heart on it, son. It may belong to somebody, although I doubt it. Poor little thing. It looks as if it needs a good feed.'

Robert watched, wide-eyed, as she put a saucer of bread and milk down on the floor, then hugged himself with glee as the puppy started a noisy lapping, its long ears trailing into the food, and its stump of a tail wagging with ecstasy.

'There's an empty box in the shed,' Nigel's mother said as the puppy finished eating, 'and I'll find you an old blanket to put in it.' She smiled. 'Then we'll see what your dad has to say.'

'Do you think he'll let you keep it?' Robert whispered, as he and Nigel watched the puppy curl up and drop instantly into sleep.

244

'Course,' said Nigel. 'Once I brought a lion home, and my dad let me keep it.'

Robert's lip curled.

'Where is it now then?' he asked.

'It died.' said Nigel promptly. 'It swallowed a nail and it died.'

Robert did not bother to pursue the subject. He was tracing with his finger the outline of the rounded head, the silken flop of ear, and the touching helplessness of the dangling paws. His heart ached with love, and he buried his face in the damp warmth of the puppy's body.

For once Nigel and he were perfectly in tune, kneeling there in adoration of the puppy, and only the crash of the front door as Nigel's father came home from work jerked them back to reality.

He was a square man with big hands and a loud boom of a voice, and Robert left him jiggling a piece of string over the puppy's head, and laughing his great laugh as the little dog leaped in the air and barked furiously.

Outside the shadows were slowly turning from mauve to purple, and people were hurrying home, heads bent against a drift of drizzle. For the first time Robert felt a twinge of conscience. He knew that he ought to have gone straight home from school but, perversely, his feet dragged, and he derived a morose satisfaction from the lateness of the hour.

What was there to hurry for? His mother would be putting the baby to bed, and it would be crying. He was *always* crying.

A woman hurried towards him down the long

lane, a woman wild-eyed and dishevelled, her coat flying open, and her hair straggling over her forehead in wet strands. Robert did not recognize her at first, and stepped sideways as she came towards him. Then he was enveloped in a pair of restraining arms, and his mother was holding him so tightly that his breath stuck in his throat, and she was laughing and crying at the same time, and patting his face as if she could not believe that he was real.

'Where have you *been*?' she asked, beginning to shake him so that his teeth rattled. 'I've been out of my mind. Never, ever do this to me again. You're a naughty, naughty boy, and I've a good mind to put you straight to bed.'

The next moment she smothered his face in kisses, and took his hand in her own. 'There's lemon curd for tea, and a cake with nuts all over the top,' she told him as they turned into the avenue, 'and we'll have it on trays round the fire . . .'

Not a mention of the baby. Perhaps it had gone away, Robert thought hopefully; perhaps they had sent it back because it cried so much. He squeezed his mother's hand, and smiled up into her face, but as soon as they walked up the garden path he knew that the baby was still there.

It was crying loudly, with furious, hiccoughing sobs, and he sighed deeply and let go of her hand, waiting for her to rush upstairs and forget that he was there.

But she walked through into the hall and into the kitchen, taking off her coat on the way. Then she started quite calmly to butter the bread for tea. She gave him the crust, the way she used to do, and he smiled at her and she smiled back and ruffled his hair.

Perhaps she could not hear the baby? Perhaps she had gone suddenly deaf?

Robert stared anxiously at her ears, but they looked just the same. His mother reached for the tray from the dresser and started to put the tea things on it.

'The baby's crying,' Robert said at last, unable to stand it any longer.

'Yes, I know, dear,' she said. 'You go upstairs and talk to him, and tell him I'm busy making your tea,' and she opened the cake tin and took out a cake that was sugary with icing and bristling with delicious walnuts.

Robert walked slowly upstairs, into the bedroom, and over to the cot by the wall. The baby was lying on his back, his two small fists clenched tightly, and his round face contorted with rage.

Robert leaned over and stared at him dispassionately. 'Shut up!' he said, then louder still, 'I said, shut up!'

The baby's chin wobbled in startled surprise, his blue eyes focused waveringly on Robert's face. A left-over sob crept up and seemed to shake him almost in two.

Robert put out a finger and traced the outline of the curved fat cheek, and gently touched the corner of the quivering mouth. A groping fist found one of his fingers, and held on to it firmly with surprising strength.

And then it happened . . .

Two unexpected dimples appeared at the corners of the baby's mouth, and as Robert gazed enraptured, it smiled straight at him, a beaming, glad-to-see-you smile.

Robert held his breath.

'Hello!' he said, and the baby chuckled and sucked noisily on his finger. Robert glowed with pride. 'Who's a little darling, then?' he said.

One day, he thought as he stood smiling down at the baby, he would tell his mother about the puppy they had found; but not yet. It was not all that important anyway.

His mother's voice spiralled upstairs, calling him down for his tea, but Robert leaned over the cot and buried his face in the milky lavender smell of the baby's neck, and tenderly touched the tuft of black hair.

'I'll come down when I've settled him,' he shouted back importantly down the stairs. Then whispering into the baby's tiny ear, he said, 'You're better than any old pup any time, aren't you?'

. . . And Never Speak of Love

Anyone could see that my sister Glynis was eating her heart out about Roy Blake who lived next door, and I could have told her exactly where she was going wrong, but she wouldn't have listened to me.

No one at home ever listened to me about anything. They just took it for granted that a girl of fourteen, going on fifteen, couldn't possibly know a thing about love and how complicated it can be. Not even though there was a war on at the moment.

It wasn't hard to see why Glynis was crazy about Roy Blake. He was tall and dark, and looked absolutely heavenly in his Pilot Officer's uniform, and since his last leave, he'd grown a neat little moustache.

'Nine a side,' Walter Davies described it as, meaning nine hairs each side of his nose. Walter was always saying really witty things like that. He was in the sixth form at the local grammar school, whilst I was at the high school of our Lancashire market town, and we'd been secretly engaged for three whole weeks.

Walter had only got keen on me when I'd pretended to like Neil Bailey, who to tell the truth I couldn't stand, on account of his spots, and his way of standing on one leg when he talked to me.

'The one sure way to get a boy interested in you is to pretend you like someone else,' I told Glynis, and she turned round from her dressing table, and told me not to be so silly.

I reminded her that there was a war on, and that time was precious, and that any day might be anybody's last, and that if Roy didn't ask her out before his leave was over, it might be too late.

'Then you'll be like Miss Carruthers, our biology mistress, whose only love was killed on Flanders Field,' I said, and Glynis asked me wearily why I wasn't doing my homework.

'Is Roy going to be at the dance?' I asked, and she said yes he was going, but that he was taking Marian Eccles from her office, a girl who bleached the front of her hair, and wore a bra that made her bosoms stick out.

'You're much prettier than she is,' I told Glynis, and watched fascinated as she spread a layer of vanishing cream over her face, then, with a pink puff fastened to a chiffon hanky, fluffed clouds of apricot-tinted powder on top.

'Do you think he'll ask you to dance?' I said, and Glynis said he might, but again he might not.

'There'll be a Ladies' Excuse Me, surely?' I asked, but she couldn't answer as she was busy drawing a perfect cupid's bow on her mouth with a purple lipstick. She pressed her top lip over the bottom, then she made little dabs on her cheeks with the lipstick, and rubbed it well in.

When she'd smeared her eyelids with Vaseline she looked beautiful, even though she still had her hair to do, and I told her so.

'I'll stay awake until you come in,' I promised, 'and you can tell me all about it.'

'There won't be anything to tell,' she said sadly, as she unwound her dark hair from its flat steel Dinkie curlers, and combed out each little sausage so that it sprang back from her fingers.

Then she dabbed Ashes of Roses perfume behind her ears, breathed into her cupped hands to check that her breath was sweet, and was ready to go.

When she'd gone I told our mother, 'I think Glynis is pining away for love of Roy Blake.'

'Nonsense, they're merely good friends. After all, they've known each other since they were children. He's just the boy next door. Granted, they went out together a few times before he got his call-up papers, but Glynis would have told me if there was anything serious.' She looked up from the Balaclava helmet she was knitting. 'Haven't you got any homework to do tonight?'

'But that's just it!' I said. 'Because Roy has always known her, he doesn't see her with the eyes of love. I've just been telling her that she ought to do something to make him notice her. I would.'

'Love isn't like that,' our mother said, knitting away furiously. 'It's like a plant; it can't be forced, and anyway, what can you know about it at your age? Go and do your homework.'

251

I remembered the note Walter Davies had passed me on the top of the tram on our way home from school, and I would have blushed if I'd been the blushing type.

He'd told me I was just like Sally Gray in *Dangerous Moonlight*, a film we'd seen together at the Rialto cinema, when I was supposed to be out with Doreen, my best friend.

There was this bit where she, Sally Gray, came down the stairs in the middle of the night, with her négligé trailing behind her, and her lover was playing the Warsaw Concerto on the piano, on account of being Polish and a concert pianist in better days, and I was training my fair hair to go the way hers went, all smooth on top, and flicked up at the ends.

'Did you remember to get any kirby grips?' I said, and our mother said there weren't any to be had, not for love or money, and even if there were, queuing up for half a pound of liver was one thing, but queuing up for kirby grips quite another.

Our father came in then, and ruffling my hair, asked me why I wasn't doing my homework, so I went upstairs to the room I share with Glynis.

She came in at midnight, and I knew she was upset, because she undressed and got into bed without removing her make-up with the top of the milk which she usually brought up in a saucer, on account of there not being cold cream about in the shops.

I wasn't going to say anything, but she started to cry softly into her pillow, and I knew I had to do something about it.

'Was he there?' I whispered.

She gave a long, despairing sob, and I switched on the light and looked at her, and she looked awful. Her eyes were all puffy, and she was letting the tears roll down her cheeks without bothering to wipe them away, so I got out of bed, and climbed in beside her, and put my arms round her tight.

'He was there all right,' she said between sobs. 'With that awful Marian Eccles, and when I got him just for a moment in a Paul Jones, he told me that he's going up to Scotland next week, to the Outer Hebrides, to start flying on operations with Coastal Command. He made a joke of it, and before I could say anything, the music changed, and I found myself dancing with a Polish airman with red hair, who trod on my feet.'

'Never mind what he looked like,' I whispered fiercely. 'I hope you looked up at him as if he was Clark Gable in *Gone With the Wind*, and offered to teach him English, so that you could sit the next dance out with him and make Roy jealous.'

'I went and sat in the cloakroom all alone,' Glynis said bleakly, 'and when I went back to the dance, they'd gone.'

'To snog on a bench in the Corporation Park, if I know Marian Eccles,' I said, and our father knocked on the wall, so I went back to my own bed, and thought how cruel life could be.

And for the next three days, Glynis came home from work and stayed in. She borrowed some of Mother's wool, and started a scarf,

253

listening to the wireless, and staring at the wall dividing our house from the one next door, as if she were willing Roy suddenly to appear through it.

The next day I met Walter Davies after school, and we walked home the long way through the park instead of catching the tram, and stood by the railings watching the ducks swimming round and round. He had stuffed his school cap into his satchel, risking a detention if he was caught by a prefect, and I thought how very good-looking he was.

'Do you think it's possible for a person to die of a broken heart?' I asked him, and he said only in books, so I told him about Glynis, and asked him if he thought she was pretty.

'Not as pretty as you,' he said, gruffly, and turned his back on the ducks so that I wouldn't see him blush. 'Me now, I prefer blondes.'

'This dreadful war,' I said, running out of conversation, and wondering what Sally Gray would have talked about, if she hadn't been so busy listening to her lover playing the Warsaw Concerto.

'Oh, I don't know,' Walter said. 'I'm going to join up as soon as I'm eighteen. Submarine Service, I expect. I can't wait to get to grips with the Hun.'

'You'll get spots,' I told him.

'Spots?' he said, reaching in his blazer pocket for the stub of a cigarette, and striking a match with his thumbnail, the way we'd seen an American gangster do in a film.

'With being in a submarine,' I explained. 'It's

to do with the lack of oxygen or something. But what matters now is how to get my sister and Roy Blake together. I'll have to think of a plan.'

'Can't see that it has anything to do with you. You're a real busybody, aren't you?'

'I am not!' I said, and he said there was no need to get shirty, but that he might as well be honest and admit he couldn't stand people who interfered in other people's business.

'I am not interfering,' I said, trying to look dignified, which was difficult on account of me wearing my box-pleated gymslip, a garment which Sally Gray wouldn't have been seen dead in, I'm sure.

'Sounds like it to me,' Walter said, and I just walked away, leaving him standing there, and when I turned round, he was leaning over the railings blowing smoke at the ducks, ignoring me.

So there were two of us sitting with our mother, listening to the nine o'clock news, and sighing alternately.

I told Glynis about my quarrel with Walter, and she said she was surprised I didn't know what to do about it.

'After all, you're the one who knows everything,' she said, and I forgave her being so nasty, because I felt rather nasty myself.

And all the time Roy Blake's leave was coming to an end, and Glynis was growing thinner and paler with every passing hour. She'd stopped eating, and I would have stopped eating too, but my broken heart seemed to make me hungrier than ever, and our mother said how she was going to make the rations go round she didn't know.

Then one day I was coming home from school the park way, just in case I saw Walter — not that I'd have spoken to him, of course — when I saw Roy Blake, sitting all by himself on a bench.

'Hello!' I said, and he smiled at me, and moved up so that I could sit beside him.

'I believe you've been posted?' I said, and he asked me how I knew.

'Glynis mentioned something just in passing,' I said. 'Did you enjoy the dance, by the way?'

'So, so,' he said, stroking the little moustache with his finger. 'I didn't think she'd taken any notice of me.'

I held my breath. There was something about the way he looked when I mentioned my sister's name, and I knew that what I was about to say might have an influence on two people's lives.

'She's very popular, my sister,' I said chattily, 'and of course, now that there are so many soldiers and airmen stationed around here, she's having a marvellous time.'

He looked thoughtful. 'That doesn't sound like Glynis.'

'Out every night,' I said.

'She always seem to be in a hurry whenever I see her. Runs away when I speak to her . . . '

'She has a lot on her mind,' I told him, just as Walter turned the corner of the path.

As he passed us, he smiled at me, and I knew he was waiting for me to join him, but the image of my sister's pale face rose up before me, and I knew that I had to sacrifice my own desires. After all, I had the rest of my life before me, but Glynis was twenty-two, and I didn't want her to end up like Miss Carruthers, dreaming about what might have been . . .

'Glynis has this Polish boyfriend,' I said, 'and you know what foreigners are like. He's trying to persuade her to marry him before he goes abroad. She says he's very passionate, and won't take no for an answer.'

'Red-haired bloke who can't dance for toffee?' said Roy, and I saw the way he was clenching and unclenching his hands, and nodded.

'He was bombed out of Warsaw, and escaped to England,' I went on, trying to remember bits from the film. 'All his family were lost. You know how tender-hearted Glynis is?'

'Played on her sympathy,' Roy said quite nastily, and I said that was what our mother had said, but with the war and everything . . .

He didn't even say goodbye. Just got up from that bench and walked away, swinging his arms as if he were on parade, and when I got to the corner of our avenue, Walter was waiting for me to tell me it was all his fault, and asking me to forgive him.

At six o'clock Glynis came home from work looking paler and wanner than ever, and I was just going to tell her that she was engaged to a Polish airman with red hair, when the doorbell rang.

She went paler than ever when she saw that it was Roy, and they disappeared into the lounge

257

together, and I told our mother that on no account must they be disturbed, and that if Roy mentioned the fact that she was going to be mother-in-law to a Pole with red hair, she had to remind him that there was a war on, and that she never interfered.

'Say that again,' our mother said, and I was trying to explain it all to her, which was difficult as one half of her mind was on the potato she was grating for the mince, and the other half was obviously on what was going on behind the closed lounge door.

Then Glynis came into the kitchen, hand in hand with Roy, and I know it sounds corny, but there were stars in her eyes, and they stood there, looking so beautiful together, and our mother wiped her eyes on the corner of her pinafore, and beamed at them.

'We had a lot of misunderstandings to clear up,' Roy said, winking at me, and our father came in from work and got out the bottle of champagne he'd been saving for the Armistice.

All that happened a long time ago, and only last week, when my sister Glynis and my brother-in-law Roy celebrated their thirtieth wedding anniversary; in spite of them having three grandchildren, and in spite of his moustache being grey now and bushy, their love was there, plain to see, just as it had been on that day when our dad had opened the champagne.

'It does my heart good to see two people so happy,' I told my husband that night. 'And to think that they might never have got together, if it hadn't been for me!'

'You're still a busybody, after all this time,' he said, teasing me, and taking out a cigarette, he struck a match with his thumbnail, the way we'd seen that American gangster do in that film, all those years ago.

A Battle of Wills

There was nothing about Henry England's appearance to suggest that he could be a violent man. On the contrary.

Thin almost to the point of emaciation, his shoulders had a permanent stoop, the result of his almost compulsive addiction to study. He was a man of letters, gentle, kind, and respected in a slightly scathing way by his pupils at the Grammar School, where he taught English and History.

At the age of thirty-four, after two relationships which didn't last long enough to become meaningful, he met Claire Garland, a young widow. They fell in love so blindly that within six weeks they were married.

Henry was so happy it seemed that all his days were now tinged with gold. Happiness, he discovered, was not so much the discovery of a new poem, but the smile on his wife's face, the sound of her quiet voice, the scent of her hair, the feel of her, the being with her that made his life complete.

But life is never perfect, as Henry knew only too well. Always, but always, there is a metaphorical fly in the mythical ointment.

And the fly in Henry's ointment was Robin Paul.

'He's so much like his father,' Claire told him one evening before the wedding, as they sat entwined on the sofa in her flat. 'It's as though he had never left me.'

Then her brown eyes widened in distress. 'I hope you don't mind me talking sometimes about Colin, darling? He was so young when he was killed, only twenty-six, and I wouldn't like Robin to forget him entirely. You do understand?'

Henry had nodded with an understanding great enough to take in four husbands if necessary.

'Robin Paul is so sensitive, so very mature and perceptive for a seven-year-old. At the beginning of term, when he comes back from Mother's, you can really get to know each other.'

Henry nodded into the fragrance of her hair, a vision of himself tramping the countryside, a small boy leaping by his side, a jam-jar threaded with string carried companionably between them.

But he resolutely put this idea to one side when he met Robin Paul. And whilst he was prepared to love any creature, great or small, who happened to be part of his beloved Claire, he did feel perhaps that the choice of the words sensitive, perceptive, or even mature could be misnomers.

Robin Paul was big for his age with hair which grew at the wrong angle from his head. And his eyes seemed to be permanently narrowed to threatening slits.

When his mother was around he treated Henry with a politeness bordering on the insolent; when they were alone he treated him with the contempt he felt his stepfather obviously deserved.

'Why are you so thin, then?'

'Something to do with my metabolism,' Henry explained in his quiet way. 'The food I eat is burned up by what they call nervous energy. I could eat a dozen cream cakes and not put on an ounce of weight, while someone of your metabolism . . . '

He stopped, averting his eyes from Robin Paul's childish paunch, and the red mottled legs bursting from the short trousers.

'My dad didn't wear glasses. Bet you'd be blind if you took them off. Bet you would.'

'Not quite, but I wouldn't be sure just who you were, unless you came within spitting distance.'

'My dad said it was rude to spit, my dad did.'

The slit eyes narrowed ominously. Henry's irritation softened to compassion and he put out an arm to draw the sturdy, menacing little figure closer to his chair.

But Robin Paul side-stepped out of his way with the dexterity of a boxer in the ring.

'Bet you can't swim nor nothing,' was the parting shot as Robin Paul made good his escape, tripping over the pattern in the carpet on his way to the door.

★ ★ ★

That night, lying in bed with a strand of Claire's hair tickling his nose, Henry asked his love if her

262

first husband had been the athletic type.

Her voice came muffled through descending layers of sleep. 'Oh yes, darling. Colin played squash and rugger, and at one time had to decide between his engineering career or being coached to Olympic standard as a swimmer.'

Henry sighed. 'Robin Paul must have been very proud of him.'

'He was only three and a half years old when his father died,' Claire reminded him sleepily. 'Why? Is something wrong, darling?'

'Nothing at all. Go to sleep, darling,' Henry lied.

He lay awake for a long time, long after her breath came slow and even, wondering how he could possibly measure up to a broad-shouldered dad whose muscles rippled beneath sun-bronzed skin. A dad who swallow-dived from the top board and did a back-crawled length at the speed of light . . .

He couldn't even begin to compete, and besides, it would be foolish to try. He knew better than to try to outshine a father who had left such a lasting impression on a child of three and a half years old.

No. If he wanted his life with Claire to be complete he must try to see her belligerent tow-headed little son through her eyes. He must search out his sensitivity and pander to the maturity his mother swore he possessed.

So he tried again.

When Claire was out shopping he pushed his horn-rimmed spectacles back to where they should have been resting on the bridge of his nose, and smiled at Robin Paul.

Busily employing his so-called sensitivity, the small boy was picking the leaves off his mother's prize geranium plant and shredding them gleefully on to the floor.

'I read a very exciting book the other day,' Henry began. 'I'm sure you'd like it. All about a monster which terrorized people.'

What could have been a flicker of interest showed for a second in the narrowed eyes.

'You mean *Jaws*, then? 'Bout a shark that bit people's legs off?'

What Henry had in mind was St George's dragon, but at least he felt it was a starting point, the first real conversation they'd had.

So he pushed aside the exercise books he was marking, and taking off his spectacles, rubbed his aching eyes. Robin Paul was just a blur as he spoke.

'Did you know that the shark they used in the film was artificially made?'

Robin Paul put his head on one side.

'Crikey! Don't you look funny without your glasses on! Bet you couldn't swim away if a shark got you. Bet my dad could've swum better than any old shark.'

Henry replaced his spectacles, bringing the aggressive little face unwillingly into focus again. Robin Paul had moved closer to him, leaning on the table.

He was so close in fact that he could smell the little boy smell of him, and see the way the narrowed eyes seemed to be flecked with gold, the way Claire's eyes were when she was excited.

Suddenly Henry thought he understood.

Robin Paul *was* excited. Excited and scared at the same time. Unsure of himself the way a bully is unsure, trying to goad Henry into some form of retaliation.

Coming even closer, Robin Paul stretched out a grubby hand and deliberately snatched away Henry's red marking pencil.

'Put that back.' Henry's voice was quiet.

'I want it,' Robin Paul answered back.

'I said, put it back.'

He had been right. The hooded eyes were wary now, assessing just how far their owner could go. Claire had been right too. Robin Paul was mature beyond his seven years — but still badly, desperately in need of guidance.

'Put that back or I'll wallop you.'

'No!' Robin Paul said, his voice cracking slightly.

He jabbed the pencil down on the table so that the point broke, leaving a scar on the surface of the polished table.

Swiftly, decisively, Henry upended the astonished small boy, face downwards across his knees.

Then he did the necessary.

The expected bellow of pain and rage didn't materialize. Instead, Robin Paul, right way up again, stared at his assailant with open-mouthed astonishment for a moment, then left the room.

No. Henry England was definitely not a man of violence. Once as a child he'd anguished over a worm his spade had accidentally cut in two, and even as a grown man his very soul cringed from the thought of corporal punishment.

How would he explain to Claire when she came back? His right hand stung and he stared at it with loathing. Wearily he drew an ashtray towards him and began to sharpen the red pencil into it.

He didn't hear the slap of crêpe-soled sandals until Robin Paul stood by his side, lower lip trembling.

Subduing his instinct to draw the small boy into the circle of his arm, Henry waited.

Meekly Robin Paul held out his hand for the pencil sharpener.

'I'll do that for you if you like, then.'

Lovingly, his tender heart aching, Henry watched as the pencil was sharpened to an exquisite point.

'Bet you can make some smashing ticks with that now, then.'

The voice was hoarse with the aftermath of tears, but the apology was there, freely given.

Henry drew his stepson close, ruffling the coarse-as-fusewire hair. Then the same voice that had tutored dozens of boys to A level in English Grammar said clearly: 'You bet I can at that, old son,' adding for good measure a most emphatic *then*.

Dear Uncle Harry

Always, around the first week in December, there was the problem of Uncle Harry . . .

It had started years ago, when Irene had found that her one and only uncle, then a bachelor in his middle fifties, was living alone. In a moment of what she now considered to be misguided sympathy she had invited him to spend Christmas with them.

It had all been because of a talk given by a well-meaning lady on the radio twelve years ago.

Irene remembered that day. At the time they had been busily engaged in stirring the Christmas pudding. First Janet, solemn and intense, even as a seven-year-old, squeezing her eyes into tight slits as she wished for the red umbrella that was already hidden in the cupboard underneath the stairs. Then Sally, stirring half-heartedly, and managing to look superior and bored with the whole procedure even at five years old.

The voice on the radio had said that if every happy family invited just one lonely person to share their Christmas there would be no lonely people crouched over gas fires in bedsitting rooms, cooking their tiny chickens over gas rings, and drinking a toast to themselves in weak tea.

Irene's warm-hearted sympathy had got the

better of her, and she'd gone straight to her bureau and written to Uncle Harry.

She was well aware that Uncle Harry would have laid down and died rather than toast himself in anything as harmless as weak tea. She also knew that he was an excellent cook, his taste turning to the exotic — but he *did* live alone, and apart from them, he didn't have any family to visit.

And so it had become a regular practice — as much a part of their Christmas as the ordering of the turkey, or the writing of the Christmas cards.

★ ★ ★

Every year for twelve years, Uncle Harry had arrived on the afternoon of Christmas Eve, dressed in hairy tweeds, and smoking innumerable cigarettes. And bringing with him the same repertoire of terrible jokes, which he repeated every year, although they'd all heard them before . . .

Uncle Harry, stepping from a taxi, laden with unsuitable presents. A black petticoat for Janet the year she was twelve and French perfume for a delighted ten-year-old Sally. And sometimes presents that even defied recognition . . .

Irene glanced towards the sideboard, where one of Uncle Harry's presents sat: a tortured effigy in cane work that had broken the ice at many a party.

'What *is* it, exactly?' an intrigued guest would say, and when Irene said that she honestly didn't know, the suggestions would come thick and fast . . .

Sighing, Irene drew a sheet of notepaper from the cubbyhole in her desk and began to write.

Dear Uncle Harry,
We're hoping you'll join us again this Christmas. It will be a little quieter than usual, as Janet will be spending the day with Ian and his mother in Kent. As you know, Ian's mother is a widow, and they didn't feel it would be fair to leave her alone, and of course I agreed . . .

Irene finished the letter, licked down the envelope, and banged the stamp so hard with her clenched fist that the chandelier lamp on top of the bureau rattled like a skeleton in a high wind.

Stephen came into the room at that moment. He walked straight over to her and ruffled her hair.

'Like that, it is, love?'

Irene leaned against him for a moment, closing her eyes and feeling the familiar ache of love.

'Christmas,' she said. 'I wonder at times if it's worth it.'

Irene had been feeling that way a lot, particularly this year.

Perhaps, in the early years of their marriage, when there had been the excitement of toys hidden on top of the wardrobe, and Stephen smuggling a tree into the house on Christmas

Eve, there had been something to say for it.

But now, Janet was nineteen and engaged to be married, and seventeen-year-old Sally, who was still at school, believed that Christmas was just an excuse for people to eat and drink too much. Even Stephen himself said it was a highly commercialized racket.

She turned round in her chair, the letter in her hand. 'I don't honestly think there's much point in getting a tree this year,' she said slowly. 'Janet won't be here, and you know Sally's views . . . She told me the other day that she considered Christmas festivities to be nothing more or less than pagan rites . . . '

Stephen took his pipe and tobacco pouch from the coffee table and sat down in his usual chair. He laughed easily.

'A phase,' he said comfortably. 'It's all talk with these youngsters. Try telling Sally that as she doesn't believe in Christmas we won't be buying her any presents this year, then see how she reacts.'

'And the tree?'

'Suits me,' Stephen said, puffing away at his pipe. 'It's all a racket anyway. Just as you say, love. We won't bother with a tree . . . '

★ ★ ★

The next day, in the shop on the corner of the High Street, Irene averted her eyes from the counter piled high with silver baubles, coloured stars and long, sparkling trails of tinsel. She

270

moved over to the section marked 'Calendars and Cards'.

She worked her way through the trays of cards. There were robins in plenty, old coaching scenes, views of the Swiss Alps, but no sign of the Nativity scene.

Surely, Irene thought, in spite of Sally's modern theories, that was what it was all about?

'Nativity cards over there,' the temporary assistant told her, brushing a tired lock of hair back from her forehead.

Irene thanked her, turned round too quickly and dislodged a pyramid of wrapping paper, so that the whole lot cascaded to the floor.

The temporary assistant made a great show of coming from behind the counter and helping to pick them up. Irene felt her cheeks burn with embarrassment.

When she arrived home, her trolley basket was loaded to overflowing and her back ached.

The sight of the Christmas cake waiting to be iced filled her with weariness, but by five o'clock it was finished. Just as she was trying the effect of a plaster Santa Claus the back door opened and Sally came in.

Her school hat was crammed deep down into her briefcase as usual and her fair hair hung like a curtain round her small pointed face. Her fringe, almost tangling with her eyebrows, gave her the appearance of a Yorkshire terrier. Irene had threatened more than once to creep into Sally's bedroom and cut it while she was asleep.

'Very arty,' Sally said as she passed the cake, tapping the Santa Claus so that he wobbled and fell, leaving a mark in the smooth spread of white icing sugar.

Irene snatched him up, feeling anger rise inside her.

'Have you any idea how long it's taken me to ice that cake?' she demanded. 'And do you think it helps any to know that you believe the whole thing's a waste of time, anyway?'

To her surprise, her voice was actually shaking.

Sally's blue eyes looked at her from underneath her fringe.

'Well, why do it then?' she asked. 'You can buy the cake and mince pies from the shops, and I'm sure they taste just as good. Sit down, Mum, and I'll make you a cup of tea. You've no idea how tired you look.

'And I wish you'd give that dress to a jumble sale. Honestly, Mum, jersey isn't right for you. You have to be slim and young to wear those jersey shifts. Not that you're fat, but you know what I mean . . . '

Irene sat down, only half listening to the chatter as Sally moved about, clattering cups and saucers on to the table.

'I mean to say, take all this Christmas business,' Sally was saying. 'You believe it because you were taught to believe it, but do you ever honestly stop and think about it in the cold light of day? I hope you don't mind me saying so, Mum, but for a middle-aged woman you're incredibly naïve at times . . . '

And Irene, sipping gratefully at her tea, had to admit that never once during the cold light of day had she really stopped to consider about Christmas . . .

'There!' Sally said triumphantly, leaning her elbows on the table, so that the hair swung forward, obscuring all but the tip of her nose. 'That's what's wrong with your generation. You live in a dream world, believing what you want to believe, and only seeing what you want to see. Andrew says . . . '

Irene knew what Andrew said. He was Sally's current boyfriend, and could, given the chance, have sorted out the economic position and put the country back on its feet in less time than it takes to tell. He was also rewriting the New Testament in the style of Hans Andersen, thus proving that it was a fairytale, he said.

There were times when Irene wished Andrew had never been born . . .

When Sally had gone upstairs, Irene sat alone in the kitchen with her fortieth birthday still two years away, feeling fat, middle-aged, and incredibly naïve . . .

She switched on the radio and an announcer warned her that Christmas was only fourteen shopping days away. She remembered that she still had Stephen's present to buy and Uncle Harry's bottle of whisky, which she gave him every year. And every year he pretended to faint with surprise when he unwrapped it . . .

* * *

The next two weeks didn't pass, they just vanished. On the afternoon of Christmas Eve Janet went off to stay with Ian's mother, and Uncle Harry arrived, clouds of cigarette smoke hanging above his bald head.

He met Andrew for the first time and insisted on showing him a few of his more complicated card tricks. He got down on his knees on the sitting-room carpet and spread the cards into position with nicotine-stained fingers.

Irene saw Sally and Andrew exchange smug glances of amusement.

'Very good, sir,' Andrew said, his horn-rimmed spectacles slipping down the bridge of his nose. 'When I was a child, my father used to entertain me for hours with that sort of thing.'

Uncle Harry stood up stiffly. As he shuffled the cards, Irene noticed with a pang of pity that his hands were trembling a little.

Not trusting herself to speak, she escaped to the kitchen. When Stephen came in from the garage, she was still there, rolling out the pastry for the last half-dozen mince pies, a streak of flour down her nose, and the light of battle in her eye.

'All this,' she said, gesticulating wildly with the rolling pin, 'the turkey stuffed, the puddings made, the pies nearly finished, the trifle waiting for its layer of cream, the ham glazed, and the vegetables prepared. And for what? And if you laugh, I'll never forgive you, never!'

Then she saw the twinkle in his eyes and the way he was biting his lips to stop them stretching into his familiar grin.

'*Voilà!*' he said, and taking Irene gently by the arm, he led her to the open door.

And there, propped against the fence, was the scruffiest, the most bedraggled Christmas tree she had ever seen.

'The only one left,' Stephen said proudly, putting his arm round her, and holding her close. 'But a Christmas tree all the same.'

He stretched out his free hand and touched the tree, and a shower of needles cascaded to the ground.

'Woodworm,' he said solemnly, and Irene leaned closer to him, smiling happily.

'But a Christmas tree all the same,' she said softly.

Then they heard footsteps behind them and there was Sally the cynic, her eyes glowing from beneath the fringe, and Andrew the genius, saying that if Irene had such a thing as a roll of tin-foil and some empty cardboard cartons he would have the tree trimmed before they could say Santa Claus . . .

Uncle Harry appeared from some mysterious errand, carrying a peculiar geometrical shape dripping with tinsel, glittering in the ray of watery sunlight that chose that moment to struggle through the clouds.

'A star,' he explained. 'A pop-art star that I kept hidden in my room when I heard there was to be no tree this year.'

'No tree!' Sally echoed, indignation making

her voice squeak. 'But Daddy always brings the tree on Christmas Eve. It wouldn't be Christmas without a tree and the Star of Bethlehem on top.'

Irene's eyes met Stephen's for the briefest of moments, but their message was perfectly clear . . .

Christmas had been a long time in coming. According to the shops in the High Street, since October at least. But now it was here.

And there, to prove it, was the tree.

You're Expected to Be There

At first he hadn't really taken it in. He simply *couldn't* be there at the birth of his own baby. Occupying a ring-side seat as it were.

Morag was talking too quickly, the way she always did when she was excited, her long fair hair falling forward over her little pointed face, and her blue eyes shining with the importance of it all.

'It's only because it's a first baby that I've got a bed in the new maternity hospital,' she was saying. 'And Keith, you should see it! All gleaming white, and so clean! And the babies sleep by their mothers' beds, in glass-sided cots, and you can visit every day, and later on I have to go for relaxation classes and breathing exercises, and they let the husbands be there when the baby is born. In fact they encourage it.'

'You mean to actually see it born?' he said slowly, reaching for one of the five cigarettes he allowed himself each day.

She smiled dreamily. 'Won't it be marvellous? We'll be able to share the most precious experience of our whole lives . . . '

Now she was getting sentimental again, he thought tenderly. He had noticed a marked tendency to this new habit early on in her pregnancy. Usually a down-to-earth, practical kind of person, now she was all hearts and

277

flowers, he thought with amusement. Soon she'd be talking about the pattering of little feet, and starting to crochet and knit.

The picture of Morag in her jeans or newest mini dress, with her false eyelashes demurely cast down, *knitting*, made him laugh, and laughing made him feel better able to cope with the situation. There were seven whole months to go yet, and anything could happen when the time came.

Surreptitiously he counted forward on his fingers. He could have an important exam. No, his finals weren't until June. He tried again. He could have a cold, and be forbidden to enter the gleaming modern hospital because of the germs. He could even make her see that to him the whole idea of being there was preposterous, ridiculous.

'Wouldn't I be in the way?' he asked hopefully, and her bright blue gaze regarded him steadily.

'You'd be a *comfort*,' she said firmly. 'If you were there, I wouldn't be afraid.'

That did it. He went and sat beside her on the atrocious brown and green faded cover of the sofa in the tiny living room of their furnished flat, and took her in his arms. Lovingly he smoothed the silky hair up and away from her forehead.

'Then I'll be there,' he said, and kissed her quickly so that she would close her eyes, and not see the despair in his own.

Living on a grant, as they were, it was essential that Morag carried on working at her job in the university library for as long as possible, and indeed, apart from the disappearance of her waistline and a tendency to consume pickled beetroot at any hour of the day, life went on exactly as before.

They still entertained their many friends to coffee in the evenings, and though Morag graduated from her usual place on the rug by the electric fire to the more comfortable position of a high-backed chair, she didn't suffer from any of the minor complaints he vaguely associated with pregnancy.

She wasn't sick in the mornings, her ankles remained as slim as before, and she returned from her monthly visits to the hospital with soothing reports that all was proceeding normally.

His mother came up from London for a week's holiday, and one day when they were alone, he told her that Morag wanted him to be with her when the baby came.

'Apparently it's the done thing,' he said, trying to make light of it. 'Would you have wanted my father to be there when I was born?'

His mother shook her head firmly, and Keith could see her struggling with her intention never to interfere, and her natural habit of always speaking her mind.

'Your father was at a football match when you were born,' she said, smiling, 'but then, things are very different nowadays. In my day, giving birth to a baby was considered to be a woman's job. But we have to move with the times.' Then she laughed. 'Your father would have fainted dead away. Do you remember the time we all went to the doctor's surgery for smallpox injections? The *fuss* he made!'

Like father, like son, Keith thought miserably, and lay awake for a long time that night imagining himself lying in an undignified heap on the floor in the hospital, whilst Morag coped bravely with whatever women did when they were giving birth.

Feverishly he tried to remember what facts relating to childbirth he had assimilated in his twenty-one years; all he could recall were television Westerns where, in the end wagon, some woman lay tossing on a bed of pain. As far as he could remember the husband always remained decently in the background, swigging back long gulps of whatever settlers swigged, and played poker — or whatever game settlers played — with the other men.

He wasn't scared. Of course he wasn't scared. It was just that the whole idea was repugnant to him, and tomorrow he would tell Morag. Quite casually, of course, and she would understand.

Beside him in the double bed she stirred and muttered something in her sleep, and he put his arm round her, half expecting the baby to kick him in reproach.

In February Morag gave up her job, and it was good to come home from college and climb the three flights of stairs to their small flat and find her there, an indisputable mother-to-be now, in her maternity dresses, her long hair cut short because, as she said, how could she feed and bath a small baby with long hair falling round her face?

Now they started crossing off the days on the calendar in the kitchen, and the baby's layette, piles of snowy bonnets, and what seemed like hundreds of matinée coats, was folded in the airing cupboard.

When March came in with cold winds blowing from the sea, she packed her case, and every morning when he left for college, he made her promise that at the first twinge, the very first twinge, she would telephone, and he would come home straight away.

He had loved her before, but now his love was all-embracing. Nothing mattered but his love for her — not the astronomical electric bills, the dinginess of their flat, the uncertainty of his future, or the almost impossible task of trying to save a deposit for a house of their own. He had forgotten that the baby hadn't been planned, and he had almost forgotten his promise to be there . . .

Then one night as they undressed for bed, Morag told him quite calmly that they had better get dressed again, as she thought the baby had decided to arrive, a full week earlier than expected.

Wings of panic beat in his chest as he climbed back into his trousers and pulled a sweater over his head.

'You're sure?' he asked her, reminding her that there were still seven days to cross off on the calendar, and unable to believe that anyone could be so calm and seemingly unperturbed.

'Quite sure,' she said, then as he picked up his car keys, praying that their unpredictable car wouldn't let them down, she started fussing because she hadn't filled the pantry with frozen foods and tins of beans and spaghetti for the time she would be away.

'For goodness' sake,' he said, 'don't worry about me, and *hurry*. Please *hurry*. You don't need to put on lipstick, surely?'

Then he was helping her tenderly into the car, throwing the case into the back, and switching on the ignition, with fingers that trembled only a little.

All the way there she talked about his shirts that only needed a quick rinse through and no ironing, and his socks that she thought he'd have enough of if he wore a pair for two days instead of one.

She took a list from her handbag and showed him the people she wanted him to telephone, and tucked it away carefully in the glove compartment. At the hospital she was whisked away by an efficient young nurse with plump red arms, mottled in a lacy pattern as if she'd stayed too long in a hot bath.

He was left to wait in a room so clinically clean that he didn't dare to light a cigarette, although there were several ashtrays dotted about on the gleaming surfaces of little tables.

'Your baby won't be born for a long time yet,' a voice said suddenly from behind him, and he jumped as if he'd been shot in the back. 'We're giving your wife something to help her sleep, so if I were you I'd go back home and get some rest. You can go in and see her for a few minutes, then we'll telephone you when things start to happen.'

'Yes,' he said. 'Yes, thank you very much,' and he followed the nurse into a room, where Morag lay tucked up in a high bed, wearing a white hospital nightdress.

'You'll hear the telephone when it rings, won't you?' she said. 'You know you never hear the alarm, so how will you hear the telephone when it rings?'

He held her hands and promised her that he'd hear the very first ring, and kissed her mouth and thought how young she looked lying there. Far younger than her nineteen years, and far too young to be a mother.

And as he drove the car out on to the main road again, he reminded himself that babies were born every day. Every minute, all over the world if it came to that . . .

The flat was cold and empty, and the pink nightdress she had worn the night before was still folded up on the pillow at her side of the bed, and he held it and it smelled of her and talcum powder, and in bed he prayed to a God he'd argued didn't exist, and he left the door open so that he would hear the first ring of the telephone out on the landing.

He wouldn't go to sleep. He couldn't go to sleep, and he'd smoke in bed, all his five cigarettes, one after another — a thing he'd promised her he'd never do . . .

When the telephone rang, he looked at the watch still strapped to his wrist, and couldn't believe his eyes. Six o'clock, and already the promise of a cold grey day seeping through the curtains, and three cigarette stubs in the ashtray by his bed.

Holding his pyjama trousers up with one hand, he heard a cool voice telling him that if he wanted to see his baby born he'd better hurry.

'Things have speeded up more quickly than we expected,' the voice went on, and once again he threw on his clothes with the speed of light, and ran downstairs to the car waiting by the kerb.

Now there were three nurses round the high white bed, and a young doctor who smiled at him and told him that Morag was being absolutely splendid. There was perspiration on her forehead, and pain in her eyes.

'I thought you weren't going to come,' she whispered, and her voice was filled with an aching tiredness, and he thought with shame of the long night he'd slept away, and vowed that he'd never confess that he didn't keep awake.

And afterwards, thinking about it, and trying to remember, it was as if he and Morag were one person, working together, breathing together, her eyes never leaving his face. It was exactly as she had said, the most precious experience, and he heard his voice comforting her, urging her on, and in the background the young doctor issuing instructions until, at last, with an effort that seemed would tear her apart, Morag pushed the baby out into the world.

It was a miracle, a wonderful, glorious miracle. Seeing the tiny red scrap of humanity lying there, still attached to his young wife's body, and being the first to tell her, 'It's a boy! A beautiful little boy!'

The cup of tea they gave him tasted like nectar from the gods. He felt seven feet tall, and they let him see her again, just for a few minutes, lying pale and tired, but blessedly at peace, with the baby tucked up in his swaddling sheet in the cot by her side.

Slowly he walked out of the hospital, into the cold early morning, with people rushing by on the pavements to catch their trains and buses, just as if it were an ordinary day.

He wanted to wind down the window and shout his news to them as he drove along, but remembering his promise to Morag, he drove carefully, and pulling up outside the tall Victorian house, he reached for the slip of paper in the glove compartment, and ran up the stairs to the telephone.

The first number he dialled was Morag's mother, and only giving her time to say hello, he shouted his news over the miles:

'Morag's had her baby,' he said, then he corrected himself.

'*We've* had our baby. A boy. Eight pounds four ounces,' he said, an enormous pride and overwhelming sense of achievement ringing in his voice.

No Need of Stars

I was quite honest with myself, and I didn't spare my feelings either.

There we'd been, I told myself firmly — Adam wandering around Europe on his long summer vacation, trying to forget his broken engagement, and me visiting my cousin Julie in Geneva, and trying to make up my mind about Miles.

Two people, unsure of themselves, vaguely unhappy, meeting in a setting more romantic and colourful than any stage-set one could imagine.

There was the blue expanse of Lake Léman, sparkling in the last rays of a summer sun; the distant fringe of snow-capped mountains, the beds of scarlet geraniums, and the smooth green spread of lawn. There were white-coated waiters, and glasses of bubbling champagne, and strung out along the lakeside edge of the lawn were the flags of many nations, fluttering in the evening breeze.

I was staying with Julie and her American husband, Hank, in their lovely apartment on the outskirts of Geneva. Hank works for the European office of a large engineering firm, and was doing a two-year stint there.

It was June, and Hank and Julie had been invited to a large official cocktail party. Hank saw to it that I was included in the invitation. Julie and I wore what we called our Ascot outfits, floating chiffon dresses and big floppy hats. Julie's was pink, and mine was lilac, and we stood together on a huge flagged terrace, sipping our drinks, enchanted by the scene, for there were people of every nationality there, many of them in traditional dress.

We talked to a beautiful young Indian girl wearing an exquisite rose-coloured sari, and she introduced us to her dignified friend from Istanbul, resplendent in pale gold brocade.

Hank talked to everyone, because that is his way, and he brought Adam over to us and said: 'What d'you know, Sabina? This guy teaches in London like you. His name is Adam. What d'you know about that?'

And we smiled at each other as Hank and Julie wandered off, leaving us together.

'He was so sure we'd know each other,' Adam said, and I looked up at him from underneath the brim of my floppy hat. It was a nice face, especially when he smiled as he was smiling now. His teeth were white and even, and his brown eyes twinkled down at me.

'On holiday?' we both said together.

'You first,' Adam said, and so I told him that I was visiting my cousin Julie, and he said that he was climbing Swiss mountains with three of his friends, and the next day they were moving on into Italy to climb Italian mountains.

The cable car was more my cup of tea, I told him, and even then I wasn't frightfully impressed. 'Mountains are cold and unfriendly things, especially when you get to the top,'

I said. 'All mist and damp, and creeping, clammy cold.'

'Sacrilege! Worse than sacrilege — heresy!' Adam said, and spotted a little round iron table, newly vacated by two of the guests.

'Don't move,' Adam ordered, and went to fetch two more glasses of champagne, and we started to talk.

We talked and talked, our sentences overlapping. I told him about the flat I shared with Lindsay, and he told me about the 'rooms' he shared with two medical students. 'A cooker on the landing, and a bathroom two flights down,' he said. 'Not posh enough to be called a flat . . . '

He told me how his engineering degree had qualified him for teaching, but how already he was becoming fascinated by the engineering side of physical medicine — plastic joints for arthritics, callipers which were feats of engineering design. His dark eyes glowed as he talked, and we hardly noticed that people were drifting away, and that the sun had almost disappeared, leaving the lake a dark shimmer of silk . . .

I told him about the children I taught — about Jimmy who came to school with his clothes buttoned wrongly, and his pullover inside out; and about Claire who stole things from the cloakroom, but I didn't mention Miles. And he didn't talk about his broken engagement. Not then . . .

Julie and Hank came towards us, still hand in hand, and Hank, without a moment's hesitation, because that's the way he is, invited Adam back to the apartment.

'Perhaps you'd rather rejoin your friends?' I said stiffly, because that's the way I am when I don't want to appear 'pushing', but Adam said that his friends were visiting a nightclub in the old part of the town, and wouldn't miss him anyway.

So we walked back through the lovely gardens to where Hank had parked his outsize car, and I sat in the back with Julie, and we drove alongside the lake, and there was the *Jet d'Eau*, floodlit and beautiful.

But I wasn't interested in the *Jet d'Eau*, beautiful and floodlit, because all I could see was the back of Adam's dark head, and the way his hair grew to an endearing point in the nape of his neck.

I suppose if I had been the type of person given to believing in miracles and love at first sight, I'd have known the way it was right from the beginning.

Hank drove at his usual breathtaking speed, on what I couldn't believe wasn't the wrong side of the road, and back in the apartment, in ten minutes flat, Julie had coffee percolating, small tables at the ready, and plates of snacks set out, because she said she had heard Hank invite at least twenty people to 'drop in'.

'That's the way he is,' she said fondly, and her eyes softened as they did when she mentioned his name, and she blew him a kiss across the room to where he crouched on the floor by the drinks cupboard, sorting out bottles with Adam as though he'd known him all his life.

And soon the enormous room, with its low comfortable chairs, and its glass-topped tables, was crowded with people all talking at once, and Adam and I, being thoroughly unsociable, and not caring a bit, found two chairs in the hall by the telephone table. There were so many questions we had to ask each other, so many things to say, and still I didn't mention Miles, and he never spoke of the girl who had given him back his ring.

Around three o'clock people started to drift away, and I went to the door with Adam. We stood together in the large tiled entrance hall, walled in mirrors at one side, and we held hands.

I could see us in the mirrors holding hands . . .

'I don't want to leave you,' Adam said. 'Not now when I've found you.'

'But you have some Italian mountains to climb,' I whispered, and he drew me close to him, and stroked my hair, at least the back of my neck, underneath my hair, and I knew that he was going to kiss me.

'You're so very lovely,' he said before he bent his head, and oh, it was a shuddering, sighing kind of kiss, like no kiss I had known before, and when it was over he held me tight.

'I'll come around about eight,' he said. 'We don't go off until the afternoon. All right?'

'All right,' I said, and drifted back into the apartment on a wave of love and longing.

Already Julie had emptied ashtrays and

plumped up cushions, and Hank was in the kitchen washing glasses and singing with pointed tactlessness a song all about an enchanted evening.

'Honey lamb, you have less than four hours beauty sleep to catch,' he teased when I told them that Adam was coming round for me. 'I have to be at the office around nine thirty, and that's bad enough.'

'All baggy-eyed and growly,' Julie said, and they went off to their room together, arms round each other, and I watched them go, loving them both and their touching adoration of each other.

I closed the door of my bedroom, and slowly started to undress. Then I tied my hair back with a ribbon and creamed my face. I could still feel Adam's caress on the back of my neck and though I knew I ought to be in bed, catching my beauty sleep as Hank had said, I sat there just staring at nothing.

At last I put out the light, drew back the long curtains, opened the double windows, and got into bed. Across the gardens in the tall block of adjoining flats, not a light showed. Sensible people were asleep. Sensible people didn't fall in love with someone they knew hardly at all.

I lay on my back, and stared out into the darkness. There was a solitary tree out there, and a star was caught up in its topmost branch. I closed my eyes. Tomorrow Adam would go off with his friends to Italy, and next week Hank and Julie would drive me out to the airport, and

I'd fly home to the flat I shared with Lindsay, and to Miles . . .

I bit my lip when I thought how nearly Miles had come with me to Geneva. If his mother hadn't been taken ill suddenly, I'm sure he would have come with me, and I would never have got to know Adam.

Miles and I were on the verge of what is called an 'understanding'. Not an engagement, because Miles doesn't believe in engagements. There are a lot of things that Miles doesn't believe in, and he told me that it had started off with Father Christmas when he was around two years old. Miles is sensible, and kind, infinitely kind, and clever, too. He does something very lucrative in insurance in a big block of offices just round the corner from my primary school.

For two years now all my Tuesday evenings, Saturdays and Sundays had been devoted to him. His kisses were sweet and undemanding, but not once had I lain in bed burning like this from the memory of his caress.

I turned over and buried my face in the pillow, and told my heart to be still. I was twenty-two, not a teenager with her first holiday romance. Holiday friendships never last anyway. Anyone would tell you that.

★ ★ ★

At seven o'clock, Julie woke me with a cup of tea — coming into my room with her fair hair tousled, and her cheeks still rosy with sleep.

She had married Hank after knowing him for

292

only a few months; she had married him without needing two years of Tuesdays and Saturdays and Sundays to make up her mind.

'Julie?' I said, but she was bustling around, picking up a discarded pillow from the floor, half closing the window, her mind already on Hank's breakfast, and her busy day ahead.

'The bathroom's empty if you want to take a shower,' she smiled. 'Hank won't come up from underneath the sheet, but I know how to deal with him! It's going to be another lovely day. Did you ever see a sky so blue, and there are little pink scarves round the top of the mountains.'

'Julie?' I said, but she had gone.

★ ★ ★

I rushed to the door when the bell rang, forgetting what was right and proper, and Adam was there, tall and thin, and so very, very serious. He'd cut himself whilst shaving, and he looked as if he hadn't slept at all.

We left Julie and Hank with their breakfast coffee and rolls and strawberry jam, and out in the forecourt Adam apologized for his car.

'It's just the job for carrying camping gear and climbing tackle,' he said, giving its shabby side a loving pat, and removing a pile of anoraks from the front seat to make room for me.

'We'll stop on the way and shop for breakfast,' he suggested. And so we did — parking the car in a side street and sallying forth with a basket to buy a long French loaf, butter, and some oranges.

Soon we left Geneva behind, and took the wide straight road to Montreux. There wasn't much time, Adam explained; he had left his three friends striking camp, and I wondered if already he regretted his impulsive suggestion that we meet again.

He turned his head at that moment, and his eyes met mine, and I read in them all I wanted to know. I sat back and relaxed.

On our right the waters of the lake danced in the early morning sunshine, and the mountains in the far distance were wreathed in rosy mist.

Adam stopped the car at the side of the road.

'No point in going any farther,' he said, and turned to face me squarely. 'We'll have a break here' — and, fumbling in a rucksack on the back seat, he found a knife for the butter and two plastic plates. He also produced hot coffee in a flask.

'I was engaged,' he told me as we sipped our coffee. 'Everything was arranged; the wedding date, and we'd paid the first down payment on a house to be built with rooms not much bigger than the inside of this car, and a garden the size of a postage stamp. You know the type?'

I nodded, and waited for him to go on.

'Then she met someone else.'

'Leaving you with a broken heart,' I said, feeling my own heart lying as heavy as lead.

Adam turned towards me, his thin face serious and intent.

'That's just it. Summing the whole thing up now dispassionately, and looking back, I can honestly say that after a couple of nights' broken sleep, a day or two off my food, and a few weeks mooning about because the whole pattern of my life had changed, it was over. Finished. Just like that. My pride was hurt, not my heart. We had become used to each other, that was all.'

'Like Miles and me,' I said.

Adam put his arm round me. 'Tell me about this Miles,' he said.

And so I told him, and his dark eyes were grave as he listened.

'Coming away like this, and meeting you,' I said bravely, 'has shown me that I can never marry Miles, because now I know . . . '

'Now you know,' Adam said softly, and pulled me close into his arms, and traced with his finger the outline of my mouth. Then he kissed me, with only the lake and the mountains and the vivid blue sky to see, and there were tears in my eyes, because that's the way I am when I'm happy.

Adam was whispering against my cheek. 'I know *my* mind,' he said, 'but then I'm older than you, and not swayed by moonlight and champagne.' He held me tighter still.

'You go home next week, and I go home in another three weeks, and by then you'll have had time to think and talk to Miles.'

'I don't need to think,' I said, but he smoothed back my hair and sighed.

'We'd have been hard put to it *not* to fall in love,' he said.

And then we drove back, and arranged to meet in one month's time outside Oxford Circus Tube station because we agreed that that was about the least romantic setting we could think of at the time.

So we said our sensible goodbyes, even shaking hands to prove that we meant it.

'There'll be no stars in our eyes next time,' I told Julie, and she laughed out loud, throwing her head back.

'When you really love someone you know you love them, stars or no stars,' she told me. 'You'll see.'

* * *

I finished my holiday, and flew back to London Airport, where Miles was waiting for me, large, matter-of-fact, kindly.

He seemed different somehow, and I told him so as his absent-minded kiss landed somewhere on my chin. He had actually forgotten where he'd parked his car, and that was so unlike Miles, who cherishes his car as if it were a piece of delicate, priceless china. Then he forgot to put my luggage in the boot, and left it standing there, and would have driven off without it if I hadn't reminded him.

All the way back into town I talked about my holiday, and Miles drove silently, making appropriate grunting noises when the things I talked about called for some sort of reply.

With far less than his usual precision, he parked the car outside the tall row of Victorian houses where Lindsay and I share a flat.

'No need to get my key out,' I told him over my shoulder, as he followed me up the linoleum-covered stairs. 'Lindsay's always in at this time.'

Miles seemed to be having trouble with his breathing, and I turned round in surprise.

'Lindsay's gone out, but she'll be back,' he said, and actually blushed. Then he followed me into the flat, and dumped my case down, and leaned against the sideboard, scowling at me, and folding his arms.

'Lindsay and I have been seeing quite a lot of each other whilst you've been away,' he said, without any preamble. 'Every single night,' he went on determinedly.

'Not just Tuesdays, Saturdays and Sundays?' I asked, and it was his turn to look surprised.

'Every single night,' he said again.

'And you've discovered that you love each other?' I said helpfully, and his mouth dropped open into a round 'O' of astonishment.

'And you've discovered that you and I had become a pleasant familiar habit,' I went on, and he came towards me then, and put his arms round me, and I leaned against him in inexplicable relief.

'Oh, Miles,' I said, and started to shake, and when he saw that it was with laughter, he laughed too, and when Lindsay came in we were sipping tea, and all was said and settled.

I went tactfully to bed, swearing that I was exhausted, and started to unpack, thinking all the time about Adam.

And that was when I talked to myself, being honest with myself, and not sparing my feelings either . . .

★ ★ ★

The next few weeks dragged by, and the day I was to meet Adam came in a mist of drizzle that turned to a steady downpour by the end of the afternoon.

I had been back at school for a week, and my tan had faded unbecomingly. It was one of those days when no amount of careful make-up would give me the effect I wanted — even my features seemed blurred into unfamiliar lines, and my hair refused to go the way I wanted it to go.

There wasn't time to go back to the flat, and I got to Oxford Circus half an hour early, wet and bedraggled, with splashed nylons, and a borrowed umbrella dripping rivulets of water down the back of my neck.

We had been right. Oxford Circus is the most unromantic place in the world, especially in the rain, especially late in the afternoon, with the home-going crowds, damp and miserable, grey-faced and pushing.

I was half an hour early, but Adam was there, standing by a newspaper stand, scanning the passing faces with a touching and terrible anxiety. He was wet, too, the collar of his raincoat was turned up, and his hair had been cut too short, but he suddenly saw me, and held out his arms . . .

There was no sunshine sparkling on a blue,

blue lake; no mountains wreathed in soft pink mist, no champagne, no stars, and no need of stars.

For it was exactly as Julie had said.

When you really love someone, you know you love them, stars or no stars.

It was as simple as that.

A Time to Surrender

The first time I met him wasn't in exactly romantic surroundings. I first saw him at one of Mother's coffee mornings. I was taking my spring week's leave from the office, and Mother, because of a sprained ankle, was unable to drive, so I'd promised to take her, then pick her up around twelve.

The coffee morning was in aid of a Worthy Cause, I honestly can't remember which, and when I arrived, most of the ladies were gathered in the hall, twittering their way into their coats, and he was in the sitting room, being pressed to a glass of sweet sherry.

Under those circumstances, one would have expected a man to behave like a hunted animal at bay, but he was sharing the fireplace — the only available space — with a pot of lilac, and obviously enjoying himself hugely.

We were introduced, and it seemed that like me, he was also on an errand of mercy, bringing *his* mother's subscription to the said Worthy Cause, and explaining that she was suffering from what she insisted was a belated dose of Hong Kong flu.

'Do they do this often?' he whispered, gazing round with unconcealed amusement at the scatter of little tables, the well-drained coffee cups, and the screwed-up paper napkins on the plates.

'Every other Thursday,' I assured him, and he whispered, 'And do they always keep their hats on?'

'Always,' I told him, and he grinned in what I decided was a superior kind of way.

I hadn't exactly taken an instant dislike to him; no, he just wasn't my type at all.

Although, to be perfectly honest, at the age of twenty-two with two broken engagements behind me, and a string of unsuccessful affairs — small 'a', I might add — I wasn't really in a position to pick and choose, and goodness knows, he was good looking enough.

The tall, rugged kind of man, with broad shoulders, and slim hips, and dark hair flopping over his forehead, almost into a pair of not quite navy-blue eyes.

One could imagine him appearing suddenly from behind a rock and shooting an unsuspecting enemy stone dead with a single burst from his speedily drawn gun. Or climbing a mountain ahead of his party, and standing at the summit, urging the others on in a loud, brave voice.

His name was Waldo, and when I looked him up later I saw it meant the Strong One, which didn't surprise me one iota.

'Where do you live?' he asked me, without the slightest preamble.

'Maida Vale, in a tower block of flats,' I told him.

I'd already seen him glance at my ringless left hand, so he didn't need to ask me that question. Instead he moved on.

'Career girl?' he asked and, lying in my teeth,

I told him that I supposed I could come into that category, and he lifted an amused eyebrow, and passed me a cigarette.

The truth was that I wasn't, and never had been, career-minded. From the age of ten, all I had wanted to be was a wife and mother, and the fact that I was the personal and private secretary to a two-ulcered managing director was purely and simply luck.

I wished that Mother would hurry up, but she had bobbed her head round the door once, seen me talking to a MAN, and whispered that she was in the dining room in her role of Hon. Treasurer, counting over the morning's takings with the Hon. Secretary.

I knew that she would take her time about it . . .

I was rather a disappointment to Mother, and she had told me quite frankly that what I needed was to meet a man who would dominate me, and thereby command my respect.

'You've been spoiled all your life, Helen,' she'd said. 'First by your father, and then by your boyfriends. When you meet a man who can show you who's boss, then you'll really fall in love. Just you wait and see.'

Well, I'd been waiting to see for quite a long time, and there were times when I suspected that she could have been right.

Harvey and Kevin, my ex-fiancés, had both been the ground-I-walked-on worshipping type, and after a while, their servile devotion had begun to irritate.

Waldo was glancing at the outsized watch

302

strapped to his rather hairy wrist, then holding out his hand.

'Enjoyed meeting you, Helen,' he said. 'Perhaps we'll meet again some day in more exciting surroundings?'

I doubt it, I thought, but I smiled up at him, and tried not to wince when he crushed my hand in his vice-like grip. 'I hope so,' I said softly, with hypocritical sincerity, and Mother, coming in at that moment, looked proud of me.

'Doing well for himself,' she told me on the short drive home. 'A computer salesman, for want of a more glamorous term. PhD. Cambridge. Not married, and lives with his mother at Hampstead.'

'He doesn't look the type to live with his mother,' I said rather nastily, and she sighed over me, and told me that his mother was a widow and not very strong, and that the house was really his, and his mother had her own self-contained flat in it, and NEVER INTERFERED.

'What colour are the dining-room curtains?' I asked, and she said that being waspish didn't suit me.

I stopped the car and helped her out, and said that I wouldn't have lunch with her as I had things to do at my flat.

She kissed me rather sadly, and I drove off, the feeling that I let her down swamping me again.

And I honestly never gave Waldo another thought, except to look up his unusual name; so that when the telephone rang almost two weeks later, and I heard his unmistakable voice at the other end, I could only stutter my surprise.

'How on earth . . . ?' I began, and his deep laugh boomed.

'We were introduced, remember? And you told me Maida Vale, in a tower block. The rest, my dear Watson, was easy.'

'Oh, I see,' I said, that being the wittiest remark I could come up with at the moment.

'Would you care to have dinner with me? I've discovered this marvellous Italian restaurant, and so apparently have hordes of other people. It's necessary to book at least a week ahead, so shall we say this coming Saturday? Eightish?'

Not a word about did I like Italian food, or did I happen to be free?

Well, I did, and I was, so in a matter of seconds I had agreed, and replaced the receiver, staring at it as though it had just delivered a message from outer space.

Waldo, the Strong One, I told my empty room, and I wished I'd had the sense to refuse, or at least to sound less keen. Instead I'd babbled on like a dateless teenager. 'That will be nice. Yes, thank you. Yes, eightish will suit me fine . . . '

I leafed through the directory, with the avowed intention of ringing straight back and saying that I'd just remembered another engagement, then I put the directory back on its shelf and went to look through my wardrobe to decide what to wear.

Harvey and Kevin had liked me in soft and floaty dresses in pale pastel shades, but I tossed a selection on my bed, shaking my head.

Black, I decided. The smartest and littlest black dress I could afford, with my hair swept back into my newly acquired false piece. Not to impress Waldo the Strong. Oh, no. Just to show him how wrong was his clear assumption that I was there all alone, waiting and willing to go out with him and eat Italian food.

For all he knew I might have been living with my lover, and preferring roast and two veg.

He was ten minutes late, and didn't apologize, but as eight o'clock had found me almost hysterical because my hairpiece wouldn't go on right, I found it in my heart to forgive him. Harvey and Kevin had always turned up much too early, anyway.

He drove swiftly but well, parked his car with admirable precision, and led the way to a table in a secluded corner. The waiter, swarthy and with curly black hair, seemed to know him, and removed the tiny reserved card with exaggerated deference.

'Shall I order?' Waldo asked, and only just subduing a childish urge to order a completely different meal from the one he had chosen, I gave in. There was certainly something restful about being dominated. It gave one a cherished feeling, I decided. So I sat back in my corner, and let him get on with it.

As soon as the waiter had gone, Waldo turned his navy-blue gaze on to me. 'Why are you wearing a wig?' he asked.

I was so astonished I could only sit there, opening and closing my mouth.

'It's not a wig, only a hairpiece,' I said at last. 'Why, don't you like it on me?'

Waldo snapped a finger at the wine waiter, also swarthy, and curly black-haired, and I had to wait for his reply until he'd given explicit instructions about the wine, stipulating the exact year.

'You happen to have very beautiful hair of your own,' he said. 'The colour of oatmeal. It's like gilding the lily pinning that thing on top of it. Will you smoke?'

I didn't very often, but I took one, feeling in dire need of it. 'I don't think I like having oatmeal-coloured hair,' I said, and he leaned across the table and lit my cigarette.

'Well, it is. My mother came originally from Cumberland, and she used to make oatcakes. Large flat things like wash-leathers, and she used to dry them on racks.'

'I believe you live with your mother?' I said.

He nodded happily. 'Marvellous arrangement. She's a semi-invalid, but fiercely independent. She cooks my Sunday lunch, and we pass in the hall now and again, but apart from that we might be entirely alone.'

I tried to guess his age, and decided to ask my mother the next time I saw her.

'I'm twenty-eight,' he said, 'and worked in Canada after I qualified. I prefer life over here. Why are *you* not engaged, Helen?'

I blushed. He really was a most unusual man.

'I've been engaged twice,' I told him, and he said that he knew. That my mother had told his

306

mother, who had confided it over the previous Sunday's lunch.

We laughed, and when the food came, he fell on it like a pack of starving wolves. The leader, of course. Not that his manners weren't perfect, but he ate with what I suppose could be called gusto, holding his knife and fork firmly, and paying undivided attention to his plate. He was, I realized, quite the most masculine man I'd ever known.

At my flat he came up in the lift with me, and threw himself down into an armchair, stretching out his long legs. I wondered when he would get around to kissing me, and the thought of him kissing me made me forget the pan of milk, and I was starting to mop it up when he came up behind me.

Now! I thought, and struggling won't do you any good, he could toss you over his shoulder with a mere flick of his wrist.

But he just took the dishcloth from me, and got on with the mopping up, then he carried the coffee through into the living room.

Feeling rather deflated I sat down opposite him, and found that he was paying far more attention to the books on my shelves than to me.

'Ah, a non-fiction reader, like me,' he said, picking up a book and leafing through it. 'But I see you also read Jane Austen. Or are they just a relic from your childhood?'

'No, I read them,' I told him truthfully. 'She had an allseeing eye, but I think some of her wit was a little cruel. She was inclined to laugh at people and not with them. Don't you agree?'

Well, he didn't, and he said so at great length, then abruptly he got up and went, crushing my hand in that mighty grip, and striding off down the corridor towards the lift.

Not a word about seeing me again, not even waiting for me to thank him for what, I had to admit, had been a most enjoyable evening.

'Waldo!' I said aloud to the empty room. 'You're the strangest man. And quite the rudest,' I told the coffee cups as I put them away.

Harvey and Kevin had always rung me the very next day after our evenings out together, and in the first flush of our engagements, sent me flowers, but it was another long week and a half before Waldo rang me again, and by this time I was ready for him.

'Shall we try some Chinese food on Saturday, Helen? Pick you up around eightish again. Right?'

The sheer assumption of the man!

'I'm sorry,' I told the telephone, 'but I have a previous arrangement for Saturday. I'm sorry.'

'Not to worry,' said Waldo, and after a few pleasantries, said a firm goodbye. No suggestion of an alternative date, nothing, just the final click of the telephone in my ear.

'Well, that's that,' I said aloud, and realized how much I'd grown into the habit of talking to myself.

All I need now is a cat to commune with, I told myself bitterly, and saw myself coming in from work, with a little bit of fish done up in a parcel, and telling Tibby all about my day at

308

the office. How beastly the managing director had been, and how frivolous the young typists were, always talking about MEN, and doing their nails when they should have been getting on with their work.

That pulled me up sharply. I had been noticing lately that the girls at work were getting younger and sillier, always leaving to get married and being superseded by younger, even sillier girls.

Or could it be that I was growing older? Soon I'd be noticing the youth of our policemen, and that stairs were getting steeper . . . !

I stayed in every night the following week, staring at the telephone, and willing it to ring. Each time it did, I could hardly bring myself to be civil to the voice on the other end, and finished the conversation as quickly as possible, just in case Waldo was trying to get through, and was sitting in a leather armchair, listening to the engaged signal.

I was sure it would be a leather armchair, in a room filled with books, mainly non-fiction books, leather-bound to match the chair.

'How childish can you get?' I asked myself out loud, and wondered if I could be falling in love.

Was this love, this feeling of walking an emotional tightrope? This feeling of great joy, interspersed with moments of bleak despair? Surely after two engagements I should have known what love was? But I'd never felt this way before.

And wasn't it human nature to feel this way because I'd finally met a man who couldn't care whether I lived or died?

At the end of the second week I stopped trying to hypnotize the telephone into ringing, and went with a girlfriend from the office to see *Gone With the Wind*.

And it was a mistake, because I positively identified. That is to say I positively identified him, Waldo, with Rhett Butler.

There was the same ruthlessness, the same air of masculine superiority, and when I wept into a tissue until it disintegrated, my friend was appalled.

'Honestly, Helen, to go to pieces about a film,' she said, and I said I'd been feeling under the weather for a while, and she suggested some marvellous little iron pills, and red-eyed and demoralized, I promised to try them.

He rang again the following week, suggesting a Greek restaurant in Soho, and this time my excuse was quite genuine. An old school friend was celebrating her wedding anniversary, and had invited me a long time ago to join a small party for dinner at the Hilton.

It wasn't the sort of engagement one could wriggle out of, and it wasn't the sort to which one could take another man.

'I'm sorry,' I said, and my heart wept blood, and I cursed my friend for enjoying wedded bliss to celebrate on that very day. 'I'm truly sorry, but I have a long-standing engagement for Saturday.'

I was going on to explain, but being Waldo he wasn't going to give me a chance. 'That's all right, Helen. Some other time, perhaps?' He was going to say goodbye and ring off, and I couldn't bear it.

I'd never run after a man before; I'd never needed to. Mother was right, I'd been spoiled. But the past few weeks had taught me that I was, after all, a complete feminist, and I respected Waldo, and was quite ready to accept a relationship of dominance and submission.

But I was prepared to fight for it first, before surrendering.

I didn't know if this overwhelming feeling I had for Waldo was love, or merely fascination for a man who treated me with a casualness I'd never encountered before.

And I had to know . . .

'Why don't you come round this evening?' I said, and my eyes in the hall mirror were dilated with horror at my audacity. 'Perhaps we could continue our discussion about Jane Austen? Maybe I could bring you round to my way of thinking?'

The silence at the other end of the line grew. Grew and lengthened.

'I'll be with you in half an hour,' said Waldo, with the air of a man emerging from a death struggle, and when I replaced the receiver my hand was trembling.

And by the end of the evening, I knew that I was in love. The really-in-love, lasting-for-ever kind; till-death-do-us-part kind of love.

Waldo took a little longer. Until three weeks later, over an Indian curry in fact.

But I didn't mind. He'd been worth waiting for.

Love is Fingers Touching

When someone stopped the music, and someone else made the announcement, Barbie stood alone, a small, fair-haired girl, wearing a flowered maxi-dress, a champagne glass clasped in her hand.

People began to crowd round the newly engaged couple — Simon whom she had loved for a whole year, and Karen, laughing, her dark head thrown back, gazing up at him adoringly.

When someone stopped the music, and someone else made the announcement, a tall, dark-haired man she vaguely knew came over to her, offering to refill her glass.

'Drink this,' he ordered, 'and the name's David. I saw you with the crowd one day last summer.'

'The summer seems a long time ago,' she said, and then she thought: I must go now. I must make myself walk over to Simon and his Karen. I must congratulate them; then I can go home.

She decided to take a taxi instead of the Tube train, and only when she was sitting in the back of the cab did she remember that she'd left her small fringed shawl behind. Now she would have to ring, and they'd guess that she had been upset . . .

How was it possible, she wondered, as the taxi drew up outside the block of flats, to care so deeply, to love so completely, and then to have it all end like this?

She would never allow herself to become so involved again. At the first sign of 'rapport', the first moment when fingers touching became more than just fingers touching, she would run away.

The lift rose silently, and at the twelfth floor she got out and walked down the dimly lit corridor to her flat. The first thing she saw was the leather swivel chair she had come to think of as Simon's, and as she tied an apron over her long dress, it seemed as if there was the slight imprint of his head on its back.

She remembered him sitting there, his long legs stretched out, a drink by his side, talking to her as she'd cooked, making her laugh with his tales of what had happened to him that day in his busy London office.

She had tried to explain it all to a close friend: 'After a year, he was a part of me. It's as though someone you were fond of has *died*. Can't you see?'

The friend, with a string of broken romances behind her, had smiled and said that when the next man came along she would forget, and why was she being so intense about it?

She wasn't hungry, but she forced herself to take a solitary chop from the fridge and lay it underneath the grill. Her day in the Regent Street store, where she worked as a fashion buyer, had been hectic. She'd skipped lunch, and now the champagne was making her feel light-headed.

When the doorbell rang, she went into the tiny hall, forgetting to take off her apron, and the tall man from the party, the man called David, was there, holding out her shawl and smiling.

'You left this draped across a chair, and our hostess gave me your address. You don't mind?'

She stood aside to let him in. She could see it all. Poor, jilted Barbie, this is just what she needs, another man to boost her deflated ego . . .

'Won't you sit down?' she said politely, and he chose Simon's chair, staring round the room with interest.

In the kitchen she turned off the grill, untied her apron, and came and sat down opposite him.

'It was a good party, wasn't it?'

'Look,' he said, and his voice, for a big man, was surprisingly quiet. 'I don't know about you, but I'm hungry. Would you give me the pleasure of taking you out to dinner? There's an Italian restaurant I've discovered by the river. Do you like Italian food?'

For a moment she hesitated. So she was to be taken out of herself. Her friends were more loyal than she'd imagined, and she ought to be grateful.

'Thank you,' she said politely, 'yes, I'd like that. Give me a minute. Would you like a drink?'

'I won't if you don't mind. Nothing much to eat all day, and a surfeit of champagne — things are beginning to float, or maybe it's the height.

Do you enjoy living way up here?'

'Once inside with the door closed and the curtains drawn, the height ceases to be. One could be anywhere at all.'

'I see,' he said gravely, and there again was the unspoken sympathy, and in her imagination she heard them say: 'Run after her, David. Take the shawl to her, and be a lamb and take her out to dinner. What possessed Simon to announce his engagement tonight? She was crazy about him. Did you see her *face*?'

And once inside the restaurant, a swarthy Italian, wearing a vivid red shirt, led them down a twisting staircase to a dimly lit room, dotted with tables covered with cloths as red as his shirt.

At a small corner table, they were handed outsize menus, and as they chose she stared around her, and saw with amusement, that the guitarist, a sad-faced Italian, was watching himself closely in a gilt-framed mirror as he sang. For the first time since the announcement had been made at the party, she felt herself relax.

'That poor little man with the guitar — no one is listening to him. Wouldn't you think it deflating to his ego to sing there night after night to an uncaring audience?'

David smiled. 'You have a kind heart, I see.'

She shook her head. 'Not all that kind. I'm in danger of becoming a cynic, you know.'

'Because of Simon Masters?'

As she stared at him without replying, their waiter arrived with smoked trout, placing the plates before them.

At a table to their right, a girl was holding hands with a fair man, and the guitarist strolled over to them and started on a serenade.

'I used to look at Simon just as that girl is looking at the man she's with. Tell me something, David. How do they know it will last? Where does love go? How can it end when people feel like that?'

'We have to take a gamble on it,' David said quietly. 'Life is a gamble, come to that, and when love ends we have to remember the good things, not dwell on whys and wherefores. It's the only way.'

'But suppose I'd married Simon when it was good?'

He grinned at her. 'Well you didn't marry him, did you? For that you should be grateful.'

Then he did a surprising thing, and stretching out his hand across the red tablecloth, he took her hand in his, tracing with his finger the tiny blue veins on the inside of her wrist.

'Stop grieving for him, Barbie. You're far too lovely a girl to waste your time suffering the pangs of unrequited love. Start to live again.'

The touch of his hand, the depth of his obvious concern for her, the kindness in his dark eyes, brought unexpected tears to her own, and she made her voice light. 'You speak from experience?'

Freely he admitted that she was absolutely right. 'I'm twenty-six and I've been in love four times, and it was marvellous every time. I have no regrets. But some day I'll meet the girl I'm going to marry, and when I know that falling

316

in love has turned to loving, I'll take her and cherish her for the rest of my life, because then I'll know the difference. You see?'

Then, answering his gentle questioning, she told him about her job, and he told her he was the accountant to a plastics firm. They discovered a mutual liking for offbeat poetry, Frank Sinatra, Yugoslavia, Dorothy Parker, walking in the rain, Italian food (especially the veal cooked in a rich wine sauce now on their plates), and guitarists who sang to themselves.

They laughed a lot, and then they climbed the winding staircase out into the dark street. A spatter of rain darkened his suit as they ran hand in hand across to his car.

When they reached her flat he said: 'You're not a cynic, Barbie. You never were, and never will be. May I ring you, soon?'

She saw once more the kindness in his eyes, and as he held her hand, she felt the quiet strength in him.

'*May* I ring you soon?'

Up in her flat, she drew back the curtains, stared across the glittering lights of London.

She couldn't be involved again; she couldn't live through the hurt again. For a long moment, she stood there, uncertain.

When fingers touch, and are more than fingers touching, then was the time to run away, she reminded herself.

Then all at once she smiled, and held the hand that he had held against her cheek . . .

317

A Time of Laughter

Only five weeks to wait now before our baby arrives, and Julian won't allow me to get up and make his breakfast. Instead I lie in bed, uncomfortably, listening to him banging around in our tiny kitchen. Before he leaves for work he brings me a cup of tea, half cold and stewed almost black, and a slice of toast burned round the edges, with marmalade glistening sickeningly on its buttered surface.

I have grown fat, and Julian has grown thin, worrying about me and the responsibilities of being a father before he has had time to be a man, and before he goes out he kisses me and reminds me to ring him at the office if anything should happen before he leaves at five to come home.

'First babies are always late,' I tell him, quoting my mother, but I know that at lunchtime he will ring me, and again during the afternoon if his boss goes out, and only when he comes home in the evening will he relax, because then he is with me, and can take care of me. I can feel him thinking that.

I know I am lucky to be loved so much, lucky to be married at all, with a baby due six months after the wedding day, and lucky to have this flat, even though the rent is so high that there is barely enough money left over to cover what are called the essentials of living. Essentials being food and fuel bills, an occasional meal out, and a once-monthly visit to the cinema.

Our flat is on the twelfth floor of a tower-built block, consisting of a living room, a small kitchen, and adjoining that a bedroom with a bathroom leading from it. The sound of heavy traffic from the main road far below is no more than a muted hum, and when the wind blows I could swear that the whole building sways . . .

There always seems to be a draught, so that my feet and legs are perpetually cold, and some days I can see the linoleum we have put down until we can afford a carpet actually lift and ripple like waves on a lake which has been ruffled by the wind.

Outside the door, the corridor leading to the lifts is as empty and bare as if the place has been evacuated for a bomb scare. The doors with their impersonal nameplates remain closed, and just occasionally, as I press the bell for a lift, a woman will join me, stony-faced, staring straight ahead as people do in lifts, striding ahead of me when we reach ground level, crossing the parquet floor of the hall, past the porter's desk and out into the street.

There is the view, of course, but views are impersonal things, and even on holiday I have always preferred to take photographs of people, leaving the beauty of the scenery to the manufacturers of picture postcards.

There was this boy I met on holiday in Austria last year. He carried a camera everywhere and was always taking photographs of the mountain peaks and the deeply wooded slopes.

319

The boy would say: 'Views are such comforting things. I wish I could get the feel of them into my photographs. They surround you, holding you safe, even the grey, forbidding kind. Can't you feel it too, Lisa?'

'To me, a mountain is a mountain, is a mountain,' I remember saying, cleverly, and he laughed. I will never forget the way he laughed, throwing his head back as if he were about to come apart at the seams.

One day he showed me a leaf with its thin thread of veins, pointing out the many shades of green, and his face came alight as he was talking. He was totally absorbed by the leaf's beauty.

I told him that he should have been an artist or a poet, not working in a stuffy insurance office, and he threw back his head and laughed again as if he hadn't a care in the whole wide world.

My back is aching, so I carefully heave myself to a sitting position, then roll out of bed. I stand by the window, shiver a little and stare without interest at the panoramic vision of roof-tops, the straight roads with cars crawling along them, the domes of churches, and over in the far distance a tall spire pointing a black finger to the grey sky.

I remember the house where I lived with my parents, an avenue where everyone knew everyone else, and people were always passing the front gate.

There were men on their way to work, children going to school, and women on their way to the shops.

I move away from the window and start to get dressed. That is what is wrong with this flat, I tell myself. No one ever passes by.

'Much chance of that, twelve storeys high,' I say out loud, and then stop, the sound of my voice in the empty silence frightening me a little.

Sometimes I imagine that if I open the door there would be no corridor outside, just space, black and empty, stretching on and on into eternity.

I tidy the living room, picking up last night's paper from the floor, emptying Julian's ashtray, and putting the textbooks he uses at evening classes into his case.

I think about going out for a walk, then see from where I stand that the window is all black clouds and drifting rain, and at lunchtime Julian rings and I tell him truthfully that I am fine.

'I am eating a poached egg because of the protein, and drinking a glass of orange juice because of the vitamin C,' I say. I sense that he is reassured and put the receiver down, feeling the emptiness and the silence once again.

I sleep in the afternoon, guiltily, in the way afternoon sleepers do, and now the rain is lashing against the window, and I know there will be no chance of going out for a walk today.

I prepare a casserole much too early, to give myself something to do, and because the music on the radio is soft and romantic, I dream again about the boy I met on my holiday . . .

How long will it be, I wonder, before I go

abroad again? What will I do when the baby comes, and I am shut away up here alone with him?

Will I talk to him then as now I talk to the empty room, asking whether I ought to put on a warm coat, and if he thinks there will be a letter from my mother in the rack downstairs?

When Julian comes in he looks pale and tired. His hair needs trimming, and I know he is putting off a visit to the barbers because the last time he went they charged him thirty new pence. I know, too, that but for the baby and me and the flat, and the essentials of living, he would be able to scatter new pence about the place just like confetti.

The casserole that has been in the oven much too long is drying up, but Julian puts his arm round me and pulls me to the window.

'Just look at all those roofs glistening grey and blue now that the rain has stopped,' he says softly. 'And see those fields in the distance. I never realized that green was a sparkling colour before, did you? I wish I could get the feel of that superb view into one of my photographs.'

He turns me round and holds me close to him, as close to him as our baby will allow. 'Do you know something, Lisa? When I'm on my way up in the lift, knowing I'm coming home to you, it's as though I'm being lifted up to heaven . . . our own little heaven. Can you understand that, Lisa?'

'To me a view is a view is a view,' I say, teasing him. He laughs out loud, throwing back his head, and in that instant he is the boy I met on holiday just last year.

Suddenly everything is all right again. I stand on tiptoe awkwardly and kiss his chin. He stretches out a hand to draw the curtains, and I tell him to leave them as they are.

'Soon the lights will be coming on,' I say, 'and we'll pull the table to the window and see it all as we eat. Views are such *comforting* things, don't you think so, my darling?'

Other titles in the
Charnwood Library Series:

LEGACIES
Janet Dailey

The sequel to THE PROUD AND THE FREE.
It is twenty years since the feud within
his family began, but Lije Stuart, son of
the Cherokee chief The Blade, had never
forgotten the killing of his grandfather. Now,
a promising legal career beckons, and also
the love of his childhood sweetheart, Diane
Parmalee, the daughter of a US Army officer.
Yet as it reawakens, their love is beset by the
beginning of civil war.

'L' IS FOR LAWLESS
Sue Grafton

World War II fighter pilot Johnny Lee had
died and his grandson was trying to claim
military funeral benefits, but none of the
authorities have any record of Fighter J. Lee.
Was the old man once a US spy? When PI
Kinsey Millhone is asked to straighten things
out, she finds herself pursued by a psychopath
bearing a forty-year-old grudge . . .

BLOOD LINES
Ruth Rendell

This is a collection of long and short stories
by Ruth Rendell that will linger in the
mind.

THE SUN IN GLORY
Harriet Hudson

When industrialist William Potts sets himself to build a flying machine, his adopted daughter, Rosie, works through the years as his mechanic. In 1906 Pegasus is almost ready, and onto the scene comes Jake Smith, a man who has as deep a love of the air as Rosie herself. But Jake sparks off a deadly rivalry, and the triumph of flight twists into tragedy.

A WOMAN SCORNED
M. R. O'Donnell

Five years after the tragedy that ruined her fifteenth birthday, Judith Carty returns to Castle Moore and resumes her flirtation with its heir, Rick Bellingham. The tragic events of the past forge a special bond between the young couple, but there are those who have a vested interest in the failure of the romance.

PLAINER STILL
Catherine Cookson

Following the success of her previous collection of essays and poems, LET ME MAKE MYSELF PLAIN, Catherine Cookson has compiled a further selection of thoughts, recollections, and observations on life — and death — together with another collection of the poems she prefers to describe as 'prose on short lines'.

THE LOST WORLD
Michael Crichton

The successor to JURASSIC PARK.
It is now six years since the secret disaster of Jurassic Park, when that extraordinary dream of science and imagination came to a crashing end — the dinosaurs destroyed, and the park dismantled. There are rumours that something has survived . . .

MORNING, NOON & NIGHT
Sidney Sheldon

When Harry Stanford, one of the wealthiest men in the world, mysteriously drowns, it sets off a chain of events that reverberates around the globe. At the family gathering following the funeral, a beautiful young woman appears, claiming to be Harry's daughter. Is she genuine, or is she an impostor?

FACING THE MUSIC
Jayne Torvill and Christopher Dean

The world's most successful and popular skating couple tell their own story, from their working-class childhoods in Nottingham to world stardom. Finally, they describe how they created their own show, FACE THE MUSIC, with a superb corps of international ice dancers.

ORANGES AND LEMONS
Jeanne Whitmee

When Shirley Rayner is evacuated from London's East End, she finds herself billeted with the theatre's most romantic couple, Tony and Leonie Darrent. She becomes firm friends with their daughter, Imogen, and the two girls dream of making their names on the stage. But they have forgotten the very different backgrounds from which they come.

HALF HIDDEN
Emma Blair

Holly Morgan, a nurse in a hospital on Nazi-occupied Jersey, falls in love with a young German doctor, Peter Schmidt, and is racked by guilt. Can their love survive the future together or will the war destroy all their hopes and dreams?

THE GREAT TRAIN ROBBERY
Michael Crichton

In Victorian London, where lavish wealth and appalling poverty exist side by side, one man navigates both worlds with ease. Rich, handsome and ingenious, Edward Pierce preys on the most prominent of the well-to-do as he cunningly orchestrates the crime of his century.

THIS CHILD IS MINE
Henry Denker

Lori Adams, a young, unmarried actress, gives up her baby boy for adoption with great reluctance. She feels that she and the baby's father, Brett, are not in a position to provide their child with all he deserves. But when, two years later, life has improved dramatically for Lori and Brett, they want their child returned . . .

THE LOST DAUGHTERS
Jeanne Whitmee

At school, Cathy and Rosalind have one thing in common: each is the child of a single parent. For them both, the transition to adulthood is far from easy — until their unexpected reunion. Working together, the two friends take a bold step that will help them to become independent women.

THE DEVIL YOU KNOW
Josephine Cox

When Sonny Fareham overhears a private conversation between her lover and his wife, she realises she is in great danger. Shocked and afraid, she flees to the north of England to make a new life — but never far away is the one person who wants to destroy everything that she now holds dear.